Community Psychology

Community Psychology

Perspectives in Training and Research

Edited by

Ira Iscoe
University of Texas

Charles D. Spielberger
Florida State University

APPLETON-CENTURY-CROFTS
Educational Division
MEREDITH CORPORATION New York

006240

To our wives, Louise and Adele, whose infinite patience, cooperation, and encouragement we gratefully acknowledge.

Contributors

JOHN ALTROCCHI, Ph.D. Professor of Psychology, Department of Psychology, and Associate Professor of Medical Psychology and Chief of Training, Division of Medical Psychology, Department of Psychiatry, Duke University. Mental Health Consultant, Halifax County, North Carolina.

MORTON BARD, Ph.D. Professor of Psychology and Director, the Psychological Center, the City College, City University of New York.

BERNARD BLOOM, Ph.D. Professor of Psychology, Department of Psychology, University of Colorado, Boulder.

EMORY L. COWEN, Ph.D. Professor of Psychology, Associate Chairman, and Director of Clinical Psychology Training Program, Department of Psychology, and Professor of Psychiatry (Psychology), School of Medicine, University of Rochester, New York.

CARL EISDORFER, Ph.D., M.D. Professor of Medical Psychology and Psychiatry, Department of Psychiatry; Lecturer, Department of Psychology; Director of Training and Research Coordinator, Center for the Study of Aging and Human Development, Duke University Medical Center, Durham, North Carolina. Program Director, Halifax County Community Mental Health Service, Halifax, North Carolina.

STUART E. GOLANN, Ph.D. Associate Administrative Officer for Professional Affairs and Secretary, Committee on Scientific and Professional Ethics and Conduct, American Psychological Association. Formerly Associate Professor of Psychology, University of Maryland.

IRA ISCOE, Ph.D. Professor of Psychology and Education; Director, Graduate Training Program in Community Mental Health, Department of Psychology; Director, Counseling and Psychological Services, the University of Texas, Austin.

DONALD KLEIN, Ph.D. Program Director, Center for Community Affairs of NTL Institute for Applied Behavioral Science, Washington, D. C., and Affiliate, Boston University Human Relations Center. Formerly Associate Professor of Psychology and Director of the Human Relations Center, Boston University.

MURRAY LEVINE, Ph.D. Professor of Psychology and Director, Clinical Psychology Training Program, State University of New York at Buffalo.

HERBERT LIPTON, Ph.D. Associate Professor, Department of Psychology and Human Relations Center, and Faculty Coordinator, Community Psychology Training, Boston University.

KENT MILLER, Ph.D. Professor of Psychology and Sociology and Director, Community Mental Health Research Training Program, Florida State University, Tallahassee.

SYLVAIN NAGLER, Ph.D. Assistant Professor of Psychology, Department of Psychiatry, School of Medicine, Yale University, New Haven, Connecticut.

Formerly postdoctoral trainee in community mental health at South Shore
Mental Health Center, Quincy, Massachusetts.

J. R. NEWBROUGH, Ph.D. Associate Professor of Psychology, George Peabody College, Nashville, Tennessee.

ROBERT REIFF, Ph.D. Associate Professor and Director, Division of Psychology,
Albert Einstein College of Medicine, New York. President, Division of
Community Psychology (27), American Psychological Association.

WILLIAM C. RHODES, Ph.D. Professor of Psychology and Education, the University of Michigan, Ann Arbor.

SHELDON R. ROEN, Ph.D. Associate Professor of Psychology and Education, De-
partment of Psychology, and Director, Psychological Consultation Center,
Teachers College, Columbia University, New York. Editor, *Community
Mental Health Journal.*

SEYMOUR B. SARASON, Ph.D. Professor of Psychology and Director, Psycho-Educational Clinic, Yale University.

JULIUS SEEMAN, Ph.D. Professor of Psychology and Director, Clinical Psychology
Training Program, George Peabody College, Nashville, Tennessee.

JEROME L. SINGER, Ph.D. Professor of Psychology and Director, Clinical Psychology Training Program, City College of the City University of New York.

CHARLES D. SPIELBERGER, Ph.D. Professor of Psychology; Director, Clinical
Psychology Training Program; Director, University Counseling Center,
Florida State University, Tallahassee.

DAVID STEIN, Ph.D. Assistant Professor for Organizational Service, Albert Einstein
College of Medicine, New York. Formerly postdoctoral fellow at Albert
Einstein College of Medicine.

ROBERT TOAL, Ph.D. Associate Professor of Psychology, Department of Psychology, Purdue University. Formerly postdoctoral fellow at Laboratory of
Community Psychiatry, Harvard Medical School.

Contents

Preface

Current conceptions of mental illness and mental health are rapidly undergoing many profound and far-reaching changes. For example, the disease model for mental illness and deviant behavior is being replaced by an interactionist orientation in which the individual, his family, his work, and his community setting are regarded as parts of a system of forces that operate in an interdependent fashion. Socioeconomic and cultural factors that were not previously associated with the field of mental health are now being considered because of their newly discovered importance. Traditional institutional approaches to the treatment of mental illness are giving way to community-based programs, and there are increasing demands for a broader spectrum of services that include genuine preventive and interventive measures.

Numerous challenges are in the air. Positive mental health, once deemed a luxury of the middle class, bids fair to become a stable product in our society. If this is to be accomplished, however, a revolution in the delivery of mental health services will be required, with a higher proportion of energies being devoted to the maintenance of emotional well-being, the improvement of coping mechanisms, and the full utilization of human potential. To meet these new challenges, it will be necessary to construct and devise new theories of human behavior, and new technologies of mental health and human relations. How is the human condition to be studied? Upon what knowledge should new theories and technologies be built? What factors must now be considered that were previously neglected?

The increasing complexity of modern life requires, indeed demands, more knowledge about communities in a complex urban technological society. Of course, recognition of the important role of the community in determining the health and welfare of its citizens is nothing new. However, the attention that is now being given to the community as a unit of social action represents a dramatic change for American psychologists whose behavioristic and psychodynamic orientations have previously constrained them to concentrate upon the intellectual and personality characteristics of individuals. There is also growing recognition among psychologists of the need to look to other social science disciplines, particularly sociology, economics, and political science, for a better understanding of the impact of communities upon people.

The growth of community psychology has been stimulated in part by widespread dissatisfaction with prevailing institutionalized mental health efforts. Serious questions are currently being raised by all of the mental health disciplines regarding the relevance of traditional clinical approaches to mental health problems. While the field of community psychology reflects the expression of dissatisfaction with other approaches, it lacks a coherent body of knowledge of its own and an established set of methods. Consequently, there are as yet few meaningful precedents upon which to base training programs. But this absence of tradition is perhaps one of the greatest strengths of community psychology as an emerging field. Hopefully, it will permit bold steps in new directions, incorporating the best from the old and embodying the most promising of the new.

This volume is concerned primarily with training in community psychology. Its contents are divided into five parts. In Part I, some of the key factors that have contributed to the development of the field of community psychology are enumerated and discussed. The chapters presented in Part II are concerned with conceptual issues relating to training and research in community psychology. Pioneering training programs in community mental health and community psychology that are developing in departments of psychology are described in Part III. In the training programs described in Part IV, psychologists have joined with other disciplines to develop multidisciplinary training programs in community mental health. Part V presents an overview of the present status of training in community psychology and provides some perspective regarding likely future developments in this field.

Through this volume it will be apparent to the reader that there is considerable discontent with existing training models and a great deal of ferment with respect to the kinds of problems psychologists should study and the nature of the settings in which psychologists should work. It will also be apparent that most new training programs in community psychology advocate activist roles in community affairs, which markedly contrast with traditional clinical approaches. Given the rapid changes that are taking place within the field of community mental health, the establishment of new and novel training programs is to be anticipated and welcomed. Hopefully this volume will help delineate and clarify some of the major issues in community psychology and bring information about existing training programs to wider attention.

Most of the chapters in this book were first presented in an informal symposium held at the University of Texas in the spring of 1967. The goals of this symposium were to explore conceptions of training and research in community mental health and community psychology, and to provide an opportunity for the exchange of information among psychologists who were actively engaged in providing training in these areas. The topics, presenters, and participants are listed in Appendix I.

We are indebted to the Hogg Foundation for Mental Health, the National Institute of Mental Health, and the Community Mental Health Training Program at the University of Texas for providing funds to support the informal symposium on which this volume is based. Special thanks are due to Mrs. Betty Cleland for her excellent work as arrangements coordinator and recorder of the symposium, and to her assistant, Mrs. Susan Roos. We are also grateful to Mrs. Cory Kelly, Mrs. Pamela Montford, Mrs. Helen Butler, Mrs. Pam Harrison, Mrs. Carletta Kassover, Sherry Payne, and Carol Hilfiker for their assistance in preparing the manuscript for publication. For coordinating communication with contributing authors and for her general editorial assistance, we are particularly indebted to Mrs. Bertha Shanblum.

I

Psychology and Human Affairs

1

The Emerging Field of Community Psychology

Ira Iscoe and Charles D. Spielberger

Community psychology is but a few years old. Only recently has the need for psychologists to get involved in the affairs of the community been recognized (Brayfield, 1967). Part of the emphasis on involvement seems to stem from the many complex social problems that confront our society. Faced with the realities of urban riots, racial conflicts, student protests and demonstrations, and an increasing disparity between the affluent and the poor, problems such as neuroses and schizophrenia that have long commanded the undivided attention and full energies of the mental health professions now pale by comparison. Evidence of social unrest—for example, school dropouts, juvenile delinquency, drug abuse, the sexual revolution, crime in the streets, civil disobedience—testify to the tremendous stresses being placed on the human condition and on the relationships between individuals and groups.

Psychology is, after all, the science of behavior, and psychologists are called upon with increasing frequency to lend their skills in explaining society's problems. They are also being asked to provide solutions to, or at least to help ameliorate, some of these problems. It is now common practice for congressional committees to request the American Psychological Association (APA) to testify on issues of social import and for community leaders to call upon individual psychologists for consultation regarding their own brand of problems. These requests for more active involvement and participation in community affairs create considerable conflict and discomfort in a discipline that has modeled its scientific work according to the traditions of the physics laboratory and that has emulated the medical model in its clinical applications.

While some psychologists have studied communities and worked in community settings, most are still unfamiliar with community concepts. Because there are few precedents for the active involvement and cooperation of university psychologists in community affairs, it is not surprising that the course content and practicum experiences provided in psychology training programs contain little that will prepare the next generation of psychologists for the new roles and the complex social demands that are already discernible. True, bridges have been extended from departments of psychology into the outside world, but crossing these and returning safely is by no means easy, and such journeys are rarely sanctioned by academic psychologists.

As an academic discipline, psychology is justifiably proud of its scientific roots and its resistance to the styles and fads of the marketplace. This is as it should be. But, more and more, psychologists who are seriously concerned with the problems of man, his hang-ups, and his aspirations, have come to believe that theories based largely on studies of laboratory animals and college sophomores must be tested in a wider context. More and more, the value of psychological theory is being judged in terms of its predictive potential in community settings.

Added pressures no doubt will continue to contribute to the growing interest in community psychology. For more than two decades a substantial portion of the financial support available for training and research in psychology has come from one government agency or another, and especially from the Veterans Administration and the National Institute of Mental Health. But it is asked more and more, "What has all this spending accomplished?" And increasing criticism is leveled at the limited applicability of psychological research to community problems. Society demands returns on its investments, and rightly so.

How do psychology's research contributions compare with those in other areas? It is well known that biomedical research has led to important discoveries that have resulted in significant improvements in medical treatment and general health care. In agriculture the applications of research findings have produced fantastic increases in productivity. In contrast, an objective evaluation of the consequences of social science research provides little evidence of tangible contributions to solving the pressing problems of our day. Certainly more is known than has been effectively used, but much more knowledge must be generated, and competent professionals must be trained to utilize this knowledge. To achieve these goals, psychologists must join with other mental health and social science disciplines to provide a better understanding of communities and how they can be made better places in which people can live in harmony as creative and productive citizens.

If psychology is to contribute to meeting the challenges of modern life, existing training programs must be modified and new programs planned and implemented. In establishing these new programs it will be important to understand where we have been and to determine, as best we can, where we are going. Earlier training efforts, particularly those in clinical psychology, should not be neglected, and new programs should recognize and retain whatever has proved effective. Awareness of past experiences should enable us to develop more adequate programs for meeting future mental health needs.

A brief review of some important factors that have influenced the evolution and development of psychology as a profession may provide a useful perspective for evaluating new training programs in the emerging field of community psychology. For more detailed treatments of historical trends in clinical and community psychology, the excellent introductory chapters in recent books by Sarason, Levine, Goldenberg, Cherlin, and Bennett (1966) and Cowen, Gardner, and Zax (1967) are recommended.

FACTORS THAT HAVE INFLUENCED THE DEVELOPMENT OF PROFESSIONAL PSYCHOLOGY

Prior to World War II, psychology was largely an academic discipline. Most psychologists worked in university settings and were concerned primarily with teaching and research. A few psychologists were associated with mental hospitals and child guidance clinics, but their responsibilities were generally limited to the administration and interpretation of psychological tests. After World War II, in response to urgent demands to provide care for thousands of military psychiatric casualties, the need to develop training programs in clinical psychology was widely recognized. Aided by financial support from the Veterans Administration, and later from the National Institute of Mental Health, clinical psychology training programs were developed at many universities, and these programs attracted large numbers of graduate students.

The rapid growth in clinical psychology after World War II led the American Psychological Association to convene a national conference on training in this area in 1949. This conference, which was held at the University of Colorado (Boulder), resulted in the establishment of criteria for a scientist-professional model for graduate training in clinical psychology. The so-called Boulder Model required doctoral programs in clinical psychology to provide training in diagnosis and psychotherapy along with training in research and basic psychology. This model has been subsequently reaffirmed at three national conferences (Strother, 1956; Roe, Gustad, Moore, Ross, & Skodak, 1959; Hoch, Ross, & Winder, 1966).

Although the Boulder Model continues to provide a basic orientation and general guidelines for more than 70 APA-approved doctoral training programs in clinical psychology, conceptions of the causality and treatment of mental illness have undergone radical change in recent years. Growing concern about mental health and mental illness, and mounting evidence of unmet mental health needs, led Congress to appoint a commission to survey the nation's mental health resources and make specific recommendations for combating mental illness. The findings in the studies conducted by this commission have profound implications for training in all of the mental health disciplines. Some of the major findings are of paramount significance for community psychology; these are briefly reviewed in the next section.

THE JOINT COMMISSION REPORTS

The Joint Commission on Mental Health and Mental Illness was established by Congress in 1955. Significantly, the central concern of the commission was in "improving the mental health of the mentally ill," rather than in preventing mental disorders (Ewalt, 1961). Furthermore, such areas as alcoholism, juvenile delinquency, mental retardation, and many other problems generally acknowledged to be associated with the mental health field were given little consideration. But despite these limitations the studies conducted under the commission's sponsorship must be regarded as landmarks of considerable significance for the development of community psychology. While several of these studies with important implications for training in community psychology are mentioned below, anyone seriously interested in this field will want to review all of the commission's publications.

Robinson, DeMarche, and Wagle (1960) compiled data on the available mental health resources in more than 3,000 counties in the continental United States and conducted intensive field investigations in 15 representative counties. Their findings were distressing, and they have not been given sufficient attention. For example, services to children were lacking in almost half of the nation's counties. In the 15 representative counties psychological services to child welfare agencies were virtually absent. Less than a quarter of the nation's counties had mental health clinics, and long waiting lists were generally encountered at most clinics. Services designed to meet the needs of racial and ethnic minority groups were lacking, and there was little evidence of coordination in the delivery of mental health services.

In another Joint Commission study Gurin, Veroff, and Feld (1960) investigated the attitudes and feelings about marriage, parenthood, and work of a representative sample of the nation's adult population. Results were reported in terms of the major crises that beset human beings at certain periods in their lives and the persons to whom they typically turn for assistance in times of trouble. Clergymen appear to be the professional group from whom people most often seek help during crises. Furthermore, the lower the educational level of the person in difficulty, the more likely he is to call upon his minister for assistance. The results of this study also revealed that the utilization of mental health resources was significantly determined by socioeconomic factors, and that mental health services were not generally available to the lower classes. One of the major implications of this study was that mental health services must be tailored to the needs of the people for whom the services are intended, rather than to the convenience of the mental health professions.

Albee's (1959) extensive and detailed survey of mental health manpower is one of the most significant studies conducted under the auspices of the Joint Commission. On the basis of his analyses and extrapolations of manpower trends, Albee accurately forecast the present shortages in mental health manpower, and he challenged prevailing conceptions regarding the delivery of mental health services. He also urged that research and preventive efforts be greatly expanded, and that the therapeutic manpower base be broadened. In Albee's words:

> What we need are techniques and methods enabling far more people to be reached per professional person. If we do not at present have such techniques then we should spend time looking for them. The logic of the manpower situation in which we find ourselves makes other solutions unrealistic.
>
> Any efficient utilization of mental health personnel probably is going to involve something other than time-consuming, face-to-face relationships between a single professional person and a single patient. The number of people who need help and the number of people prepared to give help are so out of proportion that time and arithmetic will not permit such individual face-to-face approaches to be meaningful from a logistics point of view. . . . Just as typhoid fever was never brought under control by treating individual cases of the disease, but rather by discovering and taking steps to remove the source of the disease, so we may find that time might be spent more effectively in prevention, in research, or in public health approaches to mental disorder. (p. 254)

The entire series of Joint Commission studies produced is summarized in its final report, *Action for Mental Health* (Ewalt, 1961). This title is somewhat misleading in that the emphasis is focused on the treatment of major mental illness, rather than on the promotion of mental health. However, the report did recognize the need to broaden the base of therapeutic manpower and to utilize existing knowledge more effectively. It also recommended that new psychiatric facilities be developed in general hospitals and community settings and that educational and consultative services be expanded.

Given the limitations in available mental health resources (Robinson *et al.*, 1960), the shortages in mental health manpower (Albee, 1959), and the fact that existing resources are either not readily available or not used by large segments of the population (Gurin *et al.*, 1960), it would seem that the commission's emphasis on providing treatment for the mentally ill may not be a realistic approach to meeting community mental health needs. In the past two decades, however, a number of develop-

ments within psychiatry have been concerned with utilizing more fully
the resources of the entire community in dealing with the problems of
mental health and mental illness.

COMMUNITY PSYCHIATRY AND COMMUNITY MENTAL HEALTH

With regard to the factors that have influenced community psychology, no historical perspective would be complete that
failed to note the work of two psychiatrists, Erich Lindemann, at the
Harvard Medical School and the Massachusetts General Hospital, and
Gerald Caplan, first at the Harvard School of Public Health and later the
director of Harvard's Laboratory of Community Psychiatry. As a result of
their innovative and pioneering programs community psychiatry has become an essential part of the training of many psychiatrists, psychologists,
and social workers, and mental health consultation has been added as an
important new dimension to therapeutic endeavors.

On the basis of his studies of grief reactions Lindemann developed a
"crisis theory" of therapeutic intervention. According to this theory,
human crises provide opportunities for emotional growth and for the
effective introduction of preventive mental health measures. In establishing the Wellesley (Massachusetts) Human Relations Service, Lindemann
and his colleagues were able to bring crisis consultation closer to the
community. This unique setting also provided the resources for a multidisciplinary training program that served to bring the significance of the
community in mental health into clearer focus.

Caplan has trained psychiatrists and other mental health professionals in the techniques of mental health consultation with community
caregivers such as teachers, nurses, ministers, and even parents. In his
writings Caplan has contributed significant insights into various issues
which relate to theory and training in mental health consultaton and
community psychiatry (Caplan, 1956, 1959a, 1959b, 1961, 1963, 1964,
1965a, 1965b). His approach, with its focus on the professional caregiver
rather than on their patients or clients, represents a marked departure
from the traditional clinical roles of the mental health professions. A
number of psychologists have received postdoctoral training in the programs directed by Lindemann and Caplan, and the impact of this training
on their contributions to the emerging field of community psychology is
already apparent. It is certainly no accident that the authors or coauthors
of more than half of the chapters in this volume have been associated in
some way with the programs of Lindemann and Caplan.

While Lindemann and Caplan developed procedures that extend
mental health services into the community through consultation with

caregiver groups, other psychiatrists and social scientists have been concerned with obtaining a better understanding of the community forces that produce mental disorders and social pathology. In *The Urban Condition* (Duhl, 1963), the relationship between problems of mental health and urbanization are considered in depth by psychiatrists and social scientists. The careful reader will note a tone of desperation in the discussions of breakdowns in traditional urban barriers that have resulted in civil disobedience and riots and the increasing alienation of the individual in American society. The need to generate knowledge about the psychological and motivational aspects of such problems as poverty, juvenile delinquency, and increasing crime rates is urgent, and the implications of these problems for community mental health can no longer be ignored.

In 1963, Congress passed the Mental Health Facilities Act which provided for the establishment of comprehensive community mental health centers throughout the nation. Mental health consultation was included as one of the essential services to be furnished by these new centers. The Facilities Act was later amended to provide support for staff as well as for construction. For the first time in the history of the mental health movement the focus of treatment was ostensibly to be in the community as contrasted to the mental hospital. It is one of the ironies of history that John F. Kennedy was the first President to deliver a message to Congress specifically dealing with the mental health of the nation. His assassin had, at an early age, displayed a high degree of emotional instability and a serious reading disorder.

To date, over 300 comprehensive community mental health centers have been established, but many of them have found it difficult to recruit adequate staff. Even in the face of manpower problems, however, traditional services tend to be emphasized rather than preventative and consultative roles. Many comprehensive mental health centers are now being criticized for their long waiting lists and lack of community orientation, and dissatisfaction with the relationship between the new centers and the communities they serve has been expressed by community leaders and professional groups. In fact the first position paper ever issued by the APA pointed to the need for community involvement and community control of comprehensive mental health centers.

THE APA POSITION PAPER ON THE COMMUNITY AND THE COMMUNITY MENTAL HEALTH CENTER

A position paper on comprehensive mental health centers was approved by the APA Council of Representatives in March, 1966. It was drafted by M. Brewster Smith and Nicholas Hobbs (Smith & Hobbs, 1966) after extensive consultation with numerous psychologists throughout the country. The major position taken in this paper is that community representatives must be actively involved in setting goals and determining basic policies for comprehensive mental health centers if these centers are to be effective community agencies. The need to develop approaches to community mental health problems that are substantially different from traditional clinical approaches is also stressed. The position paper states:

> . . . the objective of the center staff should be to help the various social systems of which the community is composed to function in ways that develop and sustain the effectiveness of the individuals who take part in them, and to help these community systems regroup their forces to support the person who runs into trouble. The community is not just a "catchment area" from which patients are drawn; the task of a community mental health center goes far beyond that of purveying professional services to disordered people on a local basis.
>
> The more closely the proposed centers become integrated with the life and institutions of their communities, the less the community can afford to turn over to mental health professionals its responsibility for guiding the center's policies. Professional standards need to be established for the centers by Federal and state authorities, but goals and basic policies are a matter for local control. A broadly based responsible board of informed leaders should help to ensure that the center serves in deed, not just in name, as a focus of the community's varied efforts on behalf of the greater effectiveness and fulfillment of all its residents. (Smith & Hobbs, 1966, pp. 500–501)

The emphasis on social systems and social processes within the community—for example, schools and neighborhoods—recognizes the complexity of communities and points up the need for comprehensive mental health programs to promote mental health as well as to prevent and treat mental illness. Consistent with this emphasis on prevention, the APA position paper also recommends that comprehensive mental health centers devote at least half of their services to children and youth and those who work closely with children.

For psychologists the prospect of community involvement poses both a threat and a challenge. With but a few exceptions, notably some of the programs described in this volume, the graduate training of psychologists contains little that will prepare them to understand community problems and work effectively in community settings. Consequently, if psychologists are to be involved in community affairs, as indeed they must be if the recommendations of the APA position paper are taken seriously, then training programs in psychology must provide students with opportunities to learn about social systems and the sociopolitical realities that must be confronted by those who work in community settings.

RECENT DEVELOPMENTS IN PSYCHOLOGY

Within the past decade a number of developments out-
side of the mental health fields have greatly influenced the professional
activities of psychologists. For example, legislation introduced during the
term of President Kennedy led to a greater general awareness of the problems of poverty and cultural deprivation and to the founding of the Peace
Corps, in which psychologists have had an active role. The problems of
poverty and cultural deprivation were the major concern of the Great
Society legislation introduced by President Johnson and passed by the
Congress. Under the auspices of the Office of Economic Opportunity,
which was established in 1964, a number of community action programs
were developed to combat these problems. In such programs as Head
Start, Upward Bound, Day Care, VISTA (the domestic peace corps), and
the Neighborhood Youth Corps community participation is emphasized.
Psychologists have been called upon to participate in all of these programs
and they have played an especially important role in program evaluation.

The impact of community action programs, along with the increasing
participation of psychologists in mental health consultation and community-oriented mental health programs, has highlighted the need for
appropriate training in these areas. In the spring of 1965, a conference on
the "Education of Psychologists for Community Mental Health" was held
in Swampscott, Massachusetts; it was jointly sponsored by Boston University and the South Shore Mental Health Center (Quincy, Massachusetts)
and supported by a grant from the National Institute of Mental Health.
At this conference, now generally referred to as the Boston Conference,
the participants' initial concerns with community mental health were
broadened to a more general interest in communities and their problems.
By the end of the conference the participants had concluded that the
term "community mental health" reflected a sort of "me-too-ism" and that
it was time for psychologists to accept the responsibility for defining their
own unique roles within the mental health field.

Consistent with these sentiments the term "community psychology"
was coined at the Boston Conference to apply to a broader conception of
the role of psychologists in community affairs. Within this broader conceptual framework community mental health was to be subsumed as a
subspecialty of community psychology, with clinical psychology as a
variant of community mental health. There was also strong affirmation of
the need to give attention to genuine preventive measures and clear recognition of the need to reckon with the logistics of mental health manpower.

The participants in the Boston Conference felt that in order to meet the nation's mental health needs we must back off from the incessant demands for clinical services, and that the community as a social system must be examined, as well as the problems of individual patients and clients who are casualties of the system. It also was agreed that new knowledge about communities must be generated so that effective preventive mental health measures can be instituted and innovative uses made of available mental health resources. A strong sense of futility was voiced with regard to the possibility that the nation's mental needs could be met with prevailing clinical approaches. In effect, the Boston Conference permitted the expression of accumulated dissatisfaction with traditional approaches and provided a rallying point for the presentation of many new ideas about how psychologists could participate and contribute to the betterment of the human condition.

Most conferences generate passing enthusiasm which dissipates when conferees return to their homes. The Boston Conference was different. Whether this was due to the commitment of the participants, the superb organization of the agenda, the timeliness of the issues discussed, or some combination of factors, it is not possible to determine. However, there can be no doubt that this conference greatly stimulated and contributed to the development of community psychology.

Following the Boston Conference a number of informal meetings were held to discuss the feasibility of forming a division of community psychology within the structure of the American Psychological Association. Most of these meetings were organized and led by participants at the Boston Conference. Petitions were distributed to interested APA members and a divisional organization meeting was held in September, 1966, at the APA convention. Division 27, the Division of Community Psychology, was officially approved by the APA Council of Representatives at its annual meeting in September, 1967, with Robert Reiff as its first president. It is interesting to note that the majority of the charter members of Division 27 were not Young Turks. Rather, a high percentage came from senior persons in the field, many of them with ABEPP diplomas in clinical psychology and responsible positions in institutional and university settings. By September, 1968, the membership of Division 27 numbered more than 700 psychologists, and this rapid early growth promises to continue in the future.

The report of the Boston Conference (Bennett, 1966) also greatly stimulated psychologists' interest in training for community mental health and community psychology. Courses and practicum experiences are increasingly evident in university psychology departments and in field training and internship settings. In order to provide an opportunity for the exchange of ideas among psychologists centrally involved in these training programs, an informal symposium on training in community psychology was held at the University of Texas in the spring of 1967. This symposium centered around the presentation of invited papers on conceptual issues relating to the philosophy and goals of training and research in community psychology, and descriptions of actual training programs with significant community psychology content. Many of the chapters included in this volume were first presented at the Texas symposium, which is described briefly in Appendix I.

AN OVERVIEW OF THIS VOLUME

This book is concerned with issues that relate to training and research in community psychology. It is divided into five parts. In this first Part some of the historical developments and pressing social needs that have contributed to the emergence of community psychology are described. Part II is mainly concerned with conceptual issues in community psychology and with clarification of some of the differences between traditional and community-oriented approaches to mental health problems. In Part III, five programs are described in which training in community psychology is provided within the context of doctoral programs in clinical psychology. The chapters in Part IV discuss multidisciplinary training and research programs in community mental health and community psychology. The current status and future prospects for training and research in community psychology are considered in Part V.

In the first of the five chapters in Part II, Reiff (Chapter 2) contrasts psychodynamic and community-oriented approaches to contemporary psychological problems and makes a strong case for the need to develop a body of knowledge unique to community psychology. Golann, in Chapter 3, presents an analysis of some basic differences between traditional and community-oriented approaches to mental health problems and introduces a useful model within which to consider mental health programs and services. He also presents the results of a recent survey of graduate training in community psychology. In Chapter 4, Roen examines graduate education in psychology in the light of recent developments in the community mental health field and advances a number of propositions regarding requirements for training in this area. In the final chapter in this section, Levine contends that current theories regarding the causality of mental illness and emotional disturbance overestimate the importance of intrapsychic variables and underestimate the significance of environmental events. He proposes a set of postulates to guide the practice of community psychology that give appropriate emphasis to situational factors.

Part III describes training in community mental health and community psychology that is presently provided within a number of clinical psychology training programs. In Chapter 6, Newbrough, Rhodes, and Seeman present a historical account of the development of training in community psychology at George Peabody College. This chapter provides an excellent example of the complex interplay between men and ideas in the evolution of a community-oriented mental health training program. Cowen, in Chapter 7, describes a year-long practicum experience designed to give graduate students in clinical psychology firsthand contact with important community problems. A recently established, innovative training program in clinical psychology is described by Singer and Bard in Chapter 8. In this program graduate students at the City University of New York receive intensive training in a Psychological Services Center that works with many different professional groups in dealing with neighborhood and community problems. Sarason and Levine, in Chapter 9, describe a unique community-oriented service and research facility, the Yale University Psycho-Educational Clinic. Staffed by psychologists on the Yale faculty and graduate students in clinical psychology, the philosophy of the Psycho-Educational Clinic is to work with other professionals in the settings where the problems occur, rather than to work directly with clients on a one-to-one basis at the clinic. In the final chapter of Part III, Bloom discusses a sequence of courses on community mental health recently introduced at the University of Colorado. Some of the advantages and disadvantages in the establishment of community mental health as a special area of training are considered, as is the relationship between this area and other graduate programs in psychology.

The chapters in Part IV present descriptions of multidisciplinary training programs in community mental health and community psychology. In Chapter 11, Iscoe describes a new program at the University of Texas in which graduate students in psychology and education are trained to work with mental health problems in a variety of community settings. Training in techniques of mental health consultation is emphasized in the Texas program. Altrocchi and Eisdorfer, in Chapter 12, describe a field training program in mental health consultation at the Duke University Medical Center. Based on an apprentice-collaborator model, this program provides psychiatric residents and interns and graduate students in psychology with an exciting and unusual opportunity to observe and participate in an ongoing mental health consultation program in a rural setting. The Boston University training program in community mental health, described by Lipton and Klein in Chapter 13, brings together graduate students from many different areas to work on community problems in a multidisciplinary setting. A special feature of this program is the diverse background and interests of the trainees who often come from disciplines not traditionally associated with mental health. In the final chapter in Part IV, Miller describes a program in which doctoral students in sociology obtain research training in the community mental health area. Miller also discusses a number of general definitional and conceptual problems that pertain to research in community mental health, and he provides specific examples of several dissertation problems undertaken by his students that have important implications for community psychology.

Although this volume is concerned primarily with issues and problems that relate to training and research in community psychology at the predoctoral level, the experiences of three recent graduates of postdoctoral training programs are described in Appendix II. The program at the South Shore Mental Health Center in Quincy, Massachusetts, is described by Sylvain Nagler; David D. Stein, a postdoctoral trainee at the Albert Einstein College of Medicine, describes the training that he recently completed; and Robert Toal discusses his postdoctoral training at the Harvard Laboratory of Community Psychiatry.

The reader will discern an activist orientation in the training programs described in this volume. Indeed, the enthusiasm of the various authors sometimes takes on an evangelical tone which perhaps accounts for the rapid emergence of community psychology as an exciting and vital movement within psychology. It is hoped that the contents of this book will help to clarify problems and issues in community psychology and that it will serve to stimulate thought and action with regard to training community-oriented psychologists who will have the knowledge and skills to contribute effectively to the betterment of the human condition.

REFERENCES

Albee, G. *Mental health manpower trends.* New York: Basic Books, 1959.

Bennett, C. C., Anderson, L. S., Cooper, S., Hassol, L., Klein, D. C., & Rosenblum, G. (Eds.). *Community psychology: A report of the Boston conference on the education of psychologists for community mental health.* Boston: Boston University Press, 1966.

Brayfield, A. Psychology and public affairs. *American Psychologist,* 1967, 22, 182–187.

Caplan, G. Mental health consultation in the schools. In *The elements of a community mental health program.* New York: Milbank Memorial Fund, 1956. Pp. 77–85.

Caplan, G. *Concepts of mental health and consultation.* Children's Bureau Public. No. 373, Washington, D. C.: U. S. Dept. of H.E.W., 1959. (a)

Caplan, G. An approach to the education of community mental health specialists. *Mental Hygiene,* 1959, 43, 268–80. (b)

Caplan, G. *An approach to community mental health.* New York: Grune & Stratton, 1961.

Caplan, G. Types of mental health consultation. *American Journal of Orthopsychiatry,* 1963, 33, 470–481.

Caplan, G. *Principles of preventive psychiatry.* New York: Basic Books, 1964.

Caplan, G. Community psychiatry—Introduction and overview. In S. E. Goldston (Ed.), *Concepts of community psychiatry: A framework for training.*

U. S. Public Health Serv. Public. No. 1319. Bethesda, Md.: U. S. Dept. of H.E.W., 1965. Pp. 91–108. (a)

Caplan, G. Problems of training in mental health consultation. In S. E. Goldston (Ed.), *Concepts of community psychiatry: A framework for training.* *Op. cit.* Pp. 3–18. (b)

Cowen, E. L., Gardner, E. A., & Zax, M. *Emergent approaches to mental health.* New York: Appleton-Century-Crofts, 1967.

Duhl, L. (Ed.), *The urban condition: People and policy in the metropolis.* New York: Basic Books, 1963.

Ewalt, J. *Action for mental health.* New York: Basic Books, 1961.

Gurin, G., Veroff, J., & Feld, S. *Americans view their mental health.* New York: Basic Books, 1960.

Hoch, E. L., Ross, A. O., & Winder, C. L. (Eds.). *Professional preparation of clinical psychologists* (Chicago Conference). Washington, D. C.: American Psychological Association, 1966.

Robinson, R., DeMarche, D. F., & Wagle, Mildred. *Community resources in mental health.* New York: Basic Books, 1960.

Roe, Anne, Gustad, J. W., Moore, B. V., Ross, S., & Skodak, Marie (Eds.). *Graduate education in psychology* (Miami Conference). Washington, D. C.: American Psychological Association, 1959.

Sarason, S., Levine, M., Goldenberg, I., Cherlin, D. L., & Bennett, E. M. *Psychology in community settings.* New York: Wiley, 1966.

Smith, M. B., & Hobbs, N. The community and the community mental health center. *American Psychologist,* 1966, **21**, 409–509.

Strother, C. R. *Psychology and mental health* (Stanford Conference). Washington, D. C.: American Psychological Association, 1956.

II

Community Psychology, Community Mental Health, and Social Needs

2

The Need for a Body of Knowledge in Community Psychology

Robert Reiff

When we consider how new ideas are created and developed, we are prone to think that they issue forth from some creative mind in the manner of an immaculate conception. But new ideas are often the delayed responses to social forces which have for some time been preparing men's minds to create them. The concept of community psychology is such an idea. At the Swampscott Conference (Swampscott, Massachusetts, May 4–8, 1965), where the concept of community psychology emerged, 35 colleagues from all over the country found themselves in almost unanimous agreement on a new role for psychologists, a role which each by himself had been fashioning for some time. How did this miracle occur?

If one examines the major social legislation of the last few years, particularly in the area of social services, one finds a common element running through the diverse programs. The Community Mental Health Services Act provided by law for the participation of citizen consumer groups in the planning of mental health services. The antipoverty bill soon followed with a large community action component which proclaimed that "maximum feasible participation" by the poor was an essential feature of all funded programs. Soon after there began the development of what has since become the nonprofessional and new careers movement. More recently, the Demonstration Cities Act explicitly requires that the citizen-consumer participate in all planning and program implementation. The one theme which runs through all of these programs is the involvement of the poor and the disenfranchised in determining the nature of specific social measures and in carrying them out. This idea of citizen participation in social planning is one of the central themes of the social reform movement of the last few years. It did not

This chapter is a revised version of a paper which appeared in the *American Psychologist* [1968, 23(7): 524–531], and is reproduced with permission of the American Psychological Association.

spring fully grown from the brow of social reformers, but developed as a result of social needs, partly in response to the civil rights movement and partly as a strategy to arouse an effective demand for new services on the part of the disenfranchised.

The impact of this social reform movement created ferment and change in psychology. New programs opened up new opportunities for psychologists, and the theme of citizen participation stimulated an increased desire for professional participation in social planning and social change. Community psychology became the conceptual and organizational expression of that desire.

This is a good illustration of how social forces of which we are often unaware affect our professional ideology and practice. It is well to keep in mind that psychology itself is not exempt from the principle that social forces play a role in determining human behavior, a principle which can fairly be called the basic postulate of community psychology.

CONCEPTIONS OF COMMUNITY PSYCHOLOGY

The concept of community psychology which emerged from the Swampscott Conference stressed the many new programs and roles opening up for psychologists in social action programs. These new roles often placed the psychologist in the position of a social interventionist whose primary task was to intervene at the social system level in order to modify human behavior. The social system, it was pointed out, might be a family, an organization, an institution, a neighborhood, a community, or a nation. The conference also suggested that new training programs and a new body of knowledge were needed and expressed the hope that these might eventually result in a new kind of psychologist.

There were basically three new ideas in this concept of community psychology. One was the emphasis on social system intervention to change individual behavior. The second was concern that social system intervention go beyond the individual clinical case toward modifying the behavior of many people in a system. The third new idea was the concept of the participant-conceptualizer, which stresses the activist component in professional life. It emphasized that only by participation and involvement could the psychologist enrich the theory and technology of social intervention. The intent of the conference participants was clearly that a community psychologist would be a new kind of psychologist, a generalist, skilled in all these components.

Since the Swampscott Conference there has been much discussion about the necessity for community psychology to develop a new body of knowledge. However, what is meant by the expression a "new body of knowledge" often seems vague and confusing. It is essential to clarify what kind of knowledge we are talking about because that decision may determine what community psychology is to become.

It is well to keep in mind that there are different levels of knowledge. One is the level of technology, a set of skills that can be taught to trainees who wish to function as consultants in the community. It is true that developing a body of knowledge at the practical level is essential. But we cannot be content with simply developing practical art. Community psychology must develop its own body of theory as well as unique skills and technology. At the present time community psychology can be described as a union of psychologists working in community settings, but it has the potential of going beyond this, however, and of truly becoming a school of psychology. This is not the expression of an ambitious dream or the declaration of an idea. It is the recognition of an essential need if we are to achieve our major goal of intervening successfully in social systems to unify human behavior. It is essential because the nature of the practice of community psychology confronts us at once with the inadequacies and deficiencies of existing conceptual models.

The community psychologist who comes out of clinical psychology and practices in a community mental health setting will immediately be confronted with a number of basic weaknesses in his conceptual framework. The first of these is the failure of modern psychiatric theory to give sufficient consideration to the social determinants of individual behavior. Under the influence of psychoanalysis, clinicians tend to look upon behavior as being primarily determined by the inner dynamics of the individual. Even when they have the intention of considering social factors, the word "social" is usually translated into "interpersonal" and nonpersonal social factors are left outside the realm and content of psychology. Such tangible social conditions as housing and transportation, or even such nontangible social conditions as literacy and free speech, play little or no role in the clinician's conceptualizations of individual behavior. If they are considered at all, they are thought to be nothing more than the setting or context in which the psychodynamic forces play out their vicissitudes and destinies. There may be some of us who do not think that sleeping in a rat-infested apartment is as damaging to the ego as an oedipal wish or that being illiterate in a literate society can be as tension- and anxiety-producing as the frustration of dependency needs. But we can no longer avoid taking these factors into account the moment we step into the community with the aim of intervening in a social system.

Another conceptual weakness of modern psychiatry is the tendency to extend the concepts of individual psychodynamics to all social phenomena. Wars, strikes, riots, political movements are all explained either in terms of individual psychodynamics or by analogy with them. The community psychologist is confronted with such concepts as "sick communities," "castrated peoples," and "pathological families," all of which contribute nothing to his understanding of a community, a family, or a political struggle. He is faced with the necessity of developing new concepts which enable him to differentiate the dynamics of social systems from those of the individual.

Perhaps the most important conceptual weakness that confronts community psychologists is the psychiatric illness model. The shortcomings of the illness model have been discussed before (Reiff, 1966). Alternatives have been offered and some have attractive features, but none of them takes us beyond the illness model in answering the basic problem. Put simply, that problem is "What is mental illness and mental health?" It is proposed, for example, that we substitute the concept of effectiveness for the illness model (White, 1959; Knutson, 1963). This concept is certainly helpful in dealing with so-called healthy people— people who are functioning adequately in the environment and who do not manifest the common symptoms of emotional disturbance. However, there are many, many people who come under the rubric of mental illness. People who are acutely or chronically disturbed and need some sort of help or treatment are good candidates for drug therapy and the services of a physician or psychiatrist. There is no need, therefore, to deny the fact of mental illness. The difficulty lies not in the fact but in the concept of mental illness which is contained in what we have called the "psychiatric illness model." We are using this somewhat clumsy term in order to make manifest a distinction ordinarily concealed in the more commonly used general term, the "illness model"—a distinction between the medical model of illness and the psychiatric model. Although psychiatry makes much of the fact that it is part of medicine, its conceptual system is the very opposite of that of medicine.

There are at least three basic differences between the conceptual model of medicine and the psychiatric illness model. The first difference is in their approach to illness and health. Any competent physician can tell you what the normal limits of functioning are for the circulatory system, the digestive system, and the other systems of the human body. Normality is the equivalent of health, and illness is diagnosed on the basis of a breakdown of normality. In the psychiatric model all human behavior is measured against standards derived from the behavior of the mentally ill. No other field of physical, natural, or social science derives its concepts about the nature of the phenomena it studies by extrapolating from the atypical to the typical.

The second difference between the medical and psychiatric conceptual models is in their approach to abnormality. One dictionary defines abnormal as "not average, typical, or usual, deviating from a standard, extremely or excessively large." Another dictionary defines abnormal as "deviating from a type, contrary to rule or system, unusual." But no dictionary defines abnormal as pathological, or ill. In medicine the dictionary definition generally applies: abnormality is not necessarily associated with illness. A seven-foot basketball player may exhibit abnormal growth but he is not considered ill. An obese man or woman may be abnormally heavy but not necessarily ill. It is true, of course, that certain abnormalities are the result of pathology while others may increase the potential for becoming ill but are not in themselves pathological. And still another class of abnormalities are simply deviations from the normal in a healthy organism. In the psychiatric model, however, abnormality is equated with illness, and the differences in both degree and kind of abnormality are reduced to differences in degree and kind of illness.

This brings us to the concept of deviancy. As we have pointed out, the medical model views certain deviations from the normal as abnormalities without the implication of illness. The psychiatric model has created much confusion and controversy with its formula "behavioral deviancy equals abnormality equals illness." It is precisely because of this formula that there is so much difficulty with the concept of deviancy. A conceptual system is needed that will enable us to differentiate the healthy from the ill, the normal from the abnormal, and the deviant from the typical. Furthermore, this system should not require the equation of abnormality and deviancy with illness. With such a model the juvenile delinquent, the hippy, and the criminal may be seen as different, even abnormal, but not necessarily pathological. We can thus move beyond the fruitless notion of considering them "sick" members of society and view them instead as members of social subsystems whose behavior may or may not be abnormal or deviant within these subsystems.

The best way for community psychology to begin developing such a model is to study the process by which a social system defines normal, abnormal, and deviant. Once we have learned the process by which the system defines normality we will be in a better position to understand what is meant by abnormality, and to develop more adequate concepts of the parameters of mental illness.

These are some of the problems that will confront community psychologists as they attempt to intervene in social systems to modify individual behavior. But these are not problems peculiar to community psychology. They are community psychology's version of problems in the general field of psychology, the implications of which not only set the task for community psychology but define the task for clinical psychology as well.

CONCEPTION OF SOCIAL INTERVENTION

Let us now turn to another problem which confronts the social system interventionist. As community psychologists we are interested in developing concepts and techniques for successfully intervening in a social system for the purpose of modifying the behavior of the aggregate of individuals in that system. This task is qualitatively different from the one we have been discussing.

It is one thing to intervene in a system—a family, for example, on behalf of an individual in that system, let us say a schizophrenic child. It is a totally different matter to intervene in a system—the ghetto, for example, on behalf of an aggregate of people in that system, let us say all the Negro children. In the first instance the primary object of the intervention is an individual; in the second instance the primary object is an aggregate of individuals. This is a point about which there is considerable confusion in community psychology today. We speak of social system intervention as though there were only one kind. We seem to assume that the same techniques of social intervention that have individuals as their primary object apply equally as well when an aggregate of people is the primary object. When we speak of a body of theory, a set of concepts about social intervention, we seem to imply that a single set of concepts will be adequate for both problems. But we know enough already from clinical psychology and social psychology to understand that we are dealing with different levels of behavior that require different conceptualizations.

The matter is further complicated by the fact that we are interested in many different forms of behavior exhibited by an aggregate of people in a system, ranging from institutionalized behavior such as class-based patterns of child rearing to noninstitutionalized forms of collective behavior such as riots. We are also interested in many different kinds of aggregates including mobs and crowds as well as mass movements and classes. In this area, more than any other, we are confronted with the inadequacies of existing concepts. In fact, this area of group behavior appears to be the most fuzzy and the least developed in psychology as a whole. Yet this is the particular area of social intervention in which many of us see the future of community psychology and in which there is the greatest social need. But at the present time our intent is nothing more than a promise, and unless we fill the gap between promise and performance quickly, unless we gain some elementary skills and knowledge, this aspect of community psychology is likely to fade away.

Because intervention with aggregates of people is so important to community psychology, let us illustrate how one might look at a serious social problem in order to make a beginning in identifying at least some of the conceptual tasks ahead of us. We have selected the riots of the summer of 1957 as the problem, not to provide answers as to the causes of the riots but simply to encourage a different way of looking at this social phenomenon.

The New York *Times* of Sunday, August 6, 1967, reported a number of public statements elicited from psychologists and psychiatrists about the recent riots. A number of commentators volunteered an "explanation" of the psychological factors which contributed to the riots. Some of the psychological factors mentioned were:

1. A loss of conscience and self-imposed controls because of mass hysteria.

2. The difficulty of the young Negro male in developing a feeling of self-esteem because he is the product of a matriarchal society.

3. Self-destructive or suicidal impulses generated by the attitude of "what have we got to lose?"

We can dispense with item 2 at once. The difficulty in developing a feeling of self-esteem has existed for over 200 years and therefore tells us nothing about the present riots. It is also patently absurd because even if young Negro males were the products of a patriarchal society they would still have some difficulty developing feelings of self-esteem, given the kinds of oppression to which they have been subjected.

The other two psychodynamic interpretations also contribute little or nothing to our understanding of the riots. To attribute the riots to mass hysteria is to imply that they were caused by people who were temporarily mentally ill. The same implication is contained in the interpretation of the behavior of the rioters as self-destructive and suicidal. This is the inevitable result of applying the concepts of an illness model to a profound social problem that is shaking the roots of our society.

If not by means of the illness model, how else can the psychological factors operating in the riots be understood? In order to determine what conceptual tools are needed, one must first identify the problem—that is, define the kind of behavior with which we are dealing and isolate its causes.

We have already rejected the hypothesis that the riots resulted from collective mental illness. At the same time, it is clear that atypical behavior was involved in these violent attacks on two symbols of power in our social system—the police and property. It is also clear that it was a pattern of behavior of an aggregate of Negroes. What kind of aggregate was it?

Many different kinds of aggregates engage in violent attacks on the symbols of power. There are crowds, mobs, and mass movements, to mention but a few. Crowds and mobs, for example, usually display one pattern of behavior. They are isolated, temporary, and short-lived aggregates which end as soon as they disperse. A mass movement, on the other hand, exists over a relatively long period of time. Its pattern of behavior changes from time to time. It remains an aggregate even though its members may be dispersed.

The 1967 riots, it appears, reflected similar patterns of behavior in many different cities all over the nation. They were all characterized by attacks on the power symbols of police and property. They were not short-lived; some of them continued for as long as five days. When the riots subsided, the pattern of behavior changed in form from physical to verbal assaults and threats to the power symbols of the system, but the aggregate appears to continue to exist. In short, we are dealing with a mass movement. We have now identified one of the important characteristics of the aggregate and have moved a little closer to identifying the problem. We have already noted that the pattern of behavior—that is, riots—was atypical for our system. It is apparent that it is also atypical of the previous patterns of behavior of the mass movement of Negroes in America.

One other observation can be made here. Although the aggregate appears to have the basic characteristics of a mass movement, it is lacking in two important characteristics. It appears leaderless and without formal organization. Our analysis leads us to the conclusion that the nature of the Negro mass movement in the United States has changed. Large masses of unorganized Negroes, without apparent leadership, are now actively participating in it, and their pattern of participation is very different from the previous patterns of struggle of the civil rights movement.

Has this analysis enabled us to arrive at a definition of the problem? What social and psychological conditions might account for the changes in the Negro masses' struggle for freedom as signified by the riots? The specific changes we are interested in are changes in the patterns of behavior and changes in the nature of the aggregate participating in the struggle.

We are now faced with a new conceptual problem. What social and psychological forces create and give a mass movement its particular character? Here we are dealing with the psychology of mass movements, an early but long-neglected interest of social psychologists. Although a limited body of knowledge exists, few psychologists have had the opportunity or the inclination to acquire it. Because it is a "forgotten" psychology, it needs to be further developed and refined in terms of present-day social systems. If community psychologists are to become experts in modifying aggregate behavior they should rediscover the psychology of mass movements.

SOCIAL FORCES AND THEIR PSYCHOLOGICAL EFFECTS

In the analysis which follows, we have borrowed from a work of Eric Hoffer, a longshoreman who, in our opinion, is a supreme example of the participant-conceptualizer. He has achieved great insights into mass behavior through a life of personal involvement in action coupled with a talent for penetrating observation and scholarly organization into meaningful concepts.

Hoffer (1966) quotes De Tocqueville who, in his research on the state of society in France before the revolution of 1789, found that "a people which had supported the most crushing laws without complaint and apparently as if they were unfelt throws them off with violence as soon as the burden begins to be diminished. . . . The evils which are endured with patience as long as they are inevitable seem intolerable as soon as a hope can be entertained of escaping from them." To which Hoffer adds: "Despair and misery are static factors. The dynamism of an uprising flows from hope and pride. Not actual suffering but the hope of better things unites people to revolt."

Many other students of mass movements have made similar observations. Understanding this, it becomes possible to hypothesize that the riots were not the result of oppression or despair or of mass hysteria or of self-destructive and suicidal impulses. Hope and pride may have provided the psychological dynamism of the riots. The hope we are talking about is not the pie-in-the-sky kind of hope which Negroes have been offered for decades. It is the immediate brand of hope which motivates oppressed masses to action. Let us try to understand how this hope may have developed.

The history of mass movements tells us that they are frequently initiated by middle-class intellectuals who often provide the early leadership. This certainly was the case with the civil rights movement; the active thrust provided by the middle-class educated Negro reflected his goals and desires—integration and certain concessions of a legal and social nature. The early successes of the civil rights movement, particularly the legal and social changes, began to sow the seeds of hope and had the effect of increasing the expectations of the Negro masses.

Nearly three years ago we wrote that, when working with the poor, self-actualization is an unrealistic and inappropriate goal. We suggested then that in treatment, in preventive work, and in consultative functions the guiding principle in working with the poor should be directed toward helping them to the conviction that they can play a role in determining what happens to them.

The poverty program had the effect of giving many Negroes the feeling that they could play a role in determining what happens to them. This is not to say that the poverty program is responsible for the riots, as some of its opponents are trying to assert. The poverty program helped Negroes to feel they could play a role, but the particular role they chose to play was not decided by the poverty program. One might say, in fact, that the poverty program attempted to create the channels in which Negroes could play a role. But the Negro masses are now creating their own channels.

There is evidence that certain legal and social changes brought about by the struggle of the Negro had the effect of producing hope in the Negro masses. And if that is so, we are justified in postulating that hope provided the psychological dynamism, the will to struggle, that is so evident in the riots. But while hope provided the psychological dynamism of the Negro mass movement, it does not explain its form and content. Why is the present Negro mass movement apparently leaderless and unorganized?

It is evident that the middle-class educated Negro is no longer in the leadership of the masses. There is evidence to show that the active element in the movement has changed as its major thrust has shifted from the middle-class Negro to the working-class and lower-income groups. The concessionist philosophy of the middle-class Negro has petered out. While he may have profited from concessions, the working-class and lower-income groups have gained little or nothing. In addition, concessions are getting more and more difficult to achieve with the old forms of struggle. The slogan "black power" is not a concessionist slogan. There is no concession possible to the demand for black power. It is an all-or-none slogan. It has the characteristic of a slogan of revolt in contrast to liberal reformist slogans such as "integration."

It seems clear that the die is cast. The struggle of the Negro people for freedom has reached a new phase. A new leadership reflecting the goals and desires of the lower-income Negroes is likely to be developed. The reformist solution to the Negro problem is becoming increasingly untenable. Each small improvement may bring more violence. Our social system may soon have to decide to give the Negro people complete freedom or to resort to massive repressive measures that will destroy the Negroes' hope and perhaps our country in the process.

The crucial question is how do we intervene in the social system to provide the psychological dynamisms that will minimize the danger of a massive oppressive reaction. The civil rights movement has compelled our country to take a critical look at many aspects of our system that have been taken for granted. In the course of reexamining our education system because of its failures with Negro children, we have begun to question the entire system and its effectiveness with all children. Our recreation programs, our job training programs, even our mental health programs have benefited from the self-examination imposed on us by the criticism of the civil rights movement. The shift in the class basis of the Negro struggle will result in other kinds of criticisms and self-examinations of some of the fundamental assumptions of our system. Our system of law enforcement and justice, the dehumanization of social services, and certainly some of the fundamental assumptions of our power structure are all due for critical evaluation and change. If and when psychology can make any contribution to these questions, it will truly have earned the name of community psychology.

Our analysis of the significance of the riots may not be acceptable, but it clearly indicates that no simplistic notion can be sufficient and conveys the inadequacy of trying to account for these phenomena totally in terms of social factors. If you simply measured the degree of oppression of the Negroes, you could not understand what is taking place today. That is why so many people are bewildered by the fact that the riots have taken place in the cities where they thought the greatest progress had been made.

We have tried to show how certain changes in the social conditions of the Negroes have led to certain psychological changes. These psychological changes, in turn, have led to changes in goals and levels of struggle and have changed the social forces in the Negro mass movement, thus creating a new social condition for the country as a whole. Thus, the recent riots illustrate the reciprocal, almost reverberating, relationship between social and psychological factors. Social forces have psychological effects and these psychological effects can change or create new social forces. A complete analysis requires not only identification of social and psychological factors but their interpenetration as well.

This analysis perhaps provides some notion of the difficult conceptual problems we face. We have, for example, jumped from one level of analysis to another. We used both a theoretical and a descriptive analysis simply because in some instances our thinking had advanced to the formal level and in others it had not. Although we can make the generalization that certain social forces create a certain psychological dynamism, we have no conceptual framework that explains the process by which this takes place. In fact, though the term psychological dynamism has seemed useful, we cannot actually define it.

THE NEED FOR A BODY OF KNOWLEDGE IN
COMMUNITY PSYCHOLOGY

We have indicated some of the ways in which community psychology will be compelled to face the inadequacies of existing conceptual models. It is our conviction that unless community psychology develops a body of theory as well as practice and becomes a school of psychology it will degenerate into nothing more than a new opportunities movement for psychologists. If community psychology can develop as a school of psychology it will fill a great social need. As a school of psychology, community psychology has a great future.

Undergraduate and graduate schools are filled with many able young people who do not see a professional career as the means by which they can express their need to participate in society and in social change. Community psychology with its social interventionist emphasis can attract these young people. Many already have had practical experience in the civil rights movement in the South, in the Peace Corps, and in the community action program of the poverty program. They can be drawn from law, sociology, economics, and political science as well as psychology. They are bright and dedicated. Community psychology could provide them with the means of integrating their desire to participate in society and in social change with a professional life. But it is difficult to see how we can train students as community psychologists without a body of knowledge and repertoire of skills that can be clearly identified as community psychology.

The present lack of a clearly defined set of theories and of knowledge of skills with which the student in community psychology can identify makes it necessary for community psychology trainees to tolerate ambiguities and uncertainties about their identity. Students who come from social psychology inevitably feel themselves basically social psychologists with a community focus in community roles. Clinical psychologists remain identified with clinical psychology while serving new roles in the community. Therefore, the immediate task is for more who identify themselves as community psychologists to clarify and make explicit the substantive areas that define the parameters of this new field. This could be the first step toward developing a new body of knowledge.

The key to developing a new theory and new skills is not to look for new problems, but to look at the old problems of psychology in a new way. For example, the relationship between culture and cognition is an old problem, but this problem has not been looked at from a social system framework. Each of us has an area of special interest in psychology. If we turn our efforts to rethinking the substantive problems in our areas of interest and begin to analyze these from a social system framework, we may develop concepts that could form the basis for a body of knowledge for community psychology. For example, there are psychologists whose major area of interest is human relations. A new look at human relations from the social system point of view might yield important new knowledge. And so it may be with other areas of interests such as thinking, memory, perception, etc. We should encourage our students to do likewise. Help them look at old problems from this new frame of reference.

Finally, if we are serious about the concept of participant-conceptualizer, we must begin to train our students to be participants and conceptualizers. Certain skills are prerequisites for such a role. We should, for example, teach our students how to keep a log of their activities and to develop the habit of reviewing this log much in the same way that we now train clinicians to take notes of their therapy hours and use them in supervision.

In the immediate future we are faced with two tasks so far as training is concerned. One is to develop an ideal community psychology training program. But we must start with the present situation and our present programs should be developed so that they serve as transition programs to the more ideal type when they become possible. In my view an ideal program would be a six-year doctoral program, starting the freshman year of undergraduate school. The individual would spend half time in the community and half time in school throughout his whole student career. But at the present time we have neither the theoretical basis nor the knowledge of what skills are required to do this.

We must accept the challenge and use our new opportunities for a creative burst of new concepts and skills. We must begin at once a period of dialogue with each other, colleague with colleague and faculty with students. This next period must be one of intense questioning and seeking new answers. If we cannot develop a theory of community psychology, as well as appropriate techniques of practice, we will become a once very attractive fad in psychology that will pass from the scene. If we are successful, we will have made a major contribution to all of psychology.

REFERENCES

Hoffer, Eric. *The true believer.* New York: Harper and Row, 1966.
Knutson, A. L. New perspectives regarding positive mental health. *American Psychologist,* 1963, **18**, 301–306.
Reiff, Robert. Mental health manpower and institutional change. *American Psychologist,* 1966, **21**, 540–549.
White, Robert W. Motivation reconsidered: The concept of competence. *Psychological Review,* 1959, LXVI, 297–333.

3

Community Psychology and Mental Health: An Analysis of Strategies and a Survey of Training

Stuart E. Golann

BACKGROUND ISSUES, PERSISTENT AND TOPICAL

The Joint Commission on Mental Illness and Health (1961) has stated that a national mental health program should recognize major mental illness as the core problem and that intensive treatment of patients with critical and prolonged mental breakdowns should have first call on fully trained members of the mental health professions. Moreover, the commission recommended that the "risk of false promise" would be avoided if public education for better mental health focused on disseminating information about mental illness which the public needs and wants in order to recognize psychological forms of sickness and arrive at an informed opinion of its responsibility toward the mentally ill (p. xviii). In this way the commission responded to issues which came into focus several years earlier at the National Mental Health Assembly. This assembly, which had convened to discuss education for positive mental health, revealed strong disagreement about the methods and goals of mental health education programs (Pennsylvania Mental Health, 1960).

One result of the Pennsylvania conference was that the National Opinion Research Center was commissioned to undertake a study of the scientific basis of the area of mental health education. The report was published in *Education for Positive Mental Health* (Davis, 1963). Leaning heavily on Nunnally's (1961) research, Davis concluded that "While the experts are in fair agreement on fallacies" (e.g., books on peace of mind prevent people from developing nervous breakdowns), "they have no set of practical, positive actions to recommend to the general population regarding personal adjustment and the prevention of mental illness" (p. 58).

The argument over whether to educate about mental illness or for mental health and the core problem controversy concern questions of strategy. While these are current and critical questions today, as they have been in the past (see Bockoven, 1963; Hobbs, 1964; Rossi, 1962), they will require fuller and more systematic conceptualization to highlight the salient issues. It seems unrealistic to expect to find useful answers for such goals as education for positive mental health. To state the alternatives as a choice between the uncertain and the anachronistic offers little assistance because the wording of the question preempts the changes which may be required. The basic conceptualization system is not adequate. The dilemma is not to choose between education for positive mental health or about mental illness, but rather to identify particular strategies through which selected information or services may reduce the probability (risk) that certain individuals will move toward higher levels of abnormal (devalued) behavior or increase the probability of movement toward socially valued behavior.

Goals should be based on an examination of values and the naturalistic study of human beings today, not artificially constrained by outdated language and concepts. Just as the prayers and rituals of the shaman were expressed in an appropriate idiom and strategically congruent with the belief that the disturbed person was possessed, so the differential diagnosis and chemical treatment of the physician in a mental hospital was conceptualized within the idiom of medical science and consistent with the belief that the person suffered from biologic illness. The goal of the shaman was to beat the devil out of the person—the goal of the physician is to cure the disease through a significant change in its natural history. The goal of the community psychologist is to achieve human effectiveness within a social system—to work within community systems so that they may function to develop and sustain the competence and productivity of the individuals who are part of them. Just as it would have been inappropriate to utilize the strategies of the shaman to achieve the goals of the physician in a mental hospital, so would it also be inappropriate to use the strategies of the disease model of medical science to achieve the goals of effectiveness in the modern community.

For this, and for other reasons as well, there has been increased criticism of the "medical model" (Albee, 1966). But the level of discourse remains abstract and the programmatic issues are not truly joined. Changing vocabulary will not in itself lead to programs. Professional autonomy alone will not lead to innovation (as many psychologists are committed to a medical science strategy). But what are the basic differences between traditional clinical approaches and community approaches to mental health problems? What are the dimensions along which we may effect change? It is suggested herein that the differences are associated with strategies of intervention and that these differences can be best understood by use of a single general model.

A BASIC MODEL FOR MENTAL HEALTH
PROGRAMS

Strategy, as the term is used here, involves a series of interrelated choices, made explicitly or implicitly (but made invariably), concerning a specific service or program. To be considered are the goals, locations, occasions, helpers, and recipients of mental health services and the specific characteristics of these services. There is only one basic program model, but there are many strategies of implementation which can be described or compared by its use.

In this model there are three major dimensions, and subsumed under them are seven questions at issue, six of which may be considered to be the salient decisions in the planning and implementing of services. It bears repeating that the six choices are interrelated, that one choice may inhibit a second or facilitate a third, and that all mental health services require implicit or explicit decisions for each of them. Incompatible choices lead to ineffective programs. Compatible choices are facilitated by specificity of goals. The three areas—the organizational framework, the ecological framework, and the mental health transaction—are outlined along with the dimensions of choice in the outline below.

The Basic Model
  I. *The Organizational Framework*
  - A. Resource acquisition and reduction of constraints
  - B. Responsibility interpretation and setting of goals
 II. *The Ecological Framework*
  - A. Geographic location of the transaction
  - B. Occasion or time of receipt of the service
III. *The Mental Health Transaction*
  - A. The helper
  - B. Nature of the service
  - C. The direct recipient

Every program involves the setting of goals and the use of resources to achieve these goals, and, in so doing, every program involves a series of choices about who will provide what service to whom, at what occasion or time, and in what location. These are the real dimensions along which choices are made. A few more words about them.

The organizational framework concerns resources, constraints, program responsibility, and goals. The acquisition and administration of resources and the reduction of certain constraints are part of the politics of mental health. These involve choices not treated in this model. Instead, it is assumed that at any given time resources and constraints are fixed quantities that determine the limits within which other choices can be made at that time. The interpretation of program responsibility can lead to a variety of goals. Primary prevention of new cases of personality disorder, provision of psychotherapy to low-income groups, and reduction of intrapsychic conflict are three examples of goals. These may vary in scope as well as in the clarity with which they are stated. Once goals have been stated, the agency does not automatically know what to do next. The degree to which goals are achieved is in large part dependent upon the explicit consideration of the remaining issues of choice and the priorities (strategy) adopted.

The ecological framework involves two important choices. It is important to note that wide variation is possible in the geographic or sociologic locations where a mental health transaction may occur. Examples may include diverse locations such as a community general hospital, an elementary school, a private metropolitan office, a college dormitory, or a storefront near a bus stop. The occasion or time of the delivery and receipt of the service provides another dimension of choice. Examples might include the following: after giving birth to a premature infant, upon application to elementary school, when self-referred, upon entering college, or at a time of crisis.

The mental health transaction involves three choices—the helper, the nature of the service, and the direct recipient. The question of helper is that of who will provide the service. The specific person is usually chosen as representative of a class of individuals possessing certain characteristics, training, skills, or personal attributes. Examples include a clergyman, a clinical psychologist, a general practice physician, a psychiatrist, a social worker, or a mature woman. Certain services may be impersonally transmitted, such as information in a pamphlet.

The nature of the service or the service of choice refers to the specific techniques, content, and process made available. Analytic group psychotherapy, individual mental health consultation, psychoactive drug therapy, psychodiagnostic assessment, vocational counseling, or a comic strip about the needs of infants are examples. The specific individuals who may be the direct recipients of such services constitute the next choice. They, too, may be identified as representative of classes or special groupings of individuals with whom they share certain characteristics. Examples include chronic schizophrenics, female college graduates, anxious college men, high school dropouts, industrial foremen, preadolescent boys who are thought by their teachers to be troubled, residents of a given area, and unwed mothers.

This describes the basic model and the salient dimensions of choice. If it seems that these are not actual choice dimensions, this may be because the strategies for providing services have become fixed and unquestioned. It is important to remember that once a choice has been made on any one of the dimensions, implicitly or explicitly, this may limit the freedom of choice on the remaining dimensions. Such limitation of choice often impedes the realization that choices have been made and can be changed. It is for this reason that the word "strategy" applies. Strategy in developing a mental health program involves sharpening of goals, identification of the possible choices, selection of the critical choice (the one to be made first), and decisions concerning the range of innovation. It also involves tracing the effects of initial and secondary choices on freedom of choice on the remaining dimensions.

THE BASIC DIFFERENCE BETWEEN TRADITIONAL AND COMMUNITY MENTAL HEALTH STRATEGIES

The question bears repeating: What are the basic differences between traditional clinical approaches to mental health problems and community approaches? The medical strategy has dominated the mental health field, and this has resulted in much concern about the nature of the service and the treatment of choice for disturbed individuals. Since determination of a single dimension reduces choice on the remaining dimensions, and since different goals may require different strategies, an invariant priority of choice may lead to less effective programs. Community mental health approaches require flexibility of priority and freedom of choice. For example, there has been concern, albeit belated, for providing mental health services to low-income individuals. This goal may be approached in any number of ways. The priority choice of the medical strategy typically concerns treatment, so planning for the low-income group is likely to involve thinking (often innovative) about some form of a psychotherapeutic relationship or type of medication. In the narrowest of approaches the only modification would involve some subsidy mechanism to allow the poor to apply for a service they otherwise could not afford.

The attention to treatment of choice, when combined with an institutionalized set of practices based on biomedical science concepts, so preempts the decision-making associated with the medical strategy that other issues such as those involving the location of the service or the helper of choice are infrequently considered in relation to goals. But from another point of view mental health programs for the poor may require that these same issues receive first priority consideration. Innovations such as neighborhood service centers and helping roles for nonprofessionals take on their full meaning when they are seen as the means by which a recipient-linked goal may be achieved.

The ecological framework and system of choices developed from applications of biomedical science have frequently been applied with little change to the mental health field. Consequently, many of the individuals who receive mental health treatment are not ill and many of the individuals who are ill are not treated. Szasz (1960, 1961), Adams (1964), and Mariner (1967) have written in support of the first assertion, and with regard to the second it is pertinent to note that 73 percent of the adults who were judged to be significantly impaired in the Midtown Manhattan Survey (Srole *et al.,* 1962) had never been patients in any private or public mental health treatment resource. Furthermore, only a few of the troubled people who do apply to the established mental health resources for help are accepted. For example, Hunt (1961) reported that only 25 percent of the total number of cases applying for service at an urban child guidance clinic actually entered into psychotherapeutic treatment, and only 7 percent received or remained for a full course of such treatment. Shortages of personnel at the service agencies are common and waiting lists are still generally long. Despite this, and despite more compelling arguments for innovation in the choice of the helper, the medical strategy has acted as a constraint upon the full and effective utilization of the available helping manpower.

Community psychology marks a movement away from preoccupation with the treatment of choice for direct services to patients. A reconsideration of goals of mental health programs has been coupled with a more explicit consideration of the helper of choice, the recipient of choice, the location of choice, and the occasion of choice. Innovation requires freedom to choose. The innovations stimulated by community psychology have been most apparent in the mental health field where several new strategies are apparent. A consideration of these will highlight this basic difference.

STRATEGIES OF INNOVATION IN MENTAL HEALTH PROGRAMS

Of the innovative programs being tried, some stand out as involving changes in goal-setting within the organizational framework, while others are experiments with regard to dimensions of the ecological framework or the mental health transaction. A useful way of labeling strategies is to focus on the innovative element. Thus, "helper-linked," "occasion-linked," or "location-linked" strategies denote important classes of innovative mental health programs. Certain programs are readily classifiable into one of these categories, but other programs incorporate more than one innovative element. Rioch's Mental Health Counselor Program is an example of the first type, and Walder's Parent Educators Project illustrates multiple innovations and could readily be classified as a helper-linked or service-linked strategy. Clearly, the categories, while interrelated, are not mutually exclusive. In the examples which follow certain programs have been classified in one manner or another according to what appeared to be the major innovative element. This is admittedly arbitrary, but it is not the classifications of programs into these categories that is important but the relationships between the goals of a program and the strategies and priorities of choice used to approach them.

HELPER-LINKED STRATEGIES

The manpower recommendations of the Joint Commission on Mental Illness and Health (1961) were significant in that specific proposals were made that took into account both the needs of the public and the resources and professional practices of the mental health disciplines. Three programs, congruent with the commission's recommendations, in which the primary innovation concerned the selection of the helper are summarized in Table 3–1. These are the Mental Health Counselor (MHC) Program (Rioch, Elkes, & Flint, 1965), the Child Development Counselor (CDC) Program (Lourie, Rioch, & Schwartz, 1967), and the Student Volunteer Programs (Umbarger *et al.,* 1962; Holzberg *et al.,* 1964; Holzberg & Knapp, 1965).

Mental Health Counselors. Rioch *et al.* (1965) attempted to demonstrate that carefully selected, mature women with no previous mental health training could be trained in a relatively short period of time to provide psychodynamically-oriented psychotherapy to troubled adolescents and adults in established mental health settings. It was expected that narrowly but intensively trained women could help people whose problems could not be solved by sympathetic listening alone or by common-sense advice of neighbors or friends. For example, they could learn to draw out the hidden anger of the depressed person or help the anxious person to discover the source of his anxiety. This Mental Health Counselor Program required two years of half-time training focused primarily on supervised interviewing practice and observation of individual and family psychotherapy. Theory and didactic material were included to a lesser extent. In follow-up studies of the effectiveness of the program (Golann & Magoon, 1966; Golann, Breiter, & Magoon, 1966; Magoon, Golann, & Freeman, 1969), it was found that there were jobs

TABLE 3–1   Helper-linked Strategies

	RIOCH-ELKES-FLINT: MENTAL HEALTH COUNSELORS	LOURIE-RIOCH-SCHWARTZ: CHILD DEVELOPMENT COUNSELORS	UMBARGER-HOLZBERG: COMPANION PROGRAMS
TRANSACTION			
Helper	Selected middle-aged women, specially trained	Selected middle-aged women, specially trained	College students
Service	Individual psychodynamic psychotherapy	Counseling on child development	Companion relationships; individual and group meeting about once a week
Recipient	Adolescents and adults, selected	Mothers of infants, expectant mothers	Chronic "forgotten" NP hospitalized patients
ECOLOGICAL FRAME			
Geographic	Suburban mental health clinics	Maternity clinics, urban health departments, well-baby clinics	State hospitals
Occasion	Postreferral screening and acceptance	Pregnancy—first year of baby's life	During hospitalization
ORGANIZATION FRAME			
Goals	Increase low-cost skillful psychotherapy	Reduce incidence of child behavior disorder	Improve social skills of patients; effect attitudes and career choice of students

available to the eight women throughout the three-year period of the study and that they remained employed in mental health work. Furthermore, several of these counselors were able to choose among job opportunities. For the most part they did what they were trained to do—psychotherapy. But they also learned to perform other functions, such as intake interviewing, and were very well thought of by their supervisors and co-workers in educational settings and psychiatric inpatient and, most frequently, outpatient settings. Five years after the completion of the training program and two years after the termination of the follow-up study, six of the eight women were still employed by mental health agencies, one had matriculated for a MSW degree, and one was unemployed though active in volunteer work.

Child Development Counselors. Lourie, Rioch, and Schwartz (1967) have attempted to train selected, mature women as counselors in child development. This manpower experiment was closely modeled after the Pilot Project in Training Mental Health Counselors (Rioch *et al.,* 1965), but a different role was visualized for the trainees. They were to be trained as counselors on child development and their clients were to be expectant mothers and mothers of young children. The urban health department was to provide the work setting in maternity and well-baby clinics. The goals were preventive rather than therapeutic, and it was hoped that by providing developmental information and checkups, by giving the mother a chance to talk about things, by helping her to clarify problems, and by giving her emotional support certain problems in child development would be prevented from occurring or worsening. The selection of these child development counselors was modeled after the procedures used in the Mental Health Counselor Project. Eight women were selected from 101 applicants, and they, too, were trained in a two-year, half-time program. They completed their training in February, 1966, and the follow-up of their utilization in the field was completed the next year (Golann, 1967).

Insofar as the achievement and maintenance of a career commitment and the realization of a projected role may be used as rough indices of success, there were differences in the success achieved by the two projects. This child development counselor, in contrast to the mental health counselor, seemed to have a harder time of it. Jobs were more difficult to obtain and settings in which they could develop and function in the role for which they were trained were almost impossible to find. Eighteen months after these eight women completed training, two were unemployed and two others had matriculated for the MSW degree. Three were working in a community mental health center where their roles were quite different from the focus of their training, and one was working in a day care facility.

Student Volunteers. The first student volunteer program was organized at Harvard University in 1954. Such projects, in which college volunteers initiate a friendship with hospitalized neuropsychiatric patients, often chronic or "back-ward" patients, have increased in number since that time. The social service interests of many college students are served to the benefit of the confined patient. Impressions of considerable patient benefit have been reported and the effects of the experience on the students are also noteworthy. These have included reports of increased knowledge and acceptance of mental illness (Holzberg & Gewitz, 1963), significant changes toward positive self-acceptance, and changes in moral judgments toward sexual and aggressive behavior (Holzberg *et al.*, 1964). The potential impact of such projects is underscored by the number of students who might participate. The total number of students enrolled in institutions of higher education throughout the nation is close to 6.5 million. Approximately 570,000 bachelors degrees were awarded in 1967. This included 16,750 bachelors degrees in psychology alone with an estimated 250,000 more to be awarded by 1976 (Simon & Fullam, 1966).

SERVICE-LINKED STRATEGIES

Table 3–2 briefly summarizes programs in which a primary innovation concerns the service content or process. From among a number of possibilities four have been selected: (1) Project RE-ED, (2) Parents as Behavior Therapists, (3) Interpersonal Relations Project, and (4) Group Mental Health Consultation.

Project RE-ED. The goal of Project RE-ED is the re-education of emotionally disturbed children. The children live in the school for five days each week and spend weekends at home. Selected college graduates are trained to staff the experimental schools in a special nine-month training program.

The underlying concepts and the service offered by the RE-ED school are something quite different from the predominant modes of treatment in the field of childhood emotional disorder. A clean break is made from what Levine has described elsewhere in this volume (see Chapter 5) as "intrapsychic supremacy." Psychodynamic principles of traditional psychotherapy are not used and the goal is not to "cure" the child. Instead, the many opportunities for development that occur in a

TABLE 3–2 Service-linked Strategies

	Hobbs: RE-ED	Walder: Parent as Behavior Therapist	Goodman: Activity Counselors	Spielberger-Eisdorfer: Health Dept. Consultation
TRANSACTION				
Helper	Selected young college graduates, specially trained and supporting staff	Psychologist	Selected college men	Experienced psychologist
Service	Milieu experience of 6 months stressing skill development, symptom control, coping, expression of feeling, and ceremony through trust relationships	Tutorial relationship to teach principles of behavior modification	Companion-activity relationship, 2–3 meetings/week, 1–5 hours long for 1 year	Group mental health consultation—through health department, about twice a month
Recipient	Disturbed children, age 6–12 (mostly boys) and their parents	Parents concerned about their children's behavior	Selected preadolescent boys, fifth and sixth grade	Caretaker groups—public health nurses, ministers, principals and teachers, police, welfare workers
ECOLOGICAL FRAME				
Geographic	Residential 24-hour school, home on weekends	Variable, university or elsewhere	Any place in the community—campus, boy's home, ballpark	Variable, at various agencies within the community
Occasion	Selection for special project	After child has developed behavior disorder that disturbs parent	Selection by parents as potentially troubled	Existence of work problems relating to mental health needs of recipient clients
ORGANIZATIONAL FRAME				
Goals	Improve social system functioning to above threshold	Parent becomes able to analyze and modify child behavior	Investigate behavior and attitude changes in boys and counselors	Education of above groups to better understanding of mental health problems and more effective control and prevention of disordered behavior in their clients

six-month milieu experience are capitalized upon in helping each child to develop individual skills, control symptoms and habits, and learn how to cope with their emotions and develop and practice more satisfying relationships with people. The goal of RE-ED is to make the child a working member of the social systems of which he is a part.

In order to achieve this goal, parents are involved in the process and the child is not permitted to be totally withdrawn from the home. Liaison is established with the child's regular school by a special teacher and liaison with other individuals or agencies involved in the child's life is maintained by social work personnel. The process of the re-education experience has been described by Hobbs (1966) as involving twelve underlying concepts.

Parents as Behavior Therapists. Bandura (1962) has pointed out that a problem often arises in child psychotherapy from parental requests for advice on how to alter their children's behavior. It is typically assumed by the helping agent that a disturbed interpersonal relationship is the cause of the child's behavior problem, or that the parents unconsciously desire and instigate the child's deviant behavior. Consequently, requests for advice by parents are generally ignored or evaded because of the helper's antiadvice training. Walder (1967) has developed a program in which he attempts to teach behavior control principles and techniques to parents who complain about their children's behavior. Parents learn to state their problems and their goals for the child in behavioral terms and are taught to analyze the relationship between the person and the environment. They are also helped to discern and develop reinforcers, strengthen or create desirable behaviors, extinguish undesirable behavior, and reduce aversive control and develop positive control. Preliminary findings suggest that deviant behaviors that were resistant to change when treated by conventional techniques applied by professionals have been modified by parents. Walder summarizes his current results as "very soft but very positive," and has described the initiation of a controlled evaluation study of the Parent Behavior Therapist Project.

Interpersonal Relations Project. The Interpersonal Relations Project (Goodman, 1967) involved an attempt to study behavior and attitude changes in preadolescent boys who had participated in a companion-activity relationship with selected undergraduate college men. The boys were nominated for counseling because they were regarded as troubled or potentially disturbed by parents or teachers. The selection of the counselors by group methods was also an important part of this study.

The design involved a no-treatment control group and also different levels of consultation for the counselors. Boys and counselors were first divided into "quiet" and "outgoing" types and then like and unlike pairs were formed. The activity relationship itself took a variety of forms. The dyads typically met two or three times each week throughout an academic year for a period ranging from one to five hours each meeting. These meetings took place in a variety of locations, such as the boys' homes, the college campus, a ball park, or the zoo.

Changes were reported to have taken place in both boys and counselors. The counselors, as compared with controls, gained in self-acceptance and became less defensive. Their interpersonal relationships increased in number and became more rewarding. Furthermore, nine of ten counselors reported that the project and counseling experiences were partly or primarily responsible for increased interpersonal contact (including greater sharing of feelings with their girlfriends). The counselors, significantly more than controls, showed a shift in their future work interests toward person- or community-centered roles and toward entering into service-related occupations and training programs after they completed college. They describe heightened interest in the behavior of children and emotionally troubled people in general. The outcomes for the boys are currently being analyzed, but there is some preliminary suggestion that change may be specific to dyad types. For example, quiet boys become less withdrawn when paired with outgoing counselors.

Mental Health Consultation. The development and dissemination of concepts of individual mental health consultation may in large measure be attributed to Caplan (1963, 1964, 1965). Programs of mental health consultation using group approaches have been described by Altrocchi, Spielberger, and Eisdorfer (1965), Eisdorfer, Altrocchi, and Young (in press), and Spielberger (1967). There are many similarities among these programs. The psychologists were part-time consultants to distant, small urban or rural communities. Their services had been sought by county health departments, and in each instance the question of how the limited available professional time could be used to best advantage was considered. It was decided that traditional diagnostic and remedial services would not ordinarily be performed by the consultants, but instead they would work with key groups such as clergy, police, public health nurses, school administrators, and welfare workers. The case seminar method of group mental health consultation has been described by Altrocchi *et al.* (1965) and distinguished from group supervision, seminar teaching, sensitivity training, and group psychotherapy. The goals in this form of consultation were to assist the various professional workers to carry out their own jobs more effectively by helping them to become more sensitive to their clients' needs and more skillful in their relationships with them. A further dimension of strategy here is recipient-linked in that members of the key groups with whom the consultants worked were likely to be called upon in times of personal and interpersonal crises.

It should be stated again that there are many programs in which service-linked strategies are being attempted. RE-ED, behavior therapy, activity counseling, and group consultation illustrate only some of the possible approaches. Several examples of recipient-linked strategies come next.

RECIPIENT-LINKED STRATEGIES

Table 3–3 briefly summarizes programs in which a primary innovation concerns the recipient of the service. Selected for purposes of illustration were (1) police training for riot prevention, (2) the Academic Orientation Project for anxious college men, and (3) mental health services for the poor.

Police Training. In "No Heaven for Hell's Angels," Shellow and Romer (1966) describe a novel program of service to county policemen. The situation that confronted them was one in which county police anticipated that a riot might occur at a forthcoming holiday weekend motorcycle competition. The roles performed by Shellow and Romer included information collection, conceptualization, and participant planning. First, a number of recent riots were reviewed and several common significant factors were identified. Combining this information with pertinent social science theory, it was possible to develop a set of goals that included (a) logistic planning and coordination for participants, spectators, and police; (b) avoidance of polarization of relations between different groups; and (c) inhibition of the milling behavior that usually precedes crowd disturbances. The planful collection and use of information and the dissemination of this information to the police department is of particular interest because the riot did not occur despite a number of incidents and confrontations between cyclists and police.

Academic Orientation Program. The Academic Orientation Project (Spielberger, Weitz, & Denny, 1962) attempted to evaluate the effectiveness of group process in reducing the magnitude of academic underachievement and the incidence of academic failures among

TABLE 3-3 Recipient-linked Strategies

	SHELLOW: RIOT PREVENTION	SPIELBERGER-WEITZ: ACADEMIC ORIENTATION	REISMANN: SERVICES FOR THE POOR
TRANSACTION			
Helper	Social scientists	Psychologist	Indigenous nonprofessionals
Service	Information gathering; participant conceptualization in planning and policy information	Group discussion or counseling once a week	Gets and gives information, effects referrals, finds services, expedites, helps
Recipient	County police department	Anxious college male freshmen	Low-income urban residents
ECOLOGICAL FRAME			
Geographic	Variable: police department, motorcycle shops, streetcorners, and at the races	University	Storefront facilities in the client's neighborhood
Occasion	Scheduling of national motorcycle race in the county	Freshman year	Whenever client walks in
ORGANIZATION FRAME			
Goals	Improve police crowd control skills; improve planning, avoid polarization, ensure adequate facilities	Prevent dropout and achievement loss due to emotional handicap	Provide "psychosocial first-aid"

anxious college freshmen. Previous research (Spielberger, 1962) had demonstrated that anxiety interfered with college performance as measured by academic grades, particularly for students in the middle range of scholastic ability. Underachievement and college failure were shown to be associated with high anxiety among college students.

The Academic Orientation Project involved several steps. Anxious freshmen were selected from the population of liberal arts freshmen males on the basis of their scores on the Taylor Manifest Anxiety Scale and the Welsh Anxiety Scale and invited to participate in an orientation program. Those who volunteered in response to the invitation were assigned either to one of four discussion groups or to a no-treatment control. Spielberger *et al.* (1962) described the content of the group as follows:

> Students were encouraged to bring up problems of any sort. . . . Topics included methods of study, individual academic difficulties, vocational goals, dormitory life, relations with professors in class and on the campus, and to a lesser extent, matters relating to nonacademic difficulties and problems of personal identity. The counselors attempted to stimulate group discussion, to facilitate the utilization by the group of ideas presented by individual students, to provide relevant factual information, and to summarize and clarify what was said. (p. 198)

Students who attended more than half of the sessions had a significantly higher grade point average at the end of the semester than did either low attenders or controls. Moreover, the percentage of academic dismissal was lower for high attenders than for infrequent attenders or controls.

Neighborhood Service Centers. Neighborhood service centers such as those described by Riesmann and Hallowitz (1967) may be located in storefront facilities in the neighborhoods they serve where their services are directed toward low-income, urban residents. They are planned to provide "psychosocial first aid" that may include a variety of services to the urban poor, such as giving information and simple advice, counseling, expediting services from other agencies, and environmental interventions. These centers do not require appointments. They make use of brief informal intake procedures and have no waiting lists. Anyone in the neighborhood with any kind of problem may walk into such a center and talk to someone about his concerns. The main helpers are nonprofessionals who are indigenous to the same neighborhoods and are available to help people at times of crisis. Riesmann and Hallowitz estimate, on the basis of initial service counts, that such neighborhood centers see more than 6,000 individuals in a year. They concluded that nonprofessionals can provide and expedite services for large numbers of disadvantaged families and can serve as role models for people in the community.

The projects for the urban poor, anxious college freshmen, and county police provide examples of recipient-linked strategies. It is apparent that neighborhood service centers also involve additional innovative elements including the choice of helpers (indigenous nonprofessionals), location (urban storefronts), and occasion (crisis point). Examples of further location-linked and occasion-linked strategies follow.

LOCATION-LINKED AND OCCASION-LINKED STRATEGIES

Table 3–4 summarizes an occasion-linked strategy (the suicide prevention center; Farberow & Shneidman, 1961; Shneidman & Mandlekern, 1967) and an example of a location-linked strategy (the urban agent; Kelly, 1964).

TABLE 3–4   Location-linked and Occasion-linked Strategies

	SHNEIDMAN: SUICIDE PREVENTION	KELLY: URBAN AGENT
TRANSACTION		
Helper	Mental health professionals and selected nonprofessionals	Indigenous, nonprofessional mediators—cab drivers, barbers, storekeepers, lay leaders
Service	24-hour telephone support and persuasion; follow-up interviews	Mediating link—research question as to functions
Recipient	Troubled people who call	Urban residents and health resources
ECOLOGICAL FRAME		
Geographic	Variable	Urban environment, recreation sites, voluntary associations
Occasion	Crisis point—call for help	Research question—relationship between behavior, community factors, and urban agent functions
ORGANIZATION FRAME		
Goals	Prevent suicide	Prevent individual from designation as problem needing special help

Suicide Prevention. A comparative analysis of actual and simulated suicide notes suggested to Shneidman and Farberow (1957) that persons planning suicide signal their intentions before they act. The possibility of a time-linked strategy to detect and prevent suicide was apparent and this led to the establishment of the Los Angeles Center for Suicide Prevention. This center receives about 500 telephone calls during a typical month from persons asking for help. Roughly one third of the calls are made by people who, while troubled, are not yet attempting suicide. At least 10 percent of all calls are made by people moderately to seriously suicidal and of these one out of six callers is on the verge of death.

The telephone number of the suicide prevention service is well publicized. When a troubled person calls, the staff person (who may be a mental health professional or a specially-trained volunteer) begins to assess the caller's degree of lethality. It is known, for example, that elderly single men are higher risks than young married females. The listener attempts to evaluate the current stress that the caller is under and to learn about the caller's life style, his previous suicide attempts, and the specificity of the caller's current plans to kill himself. Certain cases are judged to be more serious at the moment of the call and the telephone interview often spells the difference between life and death. If the situation is highly critical, the listener must come up with an immediate answer right there on the telephone.

Urban Agent. The use of the urban environment, including settings such as recreation sites and voluntary associations where numbers of people naturally come together, has been suggested by Kelly (1964) as an action research procedure. Taxicab drivers, barbers, storekeepers, lay leaders, and other strategically placed individuals can be the indigenous helpers at these settings. A significant research question, in Kelly's estimation, is the relationship between community factors such as the rate of population change and judgments about the behavior of individuals. The use of nonprofessionals as a mediating link to effect beneficial behavior change is suggested as a second investigation.

IMPLICATIONS FOR TRAINING IN
COMMUNITY PSYCHOLOGY

These several strategies highlight the difference between traditional and community approaches to mental health problems. It has been suggested that community psychology illustrates movement away from preoccupation with the treatment of choice for direct services to patients and that the dimensions along which change is taking place include the goals, locations, occasions, recipients, and delivery systems of mental health services. When Iscoe (1962) noted that in the community the clinical psychologist used a different approach from that taught in graduate psychology programs, it appeared reasonable to recommend that training programs take note so that psychologists might contribute maximally to the comprehensive community mental health center. What was not yet apparent was the range of innovations which would occur during the next few years and the degree to which these would move beyond the scope of the recommendations put forth by the Joint Commission on Mental Illness and Health (1961). Consequently, the range of training innovations that merit the consideration of Departments of Psychology is even greater now than it was at that time.

These considerations, while set forth as principles, are offered as suggestions for considered evaluation. The community psychologist may perform numerous applied roles. Those roles discussed in this chapter included (a) training nonprofessionals and evaluating their performance; (b) designing and evaluating new treatment modalities for disturbed children; (c) developing new strategies of mental health services to communities; and (d) developing programs of services within the educational, health, legal-correctional, and social-welfare systems for the prevention of disordered behavior. Equally important roles of the community psychologist which were not explicitly discussed include program administration and training of psychology students. The Federal regulations governing the operations of community mental health centers have recently been clarified and modified to read that "The overall direction of a center may be carried out by a properly qualified member of any one of the mental health professions" (Federal Register of June 7, 1967), thereby indicating that a qualified psychologist may serve in such administrative positions. On the basis of the foregoing roles the following principles are suggested:

> *Principle 1:* Training in community psychology should adopt a generalist, as opposed to a specialist, model.
> *Principle 2:* Training should include collaborative experience with different professions and disciplines (such as educators, political scientists, psychiatrists, and sociologists).
> *Principle 3:* Training should include consultative and educational skills to prepare psychologists to help selected individuals and occupational groups deal most effectively with job related problems of human behavior.

To a considerable extent we may have been training students in important techniques only to encourage them to apply these techniques at the wrong place or time. For example, methods of individual assessment might prove more efficacious in affecting mental health in a community when used for preschool screening than when used with a state hospital population. In part this may be due to our own institutionalized and un-questioned practices. The following principle is important in this respect.

Principle 4: Training should include a basic knowledge of social systems and supervised participant-observation in more than one of the several systems.

Through direct involvement in the educational, health, industrial-com-mercial, legal-correctional, religious, or social-welfare systems the student will obtain better understanding of the purpose and goals of such systems and the strategies and programs through which goals are pursued. This range of involvement should encourage flexibility in approach to prob-lems and commitment to values of human effectiveness, individuality, and systematic methodology. The risk of parochialism will be lessened as it becomes apparent that there are many strategies and goals that are re-lated to human effectiveness. The psychologist himself will be encouraged to develop a wider range of skills that could be made available to a larger range of recipients in an increased number of locations and upon a greater variety of occasions. As such innovation increases, the following principle becomes of greatest import.

Principle 5: Training should be reorganized to put greater emphasis on the information and skills required for the evaluation of mental health services.

Each of the innovations described in this chapter has shown some promise and potential for providing mental health services in communi-ties. While the number of innovative programs is increasing, the ability to conduct comparative evaluations of these programs is limited. In order to select from among many programs and to establish criterion-related priorities, much progress must be made in program evaluation methods and procedures. The "Declaration of Policy," which is the preamble to Senate Bill 843 (the "Full Opportunity and Social Accounting Act"), reads as follows:

Sec. 2. In order to promote the general welfare, the Congress declares that it is the continuing policy and responsibility of the Federal Govern-ment . . . to promote and encourage such conditions as will give every American the opportunity to live in decency and dignity, and to provide a clear and precise picture of whether such conditions are promoted and en-couraged in such areas as health, education and training, rehabilitation, housing, vocational opportunities, the arts and humanities, and special as-sistance for the mentally ill and retarded, the deprived, the abandoned, and the criminal, and by measuring progress in meeting such needs.

Discussing this legislation which he had proposed to the Congress, Senator Mondale (1967) stated that

The absence of adequate, *publicly announced* indicators can also veil our successes and encourage mistaken exploitation of surface indications of failure, whether it be the testing of new educational techniques, methods of fighting crime, or the administration of welfare funds. In short, we know we are destroying old structures and building new ones, *but what are we doing to people?*

It is possible in many instances to state operationally (and publicly) the goals of a new service or program in terms of one of the issues of choice described in this chapter. As such, location-linked, occasion-linked, or recipient-linked goals may provide intermediate or proximate criteria. But as to what we are doing to people, this is a question for which we have a long history of debate. The primacy of values in dealing with person-outcome criteria has been acknowledged but not yet resolved. Such questions are not readily answered, but the forum for their investigation is the University Graduate School through the development of research laboratories in the community.

GRADUATE TRAINING IN COMMUNITY PSYCHOLOGY—A SURVEY

A number of training programs have begun to incorporate community mental health and community psychology into their doctoral training sequence. The following is a brief report of a survey of the extent of such offerings. In 1967, a two-question postcard was sent to the directors of clinical training of the 72 graduate departments of psychology listed as having doctoral clinical programs approved by the Education and Training Board in 1966/67. Responses were received from 65 of the 72 departments, for a 90 percent rate of return. Table 3–5 presents the two questions of the survey and the responses that were obtained.

TABLE 3–5   Questionnaire and Responses for Survey
of Community Psychology Training

	N	PERCENT
1. Check one space which best describes your department's curriculum in Community Psychology and Community Mental Health:		
a. Comprises a distinguishable curriculum or specialization	10	15
b. Comprises the total content of one or more courses	17	26
c. Comprises parts of one or more courses	19	29
d. Comprises little, if any, part of our courses	19	29
2. Does your department make supervised field experience in community psychology and community mental health available to doctoral students?		
Yes	48	74
No	17	26

Ten departments reported a distinct curriculum or specialization and 19 departments reported one or more courses devoted to community psychology and community mental health. Combining these two categories, it would appear that 29 departments, or 44 percent of the sample, provide some focused attention within the area of community mental health. Table 3–6 lists the departments which reported (in the spring of 1967) that they devoted the total content of one or more courses to community mental health or community psychology or that they had a distinct specialization in these areas.

TABLE 3–6   Universities Reporting Focused Attention
to Community Psychology[1]

Boston University	University of Florida
Columbia University Teachers College	University of Houston
Duke University	University of Illinois
George Peabody College for Teachers	University of Kansas (Lawrence)
Loyola University (Chicago)	University of Maryland
New York University Graduate School of Arts and Sciences	University of Michigan
	University of Minnesota
Pennsylvania State University	University of Missouri
Saint Louis University	University of Rochester
University of Arizona	University of Texas
University of Arkansas	University of Utah
University of California (Berkeley)	Wayne State University
University of California (Los Angeles)	Washington University (St. Louis)
University of Cincinnati	West Virginia University
University of Colorado	Western Reserve University

[1] This list includes only those from a particular sample of universities that responded to the survey and reported course work or specialization in community psychology or community mental health. Careful note should be taken that this list does not constitute any form of evaluation and that no independent verification of the programs has been made. The list may aid prospective students interested in these fields in requesting further information from colleges and universities. It is to be assumed that there are additional colleges and universities that offer such course work, that others will increase their offerings in coming years, and that some listed here will reduce their offerings in these areas. *Note*: A more recent listing of training opportunities, compiled by APA's Division of Community Psychology, may be obtained from Bernard Bloom, Department of Psychology, University of Colorado, Boulder, Colorado 80302.

It is interesting to note that in a 1962 survey (Golann, Wurm, & Magoon, 1964) it was estimated that about one fifth of the departments provided focused attention to community mental health topics as contrasted with over two fifths in the present survey. Furthermore, only one department had reported a sequence or specialization in community mental health as contrasted with ten such reports received in the later survey. Apparently, a number of departments are moving toward the type of training recommended in this chapter and elsewhere in the volume. Certain of these programs are described in more detail in other chapters. After reading them, one may wish to reflect on the following assertion:

> Although clinical psychology is closely related to medicine, it is quite as closely related to sociology and to pedagogy. The school room, the juvenile court, and the streets are a larger laboratory of psychology. An abundance of material for scientific study fails to be utilized because the interest of psychologists are elsewhere engaged. . . . (Witmer, 1907).

REFERENCES

Adams, H. B. Mental illness or interpersonal behavior? *American Psychologist,* 1964, 19, 191–197.

Albee, G. W. The dark at the top of the agenda. *Clinical Psychologist,* 1966, 20, 7–9.

Altrocchi, J., Spielberger, C. D., & Eisdorfer, C. Mental health consultation with groups. *Community Mental Health Journal,* 1965, 1, 127–134.

Bandura, A. Punishment revisited. *Journal of Consulting Psychology,* 1962, 26, 298–301.

Bockoven, S. *Moral treatment in American psychiatry.* New York: Spinger, 1963.

Caplan, G. Types of mental health consultation. *American Journal of Orthopsychiatry,* 1963, 33, 470–481.

Caplan, G. *Principles of preventive psychiatry.* New York: Basic Books, 1964.

Caplan, G. Problems of training in mental health consultation. In S. E. Goldston (Ed.), *Concepts of community psychiatry, a framework for training.* (U.S.P.H.S. Publ. No. 1319) Bethesda, Md.: U. S. Dept. of H.E.W., 1965.

Davis, J. A. *Education for positive mental health: A review of existing research and recommendations for future studies.* Chicago: National Opinion Research Center, University of Chicago, 1963.

Eisdorfer, C., Altrocchi, J., & Young, R. F. Principles of community mental health in a rural community: The Halifax County Program. *Community Mental Health Journal,* in press.

Farberow, N. L., & Shneidman, E. S. (Eds.). *The cry for help.* New York: McGraw-Hill, 1961.

Golann, S. E. Initial findings of the follow-up study of child development counselors. *American Journal of Public Health,* 1967, 57, 1759–1766.

Golann, S. E., Breiter, D. E., & Magoon, T. M. A filmed interview applied to the evaluation of mental health counselors. *Psychotherapy: Theory, Research and Practice,* 1966, 3, 21–24.

Golann, S. E., & Magoon, T. M. A non-traditionally trained mental health counselor's work in a school counseling service. *School Counselor,* 1966, 14, 81–85.

Golann, S. E., Wurm, C. A., & Magoon, T. M. Community mental health content of graduate programs in departments of psychology. *Journal of Clinical Psychology,* 1964, 20, 518–522.

Goodman, G. An experiment with companionship therapy: College students and troubled boys—assumptions, selection, and design. *American Journal of Public Health,* 1967, 57, 1772–1776.

56 COMMUNITY PSYCHOLOGY, COMMUNITY MENTAL HEALTH, AND SOCIAL NEEDS

Hobbs, N. Mental health's third revolution. *American Journal of Orthopsychiatry*, 1964, 34, 1–20.

Hobbs, N. Helping disturbed children: Psychological and ecological strategies. *American Psychologist*, 1966, 21, 1105–1115.

Holzberg, J. D., Gewirtz, H., & Ebner, E. Changes in moral judgment and self-acceptance in college students as a function of companionship with hospitalized mental patients. *Journal of Consulting Psychology*, 1964, 28, 299–303.

Holzberg, J. D., & Knapp, R. H. The social interaction of college students and chronically ill patients. *American Journal of Orthopsychiatry*, 1965, 35, 487–492.

Hunt, R. G. Age, sex, and service patterns in a child guidance clinic. *Journal of Child Psychology and Psychiatry*, 1961, 2, 185–192.

Iscoe, I. Editorial: The final report of the Joint Commission on Mental Illness and Health: Implications for clinical psychology. *Journal of Clinical Psychology*, 1962, 18, 110.

Joint Commission on Mental Illness and Health. *Action for mental health*. New York: Basic Books, 1961.

Kelly, J. G. The mental health agent in the urban community. In Group for the Advancement of Psychiatry, *Urban America and the planning of mental health services*. Washington, D. C.: Author, 1964.

Lourie, R., Rioch, M., & Schwartz, S. The concept of a training program for child development counselors. *American Journal of Public Health*, 1967, 57, 1754–1758.

Magoon, T. M., Golann, S. E., & Freeman, R. W. *Mental health counselors at work*. Oxford: Pergamon Press, 1969.

Mariner, A. S. A critical look at professional education in the mental health field. *American Psychologist*, 1967, 22, 271–281.

Mondale, W. F. Some thoughts on "Stumbling into the future." *American Psychologist*, 1967, 22, 970–973.

Nunnally, J. D., Jr. *Popular conceptions of mental health*. New York: Holt, Rinehart, and Winston, 1961.

Pennsylvania Mental Health. *Mental health education: A critique*. Philadelphia: Author, 1960.

Riesmann, F., & Hallowitz, E. The neighborhood service center: An innovation in preventive psychiatry. *American Journal of Psychiatry*, 1967, 123, 1408–1413.

Rioch, M. J., Elkes, C., & Flint, A. A. *Pilot project in training mental health counselors*. (U.S.P.H.S. Publ. No. 1254) Washington, D. C.: U.S.G.P.O., 1965.

Rossi, A. M. Some pre-World War II antecedents of community mental health theory and practice. *Mental Hygiene*, 1962, 46, 78–94.

Shellow, R., & Romer, D. No heaven for hell's angels. *Transaction*, 1966, 3, 12–19.

Shneidman, E. S., & Farberow, N. L. (Eds.). *Clues to suicide*. New York: McGraw-Hill, 1957.

Shneidman, E. S., & Mandelkorn, P. *How to prevent suicide*. Public Affairs Pamphlet No. 406. New York: 1967.

Simon, K. A., & Fullam, M. G. *Projections of educational statistics to 1975–76*. Office of Education, National Center for Educational Statistics. Washington, D. C.: U.S.G.P.O., 1966.

Spielberger, C. D. The effects of manifest anxiety on the academic achievement of college students. *Mental Hygiene*, 1962, 46, 420–426.

Spielberger, C. D. A mental health consultation program in a small community with limited professional mental health resources. In E. L. Cowen & M. Zax

(Eds.), *Emergent approaches to mental health problems.* New York: Appleton-Century-Crofts, 1967.

Spielberger, C. D., & Weitz, H. Improving the academic performance of anxious college freshmen: A group counseling approach to the prevention of under-achievement. *Psychological Monographs,* 1964, **78** (3, Whole No. 590).

Spielberger, C. D., Weitz, H., & Denny, J. P. Group counseling and the academic performance of anxious college freshmen. *Journal of Counseling Psychology,* 1962, **9,** 195–204.

Srole, L., Langer, T. S., Michael, S. T., Opler, M. K., & Rennie, T. A. *Mental health in the metropolis.* New York: McGraw-Hill, 1962.

Szasz, T. S. The myth of mental illness. *American Psychologist,* 1960, **15,** 113–118.

Szasz, T. S. The uses of naming and the origin of the myth of mental illnesses. *American Psychologist,* 1961, **16,** 59–65.

Umbarger, C., Dalsimer, J., Morrison, A., & Breggin, P. *College students in a mental hospital.* New York: Grune & Stratton, 1962.

Walder, L. O., Cohen, S., Daston, P. G., Breiter, T., & Hirsch, I. Behavior therapy of children through their parents. Paper presented at the American Psychological Association Convention, Washington, D. C., September, 1967.

Witmer, L. Clinical psychology. *Psychological Clinic,* 1907, **1,** 1–9.

4

New Requirements in Educating Psychologists for Public Practice and Applied Research

Sheldon R. Roen

Psychologists who have allowed "community" to enter their research and practice have experienced an exhilaration in finding a model of activity more congenial to their disciplinary interests. There is now no doubt that the contemporary idiom reflecting an interest in contextual issues portends major reconstructions in the entire field of social well-being. The noun "community" has become also an adjective; the subject or object a descriptive modifier. Important segments of society, it would seem, have made a determined commitment to work toward ameliorating recalcitrant social problems.

Community psychology is one organization's response to a movement that in a very short time has come to include community health, community action, community pediatrics, community psychiatry, and several other efforts that, although similar in concept, have resisted the communal label. At this point in time, psychologists seem to have accumulated most of their community experience in the community mental health field where their roles have been rather general and diffuse. Spotlighting this aspect of community work may allow leverage on the broader issues of new training models for psychologists. It will, therefore, be the object of this chapter to pose questions in relation to community mental health and deduce implications for new educational requirements.

Among some of the questions that immediately come to mind are the following: Is the level of change reflected by community applications of psychology of sufficient depth to justify attention to basic changes in training models? What, if anything, can be specified as special or unique about the contributions of psychology to this new movement? Has the community field developed sufficiently to be amenable to definition? Are community affairs in general, and mental health applications in particular, germane to the main stream of psychology, or should they be left to other disciplines and the opportunity taken to retrench and reconcentrate the field of psychology?

These questions, among others, should be attended to if an intelligent contribution to the problem is to be made. However, for purposes of the present exposition, only limited aspects of some of the questions will be reviewed.

HOW TO POSE THE INITIAL QUESTION

As we tell our students, the way in which a question is asked is one of the more important aspects of scholarly strategy. If, in a descriptive pursuit, we emerge with an operational definition of what psychologists in the community are currently doing, we risk falling into the technocratic bind that, for example, currently plagues clinical psychology, which tends to be defined in terms of psychotherapeutic and diagnostic technique. Let us take courage and aim for the very core conceptualization—that which is at the root of the new movement—and, if successfully specified, juxtapose it against the discipline of psychology to see at which point they intersect.

An approach to the core question can be made for present purposes from three perspectives. First, there are the guidelines of Federal legislation, which have, with great financial and promotional impetus, ushered in the movement as it is generally known today. Second, community mental health can be looked at in practice in agencies where psychologists play active and innovating roles. Third, we have the opportunity to look at the presumably more thoughtful products of mental health professionals who have taken time out from their busy schedules to submit articles to a journal that has community mental health as its title.

FEDERAL IMPETUS

There is no need here to detail the Federal guidelines for community mental health; these are by now fairly well known. However, in reading the Federal literature one is struck generally by the implied impatience toward both administrators and practitioners—the constant, not always subtle, reminder that in the field of mental health society demands more than what had been offered previously. Besides insistance on efficient, equitable, and flexible delivery of service, there are requirements for manageable catchment areas and commitments to deal with problems of total populations. By advocating greater contiguity with the environmental well-springs of emotional problems, and by asking that more attention be paid to urgent demands for expedient remediation, the general aim of government appears to be the securing of a feeling of responsibility on the part of the mental health profession for population groups. It follows that with this leverage preventive strategies would emerge for the promotion of positive mental health—that precious commodity having correlative influence on other stubborn social problems.

The stakes are therefore extremely high and the mobilization of forces relatively great. In this call for total commitment, government seems to be saying to public practitioners: "Get interested in the larger picture. There is a job to be done for which we will furnish the materials. You take an educated look, define the problems, and commit yourself to their resolve. In the process, however, you will find it necessary to give up those previously comforting service arrangements which may have met professional and institutional needs but were not attuned to the public at large."

COMMUNITY PRACTICE

With regard to what can be discerned about the core question from practices of community mental health centers in which psychologists play an active and innovating role, this too need not be overly elaborated upon here. Those acquainted with such programs know of their hectic pace and their entanglements in all manner of community intervention. In terms of individual clients there seems to be a shift in ideological emphasis from uncovering latent conflicts to meeting manifest needs. The routine processing of clients is discouraged, and flexibility, experimentation, and efficiency are valued. In reaching out to the community, the old constraints of "professionalism" have been discarded; collaboration with anyone is a plus, physical mobility of staff is encouraged, new semiprofessional or nonprofessional manpower pools are sought, and inventive programs for dealing with mental health problems are rewarded. In case conferences alternative suggestions for dispositions are carefully evaluated: crisis intervention; short-term limited goal treatment; conjoint family therapy; collaborating on the case with other than a mental health professional; promoting coping skills, as in therapeutic tutoring; placement in a group; and referral to a more directly pertinent agency or community service. Community conferences are scheduled on a regular basis to discuss such issues as consultation, unmet community needs, and dynamics of local social systems.

From the perspective of the community mental health center, then, there would seem to be a seeking for new satisfactions. By opening their doors to all within a defined region, and by valiantly accepting a role in immediate problem solving, their stance is one of responsiveness to as many community problems as the energy of its staff allows.

PUBLICATIONS

The third available perspective for shedding light on the core question is an analysis of articles submitted to the *Community Mental Health Journal*. Although psychologists are on the low end of subscribers, they are by far the major source of contributed manuscripts. The situation obtains even though the journal sometimes bends over backwards to encourage multidisciplinary participation. There are, of course, obvious reasons why psychologists write, but the fact that they do is sufficient. Assuming that they get read, considerable influence is thereby exerted by psychologists in terms of what they decide to write about, and what a board of consulting editors decides is a worthwhile contribution.

The range of topics published appears as wide as imagination allows. One attempt at classification of articles produced the following: (a) analysis of social structures and environmental forces; (b) efficient and innovative administration of the mental health enterprise; (c) training and utilizing professionals, semiprofessionals, and nonprofessionals; (d) new techniques of practice and programming; and (e) special procedures relevant to selected "high risk" groups. These categories still left a large miscellaneous group of manuscripts where topics reflect further the range of diversity: Effect of Residential Change on Adjustment, Bussing of Negro Children, Alternatives to Hospitalization, Political Science and Mental Health, Physical Abuse of Children by Parents, Training the Poor for New Careers, Tenant Participation in Public Housing, Employment of the Mentally Restored, Dealing with Hard-Core Handicapped, Amicatherapy, and a variety of other titles relating to previously neglected population groups in terms of innovative programming for prevention, treatment, and rehabilitation.

The vision of authors submitting papers seems not to be focused on individuals or on issues of predominantly academic interest. Instead, they seem to be looking mainly at the context of problems and formulating the issues in terms of direct action notions for remediation.

From this short and certainly inadequate discussion of three perspectives one might be wiser to beg the core question and view the current frenzy as merely a result of reconsideration and reintegration of old ideas in a more congenial *zeitgeist*, or, even less generously, call in the unexplanatory professional "fad" argument. These responses will only take us up a dead end, however, and do no justice to the marshaling of impressive human economic resources. Although scholarly presentation of the theoretical underpinnings and historical roots of the community movement is certainly in order, and hopefully this is being carried forth by those in a sufficiently authoritative position to do it, the task here is to try to derive a reasonable conceptualization of the core issue to be used for training recommendations.

HAS THE QUEST CHANGED?

It seems to this writer at least that the field has dropped the historic question most typically posed as "What is the nature of man?"—gone beyond the more contemporary question of "What is the nature of the problems faced by man?"—and synthesized the two by posing the contextual question of "What happens at the interaction of inner man and problem world?" As pointed out by Kagan, absolutistic psychology is in demise as the result of not having incorporated the crucial discoveries and formulations made by other sciences regarding the relativistic nature of phenomena.

> Biology began to drift from the constraints of an absolute view of events and processes when she acknowledged that the fate of a small slice of ecto-dermal tissue depended upon whether it was placed near the area of the eye or the toe . . . [and in physics] . . . the simple notion that whether an object moves or not depends on where you are standing has lead to such significant reversals as defining mass as relative to the speed of light. (Kagan, 1967, p. 133)

Similarly, in the clinical realm, although it has long been obvious that "human nature" as an absolute concept is without substance, there continued to be some carry over in "set" as a result of the limiting technique practiced in isolated consultation rooms that demanded sharply specific focus on the infantile machination of human motivation as related primarily to family. There can no longer be any doubt that human nature contains "instincts," if you will, that are libidinous and aggressive, and that their distortion plays a significant role in certain kinds of psychopathology. Equally useful as a concept, however, is the observation that man also has "instincts" toward self-preservation, gregariousness, familial loyalty, and the application of logical thought, curiosity, competence, esthetics, and much more. In different individuals, and in different cultures, and in different historical epochs, and in different stages in the life cycle, any one of these "basic natures" may become dominant.

From this point of view, situational requirements may well be the single most important factor in understanding a behavior. Personality trends certainly supply important elaborations of our understanding, but may not, in the final analysis, be of prepotent significance. About all that can be said with confidence regarding "human nature" is that it is extremely adaptable and inherently ambiguous. If physical matter itself is not amenable to absolutistic notions, can that which is complexly composed of it be any less relative? How else can we convincingly explain the role of exterminator in a concentration camp, soldier on the battlefield, and terrorist within a cause in light of the behavior of these same individuals a decade later as exemplars of urbanity and devotees of humanized civilization?

In its attempts to understand and intervene effectively in the lives of troubled people, community mental health would seem to be asserting that the context in which the problem at hand is imbedded is of great, if not pivotal, significance. Not content with the underpowered concept of behavior being overdetermined, it looks seriously at the hospital as an institution, the school as an environment, the neighborhood as a molder, the symptom as a hang-up, the timing of the intervention as a tactic, and at social forces as handles on prevention.

If you allow this construction of the issues, training strategy might then be best broadened to include contextual problem solving: problem-oriented intervention as well as personality-centered analysis.

SOME PROPOSITIONS ABOUT TRAINING

An activist beat lies in the heart of the community orientation. It is not then surprising that first thoughts of training reach out to where the action is—the practicum center. The history of this aspect of psychological endeavor in the United States can be traced to the establishment of psychological clinics at the end of the nineteenth century. The choice of the word "clinic" for this type of facility must have been of significant influence in fostering a medical model with consequent interest in diagnosis and treatment of what was to become defined as psychopathology.

As other psychologists interested themselves in application, a variety of applied specialities emerged as a function of the setting, problem, or social institution toward which the application was directed. Compartmentalizing in these terms can now be seen as having been too arbitrary since it has given rise to serious professional problems and has factionated graduate education. In order to meet the needs of subspecialities and interest groups, practicum facilities were often organized as laboratories in which clients were selected for study and for the practice of technique according to predefined notions as to the proper subject of focus and the intervention of choice. The facility could neither be a model of what students would subsequently experience in their work after graduation nor a purveyor of innovation based on sound inquiry. The hierarchy of values engendered by a clinic model favored depth of study of personality characteristics of individual clients, lengthy intervention techniques aimed at changing long-standing personality traits, a predilection for working with select persons who exhibit certain kinds of symptoms, a greater feeling of responsibility toward persons who happen to become clients rather than people with common social problems, and a narrowing of definitions regarding those who could be helped and the appropriate techniques for helping. Perhaps as a reaction formation, academic values also narrowed and clinical and research loyalties divided. Applied psychology neither fulfilled its mission to help with the general problem of mass maladjustment nor was it a catalyzer for application of scientific psychological knowledge.

With the above as background, the following propositions about education and training are offered:

1. The range of problems with which professional psychologists have dealt can now with benefit be broadened. Unless exposure is obtained in graduate school to the full range of plausable applications of psychological knowledge, flexibility in subsequent practice will be hampered and the range of human problems attended to by psychologists will remain narrow.

2. The in-house practicum facility at which graduate students train serves a better educational purpose if it exemplifies sound, broad, public practice and is similar or advanced in structure and operations to what the student will be exposed to upon graduation.

3. The approved current trend in professional preparation of psychologists seems to be specialization postdoctorally in similar manner to medicine and other substantive professions where after graduation the new professional enters a residency, apprenticeship, or postdoctoral fellowship. Our own ABEPP rules are in harmony with this proposition by implying that unless specialized, supervised experience is obtained postdoctorally, the practitioner is not completely qualified. Adherence to this view would leave graduate education free to offer more broadly based general education emphasizing interdisciplinary cross-fertilization, greater appreciation for other applied specialties and intervention technologies currently in practice, exposure to wider assortments of human problems toward which psychologists could contribute insightfully, and greater commingling of the psychological subspecialties.

4. Significant research is nurtured in applied psychology when the student is meaningfully immersed in timely problems of people as manifested in natural human environments. Conceptualizing problems in the isolation of a "laboratory" or the academic classroom may contribute to solving issues relevant to the theoretical concerns of the discipline, but is less likely to lead to research breakthroughs needed in professional practice.

5. Practicum work should be a graded experience that begins at the earliest moment in graduate training and should be meaningfully integrated with the total curriculum. Theory, research, and practice would all be strengthened if approached coherently.

6. Role models of the scholar-professional should be available to the graduate student continuously. More active affiliation and participation of faculty in the practicum facility may serve this end, especially if the faculty exhibits the combined elements of the role to be emulated.

7. Currently, the old formula of behavior being a function of the

person and his environment is being resurrected in professional practice. If a student is to appreciate fully how environments impinge on people, he needs guided experience with environments. Previous neglect of the physiological and neurological aspects of behavior eventuated in specific course requirements in these subjects. This precedent can be followed with some modification in regard to environmental components of behavior. Community, as a concept for environment, is particularly viable in this regard. Departments of psychology should choose to "affiliate" with particular, defined communities, proximal to the practicum facility if possible. These communities could then be cumulatively studied historically, topographically, demographically, and clinically so that a pool of "environmental" data can be fashioned against which the personal and social problems of residents can be better understood.

TRAINING PROPOSALS

Let us have fun with a fantasy. Suppose the above propositions were sufficiently agreeable as to serve as guidelines for changing some of the current educational practices. The major task would be gradually to reconstruct the mission and style of applied psychology. Toward this end the following thoughts regarding implementation are offered.

THE PRACTICUM FACILITY

Departments of psychology would give serious consideration to Albee's (1964) proposal for Psychological Centers which was strongly supported by the Chicago Conference on the Professional Preparation of Clinical Psychologists (Hoch, Ross, & Winder, 1966). The facility itself should be oriented to practical problem solving in the general field of social well-being. It could specialize in problems emerging from the community with which it is affiliated and about which it will be continuously gathering information, adhering more to a neighborhood service center model than a medical clinic model. Links of collaboration could be fashioned with other community service facilities through workable patterns of communication and interchange so that clients could be comprehensively served. Likewise, other university-sponsored service programs related to social welfare would be invited to affiliate in whatever manner proved feasible. Distinguished specialists with competencies not indigenous to the regular faculty would be adjunctively appointed to the staff of the facility which would endeavor to function all year round through special arrangements with students.

STUDENTS

Rather than enroll in specialized practicum courses, students would be assigned for practical experience on a continuous basis from the very first semester of their graduate training with gradation in time commitment. The staff of the facility would be responsible for providing appropriate experiences either in the facility or in proximal community agencies with which it would establish affiliations. Internship credit could be given to this type of experience especially when students enroll over the summer months. What now goes by the label of diagnostic testing would be conceived as data-gathering in relation to the specific human problems assigned to students. Initial data-gathering experiences might include individual test administration but would go much beyond; for example: to diagnosis—the amassing of information relevant to the reasons for poverty in a given family; path to the institution—the reasons for breakdown in communication between the individual and an institution from both points of view; referral—delineating the forces causing frustration in obtaining needed services; disposition—a systems analysis of probable success vs expenditure of effort for a variety of service approaches and intervention techniques.

Advanced students would engage in specific interventions after careful analysis of a problem. Intervention would be guided by the formulation of practical goals in keeping with a commitment to society as a whole. Intervention experiences might include traditional modes of psychotherapy, consultation with teachers and others who are in a position to do something about the problem, desensitization or other emergent behavior modification techniques, crisis intervention, short-term or limited-goal problem solving, consultation to social action groups, and the array of group methods including conjoint family therapy and sensitivity training. Experiences would also be offered in promoting competence, establishing more wholesome milieus, and negotiating with social forces. Conceptualizing plausible notions of prevention would be valued.

FACULTY

Faculty, in lieu of teaching or supervising in particular practicum courses, would hold appointments as senior staff members at the practicum facility. They would conduct case conferences emphasizing the generalizable problem case and could devote a portion of the conference to emergent research issues. Their supervision would be in their area of interest and specialization, and students for a portion of their caseload would move flexibly from supervisor to supervisor according to the problem assigned. Faculty would also serve as practicum advisors to students for the purpose of guiding them to a balanced experience. Faculty would be encouraged to see a limited number of cases in their own right at the facility under special service fee arrangements as a way of keeping up their own professional skills and experimenting with the development of new skills.

EXAMPLES OF INNOVATIVE TRAINING EXPERIENCES

Within the framework suggested, it would be possible to test the value of special kinds of experiences. For example, at the beginning of their graduate career students could be assigned to the role of "case administrator" for, say, ten to twenty cases. They would involve themselves with the client somewhere early in the intake phase and function a little like an ombudsman in getting feedback two to four times a year from them about how they were progressing through the various channels of intervention. The clinical responsibility for this aspect of the students work would, of course, belong to others. The student would stick with his caseload throughout the graduate education period in this quasi-administrative relationship with these particular clients and hopefully obtain a worthwhile longitudinal experience of vagaries *in vivo* to balance his experience of people "in treatment."

Another early experience that might be worth testing is the point of contact with the facility. Telephone answering and initial letter reading could go a long way to help the student to appreciate fully the range of problems for which people look for help and which often get screened before intake. This receptionist function for, say, four hours a month could be buttressed by an application period (not intake) in which students in personal interview ask the application questions and record the responses.

SUMMARY

An attempt was made in this paper to delineate some of the newer thinking about the education of applied psychologists relative to the community movement. It was suggested that the basic question for psychology has been changed from "What is the nature of man?" to the contextual question of what happens at the interface of inner man and problem world. The practicum experience at the graduate level seems to have most potential for reorienting the field in this regard.

REFERENCES

Albee, G. W. A declaration of independence for psychology. *Ohio Psychologist,*
　　1964, 10(4), p. 3
Gladstone, S. *Concepts of community psychiatry: A framework for training.*
　　PHS PJ, No. 1319. Washington, D. C.: U. S. Dept. of H.E.W., 1965.
Hoch, E. L., Ross, A. Q., & Winder, C. L. Conference on the professional prepa-
　　ration of clinical psychologists: A summary. *American Psychologist,* 1966, 21,
　　42–51.
Kagan, J. On the need for relativism. *American Psychologist,* 1967, 22, 131–142.

5

Some Postulates of Practice in Community Psychology and Their Implications for Training

Murray Levine

Community psychology is emerging from a set of social and professional pressures which have been reviewed elsewhere (Sarason, Levine, Goldenberg, Cherlin, & Bennett, 1966). These pressures have to do with the demand for new patterns of treatment which will not remove the mentally ill or the deviant from the community (Joint Commission, 1961), with the demand for preventive patterns of help (Eisenberg, 1962), with the inevitable shortage of professionally trained treatment personnel (Albee, 1959), with dissatisfactions with the efficacy of current patterns of diagnosis and therapy, (Meehl, 1960; Eysenck, 1961), and with dissatisfactions concerning inequities in the distribution of services to all levels of society (Hollingshead & Redlich, 1958; Furman, 1966).

Contemporary concepts of illness and of therapy may be summed up in the descriptive, albeit somewhat inflammatory, term "intrapsychic supremacy." Contemporary practice is based on an assumption that the important events involved in problems of living are invariably intrapsychic ones. If a person was having difficulty, it was because of events within him; no change in the outside world would have very much of an important effect because the intrapsychic events were fixed in earlier experience. The assumption of intrapsychic supremacy also holds that important changes in intrapsychic events could take place only within a certain set of narrow conditions, conditions normally produced only in a psychotherapeutic relationship, with a skilled, professionally trained psychotherapist. Psychotherapy became the treatment of choice on the assumption that all one needed to do was change the intrapsychic events, and then other matters would take care of themselves.

The assumptions of intrapsychic supremacy tended to overlook the situational determinants of problems in living, tended to underestimate the strength of environmental events to foster constructive change, and, most importantly in relation to the near exclusive reliance on psychotherapy, the problem of transferring gains from psychotherapy to the life situation was largely ignored. The concept that people lived in social systems and that their behavior and feelings were importantly influenced by the settings in which they lived and worked was given only peripheral attention.

In the course of thinking about the various methods of approach evolved by members of the Yale Psycho-Educational Clinic (Sarason et al., 1966), it seemed that a variety of programs operated with a relatively limited set of postulates.

The postulates of community mental health practice seem to be five in number. In what follows, the postulates shall be stated as formal propositions without elaboration. A more detailed discussion of the postulates can be found in another place (Levine, in press).

> *Postulate 1:* A problem arises in a setting or in a situation; some factor in the situation in which the problem manifests itself causes, triggers, exacerbates, or maintains the problem.

Example 1. An aggressive and hyperactive child in a classroom tends to become a problem primarily when the teacher is overly permissive, inconsistent, or threatened by the hyperactive and aggressive behavior. The same child may be placed with a firmer, more definite, more demanding teacher with the consequence that objectionable behavior frequently disappears, often immediately. If a substitute teacher comes in, or if the child is again placed with the "wrong" teacher for him, the problem reasserts itself. The first teacher cannot be said to be causing his behavior any more than the second teacher can be said to have "cured" him. It is simply that characteristics of the situation elicit different behaviors from the same individual.

The postulate reflects the well-known consideration that people, even severely deranged psychotics, act differently in different situations. If anything is true, it is that situational factors account for the bulk of variance in human behavior.

A second postulate related to the statement that the situation is always involved is necessary.

> *Postulate 2:* A problem arises in a situation because of some element in the social setting that blocks effective problem solving behavior on the part of those charged with carrying out the functions and achieving the goals of the setting.

The postulate strikes at an important set of issues. It implies that human behavior poses an issue in a setting only when the social system of deviance control or of conflict resolution is ineffective for whatever reason. Just as the situational postulate implies that there is no such thing as a purely intrapsychic problem divorced from a social or interpersonal context, so this postulate implies there is no such thing as a problem divorced from the systems of deviance control and conflict resolution which would ordinarily serve to control it. A person becomes an issue, so to speak, when the situation does not provide for him satisfactorily, or for those who also live or work in the setting with him.

The postulate permits the deduction that an agent who attempts to intervene in the situation will learn something about the constraint in the social system which led to the inadequacy of the typical mode of deviance control, or to the failure to consider alternative solutions to the problem presented by the given individual. We shall return to this point later on in discussing the problem of institutionalizing innovations in helping services in given settings. Suffice it to say that attempts to intervene will reveal much about the nature of the social system in which the individual is considered a problem. In order to intervene effectively, one needs to take into account variables related to the total social system.

The issues relevant to the postulate vary markedly from relatively innocuous matters which can be cleared up easily to concerns which reveal the vitals of the particular setting. If one intervenes in a setting to help the setting deal more effectively with its problems—a frequently stated goal of consultation, for example—one can be assured that the problem will involve more than simply a lack of skills or knowledge on the part of people in the setting. Mental health personnel are accustomed to thinking about all problems as consequences of emotional blocks. Problems related to role, or to system constraints, or to inadequate cooperation within settings are equally important. For example, if one asks the aides in a mental hospital what ought to be done for the patients, many excellent therapeutic suggestions emerge. If one asks why the suggestions are not implemented, system problems emerge.

> *Postulate 3:* Help, to be effective, has to be located strategically to the manifestation of the problem, preferably in the very situation in which the problem manifests itself.

This postulate follows from the first that the situation is always involved in the problem in some way. If the situation is directly involved, then the form of help must be brought to bear directly in the situation. Help should be located strategically to the manifestation of the problem because of the tendency of settings to deal with deviants by getting rid of the deviant in some way. A variant of the method of getting rid of the deviant is the "hands off" phenomenon (Sarason *et al.*, 1966) noted in the schools. (When a child is identified or labeled as mentally disturbed or mentally retarded, there is a tendency for the teacher to feel incompetent to deal with the problem and to avoid dealing with the child in any way at all.)

The concept that help should be located strategically to the manifestation of the problem is also designed to overcome the problem of transfer of gains from the therapy situation to the life situation.

A major example of this third postulate is found in Ira Goldenberg's development of a Residential Youth Center (RYC) in New Haven, as part of the Community Progress, Incorporated (CPI) manpower program. The RYC was located in a downtown area, at the edge of one of the poorer neighborhoods. Part of the manpower program, it accepted for residential help only those who were also engaged in some manpower program. The center was staffed by workers who took part in the training and education of the residents in other CPI settings. Several beds were always kept open for short-term emergency admissions from others in the program. Workers from the RYC also worked with the families of residents, helping to change the family if at all possible. Routine work with families would not have been possible had the center been located away from where the families lived. Similarly, workers in the center were always available to boys who had successfully completed the program to provide additional and continued support as necessary.

One can contrast the Job Corps concept with the RYC concept. The Job Corps camps, frequently located in isolated and rural areas, operate with the assumption of intrapsychic supremacy. The Job Corps was established on the premise that it would be possible to take people away from their normal environments, retrain them, and then return them to the environments in which they had had difficulty to begin with, with no attempt to change the situation or to pave the way for the new skills to be used, if indeed they were learned. In a sense, the Job Corps is the analogue of the large training school for the retarded, or the huge state mental hospital located a considerable distance from the population centers which provided the patients.

The concept that help be located strategically to the manifestation of the problem cannot be interpreted in spatial or geographic terms alone. Community mental health centers are now being located in large population centers. However, if the intake procedures are complex, then the institution may well be isolated even if in the midst of a population center. There needs to be accessibility in attitude as well as accessibility in a physical sense.

> *Postulate 4:* The goals or the values of the helping agent or the helping service must be consistent with the goals or the values of the setting in which the problem is manifested.

This postulate assumes that settings have important major purposes, and that the achievement of these purposes is vital to the continuance of the setting. It further assumes that the setting will act to expel, or otherwise isolate or make ineffective, helping agents who promote goals or values at variance with the major goals and values of the setting. A classic example of the failure of an effort at community mental health education and the expulsion of a project is found in Cumming and Cumming's book *Closed Ranks* (1957). Another perennial conflict arises when mental health and school people meet. E. K. Wickmann's classic research (1928) admirably depicts the difference in orientation between mental health workers and school teachers in their views of what constitute significant mental health problems, and why.

Help has to be offered in terms meaningful to the setting in which the problem manifests itself.

The postulate poses a severe problem for the community psychologist, and it poses a distinct problem in self-examination (Gouldner, 1965). The community psychologist may have to decide whether he can conscientiously support the goals of a given setting, even though he may feel he can be of help in that setting, in a technical sense. In a Psycho-Educational Clinic seminar, Ira Goldenberg posed the *reductio ad absurdum* for the group by asking what the community consultant would do if approached by the local KKK to help them with their interpersonal and organization problems so that they could more effectively carry out lynchings, terrorism, and other attempts to prevent minority groups from exercising civil rights.

In many instances the community psychologist's goals are not only to provide a helping service, but also to modify aspects of the settings in which people live and work. Since this is the case, the community mental health worker will obviously become deeply involved in value questions, and it behooves him to know his own values and to respect the values of others. In principle the problem is no different from one faced by psychotherapists, but the problem needs to be restated and faced in this new context. The community psychologist is an agent of deviancy control in settings whose goals he values, and he can be a change agent in settings whose goals he questions. It is important that the community psychologist understand what his own goals and values are, for the postulate suggests that different tactics and approaches are in order in different situations. It is unwise in the extreme to assume that community psychologists and the rest of the population share common values and common goals. It is a question which requires deep thought and serious evaluation in each new situation.

> *Postulate 5:* The form of help should have potential for being established on a systematic basis using the natural resources of the setting or through introducing resources that can become institutionalized as part of the setting.

The postulate covers several needs at once. First, it extends the concept that help should be located strategically to the manifestation of the problem, and the concept that the situation is always involved. Second, the postulate formalizes the community psychologist's concept that settings ought to be able to care for their own problems rather than have to remove the problem from the setting. Third, the stipulation that the form of help use some natural resource in the setting, or that it make use of helping agents who can be introduced into the setting on a permanent basis, recognizes the shortage of professionally trained personnel as well as the problem of transferring gains made in the therapeutic setting to the life setting.

The role of the community psychologist in these instances is in helping to identify the problems, helping to develop solutions which are meaningful within the structure of the problem setting, training the workers, if that is indicated, and helping to institutionalize the solution as a means of dealing not with a single problem, but with a class of problems. Where the traditional helping professional is interested in dealing with individual problems which come to his attention, with helping those individuals, and then removing the help, the practitioner of community psychology is interested in establishing quasipermanent solutions which will help a class of problems in settings.

The second postulate suggests that the problem of institutionalizing a solution will not be simple. If there are some blocks to the deviance control system or to the conflict resolution system, it is very likely that the proposed solution will in some way encounter the same elements of system problem that led to difficulty in the first place. One can cite any number of examples of important innovations in practice which were subverted by systems the practice was meant to change.

IMPLICATIONS FOR TRAINING

If these postulates have any generality, then they suggest that the relevant theory has to do with group dynamics, with concepts such as role, with the study of institutions and organizations, particularly as these involve the control of deviancy, the study of the goals and values of a variety of social institutions and settings, the organization of helping services, the introduction of services into ongoing systems, the development of new service organizations, and the concepts of social and institutional change. The community psychologist will need experience in understanding institutions and settings, in providing leadership, in developing organizations, in understanding governmental agencies and sources of funding for programs, in training procedures, as well as understanding personality theory and psychodynamics. It becomes apparent that the techniques of individual diagnosis become somewhat superfluous for most problems, and that techniques for diagnosing problems as reflections of the dynamics of settings and social organizations need to be developed. Techniques of individual therapy based on concepts of intrapsychic difficulty become less important, and techniques of help which depend upon variations in relationships possible within settings become more important. Concepts of work, play, and education, as systematic areas of study, become more important, while the detailed and microscopic study of drives and their vicissitudes becomes less important. However, the community psychologist needs to remember that he is always the agent of the individual, the agent of human growth and development, and not the agent of a system.

A MODEL TRAINING INSTITUTION

In what follows, I will criticize some current trends in the field of clinical psychology and describe a model training institution for community psychology. The program of this hypothetical training institution is loosely derivable from the set of postulates. Since the first postulate also applies to the training institution (the setting is always involved), the discussion will center on the organizaton and feeling tone of the training institution itself.

Training programs in clinical psychology in university settings have had several important deficiencies—deficiencies which reflect problems in academic fields generally. If we face facts frankly, we must admit that university training has too often proven to be irrelevant. If we can get agreement on any point, it is that people who are in the field, with near unanimity, will say that little or nothing they learned within the university adequately prepared them for tasks in the world, either shortly after graduation, or in terms of the demands placed upon them five and ten years after graduation. The complaint has to do not only with rapid changes in knowledge which produce obsolescence, but also with the bankruptcy of academic disciplines which have become so much more concerned with method than with substance that the disciplines themselves are in danger of withering away.

Were the social and psychological sciences dealing with problems of substance, and with theories which have powerful constructs, the professional in the field would have found the formal discipline very relevant to his work. The greatest indictment of much university-based social and psychological science is not that the concepts and empirical underpinnings are weak, but that they are esoteric and irrelevant because the problems with which they deal are trivial. We have only to pick up the most recent journal, or speak in public as we do in private of our feelings about students' dissertations, or more difficult yet, take seriously our feelings about much of our own research efforts, to acknowledge the correctness of our questions about the state of the research art.

University training not only is encumbered with the irrelevant and the trivial, but also is frequently lifeless in that the students real needs to develop and grow are not met and sometimes, perhaps too often, are stultified. We take our students, and in Jane Addams words (1910):

> . . . we spread the snare of preparation before the feet of young people, hopelessly entangling them in a curious inactivity at the very period of life when they are longing to construct the world anew and to conform it to their own ideals.

Our students too often view their university training as a means of marking time, of getting their union cards, or as a necessary evil on the way toward freedom; and when they finally do go out to clinical settings where they become engaged with the work of the world, we lose them to an unthinking commitment to ideas and forms of practice we know can lead only to a dead end.

Should our students be cut off from contact with the real problems of living? Should we train them to be so aggressively critical and so demanding of certainty that they are unable to entertain large ideas and large problems without feeling either guilty or dilettantish?

What of our professional colleges? Is there not a danger that many are so concerned with respectability and with the trappings of professional credentials that they no longer look at what anyone actually does? Too often what seems to be important is not demonstrable competence, ideas, or empirical verification, but degrees, number of courses, amount of supervised experience, and legal and paralegal certification, without any evidence that any of these things, in any quantity or combination, produce better practitioners. In point of fact what these trappings do is to close options for individuals and for the field. I am appalled when I hear some of my colleagues ask for a diploma in community psychology, as if the diploma would provide any help in the development of new ideas, of desperately needed new ideas. If we can predict anything, it is that the existence of formal requirements and formal certifications of "goodness" will result only in a form-oriented obstacle course which will direct effort and imagination away from dealing with substantive problems.

The idealized training model I am about to describe will be oriented toward the urban problem, but I see no reason why some modified version could not be established for almost any kind of situation.

I envision an institution which will be a residential center, located in the midst of a densely populated, heterogeneous urban area, perhaps a ghetto, but in a neighborhood in which there are many children. The center will house two or three senior staff members, perhaps with their families, and about twenty other people, most of whom would be graduate students, but not necessarily all. The graduate student resident population would include people from a variety of disciplines, and would by design include not only community psychologists but also sociologists, city planners, industrial administrators, law students, economists, and English, medical, nursing, and teaching students as well. I would have a few places reserved for some indigenous workers, and I would want a budding journalist, novelist, artist, or poet to reside there. I would want a mixed group of people in residence in order to avoid the insularity that so characterizes our various fields and makes it so difficult for people in different disciplines to talk together.

Each individual living in the center would have the responsibility of developing some kind of relationship with some aspect of the surrounding community, and if feasible, of studying or developing some kind of programmatic solution to a problem in living encountered in the area. It would be the responsibility of the senior resident staff to see that each student who develops a program treats the program as a research opportunity and attempts to relate what he is doing to some broader conceptual base. If the system of postulates has any validity, attempts at intervention will shed light on some aspect of social organization. Attempts at intervention can be viewed as experiments in varying the social order and as a means of understanding the behavior of people in their social order. Many undergraduates are now organizing or participating in a variety of efforts—action oriented, educationally oriented, recreationally oriented programs—and this model of training would simply harness that energy and give it purposeful direction. Below, I shall discuss the social organization of the residential center which would provide students maximum freedom to develop in their own ways and maximum freedom to study whatever problem seemed worthy of study.

I would hope we could talk graduate departments into working up a reading list and certifying students on the basis of their taking exams, leaving a minimum of courses, perhaps with those limited to formal statistics and research methods. Faculty members would be available for small group discussions, tutorials, and other informal conversation, largely as the students feel the need for additional help. Faculty would be used at their best, and would not have to prepare or repeat lectures which all too frequently interest neither faculty members nor students.

There would be three experiences at the heart of the training program. First, there would be a working seminar in which the students would present and discuss their work and their ideas. Everyone would be expected to participate equally. University faculty members and other experts would be invited when the group felt there was someone who had something relevant to say to them, or when some expert direction was needed for some particular problem. The seminar would not be a course with credit, but would be part of the requirement for anyone who wanted to live and work in this situation. Intellectual exchange would become a vital part of living. A norm of vigorous intellectual exchange would be encouraged, in contrast to the paradoxical situation which now prevails in which ideas are anathema to students!

The second experience would involve a combination of group therapy and sensitivity training. Its basic purpose would be to aid in the self-development of the members of the group, to aid in self understanding, and to provide a method for continuous evaluation of one's self in relation to present functioning and in relation to one's plans for the future. Contemporary training programs give students very little basis for deciding on a career, for exploring alternatives, or even for learning about what activities they do well and poorly. Most individuals more or less slip into their futures, and do not actively strive toward some more or less clear-cut goal. This kind of open and continuous evaluation would be extremely important for those who made a career in community psychology, since an adequate understanding of one's own impact on others is critical in appreciating one's style as a leader.

The third experience would be a staff meeting in which all present would participate equally in deciding policy, in allocating resources, in arranging for the care and maintenance of the building, and in dealing with all other problems of group living which arise. The staff meeting would provide each person with the opportunity to experience and understand the practical administrative problems any leader necessarily encounters, and to understand group process, not with simulated but with real tasks.

Residents would be selected on the basis of expressed interest, the approval of the group, the willingness of their department to set up a degree-granting program through the center, and the willingness of the department to accept that it will get no feedback concerning individual performance without the consent of the student. Each resident would start on a probationary basis the summer before his school semester begins, and if he and the group decide this is not a suitable program for him, he could still enter a standard graduate program without loss. Once in the program, decisions about continuation would be made by the group itself, with two norms encouraged—the group is to encourage each individual to reach out and grow, and second, if the group decides that a member cannot function, it also accepts responsibility for finding a suitable placement for the person. The purpose of such norms would be to guarantee an atmosphere in which one's security is not threatened and in which failure becomes the basis for growth experiences, and not something to be concealed.

All residents would receive their salaries and expenses from some relatively independent source. Hopefully, an independent board would take responsibility for granting fellowships and for raising the funds, but they would ask for a minimum of control. Fellows could be recommended by university departments, but once through the probationary period, the fellowship should be automatically renewable for a period of several years. The board should require no other evaluation than that the individual continues in residence at the center. Since we would hope that students would get involved in meaningful—that is, potentially controversial—issues, we would want the student to have the maximum of financial freedom. We would hope that students would make some modest contribution toward room and board, so that even here they would not be dependent, but would be paying their own way. I would demand that the board accept funds that were given without strings, and that the board's sources of funds be sufficiently diverse so that it would not be dependent upon a single government agency or upon some single patron who could destroy its effectiveness by suddenly withdrawing financial support.

The residential center itself ought to have some endowed fund large enough to pay its basic operating expenses and to provide a modest amount of internally controlled funds for programs and for research. The funds ought to be disbursed by the residents or by some subgroup which rotates. By no means should the center allow itself to become dependent upon outside support, nor should it let its basic interests be developed because of the availability of funds for certain purposes. Contracts with governmental agencies might be accepted, provided these contracts clearly served the research or program needs of some of the residents. Funds should not be accepted or sought only for the power and prestige accruing to holders of grants and contracts. If the center is to promote a concept of integrity and incorruptibility then it must begin to have integrity and to be incorruptible itself, traits of institutional character one does not find too often in these days of spasmodic government financing. Eventually, some proportion of the institution's funds ought to be raised from people who are served by its programs, another way of guaranteeing relevance in programming.

I emphasize financial independence, because too often we have seen people and ideas subverted in a search for funds. Funds ought to be accepted and sought with the understanding that funds are the nutriment for the vitality of the training center, but they cannot be accepted as the controlling force. We accept the principles that those in direct touch with the issues are in the best position to know what they need and that a relative scarcity of funds is a stimulus to ingenuity.

While the residential center would have a general mission, it would be organized on the principle that within the general mission each individual has ultimate responsibility for whatever program he develops. The power of decision should rest with the individual, and the group would act in an advisory capacity only. Each member would use the group as a resource for ideas, for sharing problems, for encouragement, and for criticism, but basically the person responsible for the program would decide what he wanted to do. There would be some group control in the sense that funds and other resources would be allocated to programs on the basis of some consensus, but there would be no other restriction, and an individual would still be free to utilize other resources if he had been unable to sell his idea to the group.

The issue of responsibility is introduced for a number of reasons. I believe that current graduate programs keep students in a state of dependence, treating them as if they are not responsible and not competent. [See Rogers (1967) for an expression of similar ideas about graduate training.] We handpick cases, watch the students' every move, whisper in their ears with hidden microphones, frighten them by insisting that they will ruin someone else's life forever if they say the wrong word, and encourage them in the fantasy that somewhere there is some magical way of doing business, which, if only they would find it (we keep it from them), they would handle everything perfectly. In research we give them the drippings of our squeezed out problems, and tell them they are brilliant when they take up our scut work as their central research interest. We do not encourage our students to reach, to think, or to try so that they can risk failure and learn from it. We tell them to be exactly like us, and if they protest, or if they question us, we tell them they have personal hang-ups which, if not corrected, will get them thrown out of school or worse. I maintain that one cannot encourage others to accept positions of leadership unless we make it possible for a student to try and to risk failure in the knowledge that he will be a better, fuller, wiser, and more courageous person for having tried, and tried again.

THE NEEDS OF THE FUTURE

I do not believe there is any such profession as a community psychologist. I do not believe that we will now, or in the foreseeable future, have service people to deal with the multitude of problems in living which will be continuously generated because of our rapidly changing society. The issue then is not service people; rather it seems to be one of providing people who will be able to fulfill several functions. We will need people able to exercise leadership within settings to help those settings become more viable for all the people within them, and to deal with the problem of deviance in ways other than removing the deviant from the setting. The leadership of the future needs to be much more deeply concerned with human values in any setting.

Second, we will need people who see it as their function to be the observers of social trends, to be the ones who plan for and anticipate changes in living, who anticipate the growth of problems, and who will be in a position to advise leaders in government and in various social groups of what the developing human problems are and what needs to be done to come to grips with the problems. These will be research and conceptually oriented people, for in the kind of position we foresee nothing will be more practical than sound theory.

Third, we will need popularizers who are informed and responsible. The popularizers will be those in touch with the communication media and the educational system. They will begin to spell out the problems at a very early stage to prepare for the acceptance of change. Government cannot move to achieve changes any more quickly than people are aware of the need for change, and hopefully, with scientifically trained popularizers used to talking with social scientists, we will have the basis for influencing, or at least mobilizing, opinion and attitudes concerning necessary changes. The war on poverty, for example, which is really an effort at social engineering, has been handicapped by inadequate popularization of the real problems, by inadequate understanding of the real problems, and by a lack of leadership in institutional settings attuned to change.

We have learned that money alone does not make for change, although it helps. People who are prepared to state the problems, who are prepared to discover the problems, who are prepared to institute solutions tentatively, and who have an empirical and not a power orientation and are prepared to work cooperatively—these people will fill the needs of the future.

I can speak with great confidence concerning this model, and I can describe it in great detail, not because it exists anywhere that I know about at the present time, but because it represents an updated version of the better settlement houses of the pre-World War I period. There are lessons to be learned from that group of early workers who influenced the lives of many in diverse ways. They not only helped in the development of specific forms of assistance, but also helped by influencing the power structure, by influencing legislation, and by influencing its enforcement. Later many people who had experiences in the settlements came into positions of power and responsibility in government where they were able to implement many of their views on a very wide scale indeed (Levine & Levine, 1970).

The lesson of history tells us that we cannot develop helping models which are uniformly effective. What we can develop are models which enable us to learn about how people live and which can help us to see how people might live. I believe that in the long run the greatest payoff lies in the development and implementation of utopian visions of what the world might become.

REFERENCES

Addams, J. *Twenty years at Hull House.* New York: MacMillan, 1910.
Albee, G. W. *Mental health manpower trends.* New York: Basic Books, 1959.

Cumming, E., & Cumming, J. *Closed ranks*. Cambridge, Mass.: Harvard University Press, 1957.

Eisenberger, L. If not now, when? *American Journal of Orthopsychiatry*, 1962, **32**, 781–791.

Eysenck, H. J. The effects of psychotherapy. In H. J. Eysenck (Ed.), *Handbook of abnormal psychology*. New York: Basic Books, 1961.

Furman, S. S. Suggestions for refocusing child guidance clinics. *Children*, 1965, **12**, 140–144.

Gouldner, A. W. Explorations in applied social science. In A. W. Gouldner & S. M. Miller (Eds.), *Applied sociology: Opportunities and problems*. New York: Free Press, 1965.

Hollingshead, A. B., & Redlich, F. C. *Social class and mental illness*. New York: J. Wiley, 1958.

Joint Commission on Mental Illness. *Action for mental health*. New York: Basic Books, 1961.

Levine, M. Some postulates of community psychology practice. In F. Kaplan and S. B. Sarason (Eds.), *Collected Papers of the Psycho-Educational Clinic*. Springfield, Mass.: Massachusetts Department of Mental Health, 1969.

Levine, M. & Levine, A. *A Social history of helping services: clinic, court, school, and community*. New York: Appleton-Century-Crofts, 1970.

Meehl, P. E. The cognitive activity of the clinician. *American Psychologist*, 1960, **15**, 19–27.

Rogers, C. R. Graduate education in psychology: A passionate statement. *The Clinical Psychologist*, 1967, **20**, 55–62.

Sarason, S. B., Levine, M. Goldenberg, I. I., Cherlin, D. L., & Bennett, E. M. *Psychology in community settings: Clinical, educational, vocational, social aspects*. New York: J. Wiley, 1966.

Wickman, E. K. *Children's behavior and teachers' attitudes*. New York: Commonwealth Fund Division of Publications, 1928.

III

Training in Community Psychology
Within Clinical Psychology
Programs

6

The Development of Community Psychology Training at George Peabody College

J. R. Newbrough, William C. Rhodes,
and Julius Seeman

The development of the community psychology program at George Peabody College will be discussed in this chapter. Since community psychology as an identifiable area of interest is of such recent origin, it was thought to be useful to preserve the historical value of this account by presenting events with some attention to their chronology as the program evolved and to the persons who participated in them.

The first course, a seminar in community mental health, was offered in 1957. A year later this seminar was incorporated formally into the doctoral program in clinical psychology. Two sets of forces combined to bring the program into being: (1) the personal histories and viewpoints of individual faculty members at Peabody (and their conceptions of national directions which were needed in psychology), and (2) the climate within the psychology department to support what was then a rather esoteric offshoot from psychology.

The first step in the evolution of the program came in 1951, when Nicholas Hobbs was appointed chairman of the Division of Human Development. George Peabody College had at that time an established reputation for its programs of education. Hobbs (1964) took the view that a clinical psychology program most relevant to Peabody College would be one which was oriented both toward children and toward a community perspective. Two years later, in 1953, he brought in Julius Seeman as coordinator of the clinical psychology training program. Seeman's background in work with children and his prior experience as a teacher in the public schools assured an emphasis upon developmental and community processes in clinical psychology.

At this point the most urgent need for the program was a person who could further the desired community emphasis. To this end William C.

Appreciation is extended to James Cooper, Nicholas Hobbs, Phil Schoggen, and Charles Spielberger for their interest and help in the preparation of this account.

Rhodes was appointed to the faculty in 1956. His background of experience in the Georgia State Department of Mental Health and his social-psychological perspective in clinical psychology provided a pertinent background for the developmental task he was to assume in the community psychology program at Peabody.

The directions of community psychology at Peabody College were thus shaped in considerable degree by the people involved in the program. To these personal influences must be added the effects of broader movements in psychology. In 1954, Hobbs was asked by the Southern Regional Education Board to conduct a study of mental health manpower needs in the Southeast region. This study supported Hobbs' recognition that sole reliance on individual professional treatment for emotional disturbance was an inadequate national policy.[1] Rhodes' view, compatible with the foregoing one, led him toward studies of discordant behavior as a sociopsychological phenomenon, toward studies of early intervention in behavioral pathology, and toward planning and evaluation based on quantitative data. Seeman's earlier research on outcomes of psychotherapy led him to a view that criteria of therapy outcome needed to be formulated in terms of adaptive behavior and personality integration. This interest led away from studies in psychopathology and individual treatment and toward more general studies of effective behavior and psychological integration.

All of these conceptual influences combined ultimately to make community psychology an integral and inevitable part of the Peabody clinical program. The inevitability of this development, however, can be seen most clearly in retrospect. It was certainly not that clear to the faculty in 1957. The general definition of clinical psychology in that year consisted of the usual threefold function of psychodiagnosis, psychotherapy, and research. There was no precedent clearly evident for community oriented functions.[2]

Nevertheless, it was during that year, 1957, that the clinical staff began to crystallize its conception of community psychology as an integral part of the doctoral program in clinical psychology. Although the first course was called "Seminar in Community Mental Health," there was, from the beginning, an attempt to clarify terminology. In the course outline Rhodes stated:

> The first assumption which is made here is that all of the material with which the mental health worker is concerned is neither mental nor is it

[1] This was at a time when the leaders in the mental health professions were becoming increasingly concerned about the national mental health needs and the resources needed to meet them. Hobbs was active in national affairs and provided an important, continuous inflow of information about national issues and national trends affecting psychology.

[2] Many clinical psychologists were active in community work, but specific training was to be found mainly at post-doctoral levels at such places as the Massachusetts General Hospital program of Erich Lindemann.

health. Only if one wishes to stretch the net of both of these words far beyond the logic of meaning, or the possibility of point-at-able definitions, can they be used at all by the variety of disciplines active in this field.

In a 1958 address to the Tennessee Psychological Association, Seeman (1959) said,

> Let me say first how I shall not conceptualize the problem. The term "mental health" is in some ways a useful one. It contains a big idea in two words. It has also been a basis on which many of our colleagues have organized their careers. But the term does not help very much at a conceptual level. For one thing, it places the focus on an often irrelevant dimension of illness and health when that is not what we are talking about at all. For another, it is so far removed from behavioral reference points that it has limited utility for psychological description. And so this paper will employ terms more immediately derived from the language of psychology.

These efforts at conceptualization made it clear that two levels of discourse could be distinguished. At one level were processes that could be classified as within the definitional framework of psychology. For these processes it was not regarded as necessary to use the term "mental health," so starting in the 1959/60 academic year, the term "community psychology" was chosen to describe the offerings. The second is a more complex level of discourse which includes man failing to adapt to particular settings. At that level are phenomena not unique to psychology but applicable equally to other disciplines and to interdisciplinary discourse. It is for such phenomena that the term "community mental health" has been reserved.

The program has gone through three phases in its development. They are described below, beginning with the early developmental work by William C. Rhodes, who became director of the Community Psychology area within the clinical training program.

PHASE I, 1957–1963

In the years between 1957 and 1963, the offerings in community psychology underwent continuous evolution. The first seminars were confined to the presentation of content material. By 1960, there was an increasing emphasis on practicum experiences as well. The nature of the work is illustrated by setting forth a typical seminar outline of that period and by listing the kinds of practicum experiences developed for the students. The typical course covered the following topics:

I. Major historical influences on community psychology
    A. Growth and development of social psychology
    B. Influences from the development of clinical psychology
    C. The development of the mental health movement

   II. Conceptual models of community psychology
      A. The influence of ecology
      B. Demography and epidemiology
      C. The concept of discordance
  III. Understanding the community
      A. Behavior shaping systems
          1. The legal-correctional system
          2. The medical system
          3. The social welfare system
          4. The educational system
      B. Power and the community
          1. The structural basis of power
          2. The personal basis of power
          3. Power-oriented behavior
      C. Poverty, social class, and culture
      D. Discordant behavior and community response
          1. The classes of discordant behavior (e.g., delinquency, crime, suicide, maternal deprivation, alcoholism, etc.)
          2. Community patterns for coping with discordance
             a. Patterns of exclusion
             b. Patterns of rehabilitation
  IV. Methodology of community psychology
      A. Program research
      B. Communication theory
      C. Group psychology and group processes
      D. Psychological change techniques
          1. System-change techniques
          2. Person-change techniques
             a. Therapeutic techniques
             b. Consultation

Consultation was viewed as the major technique in community psychology. A specific practicum course in consultation was devised with field placements, seminar-type presentations and the writing of student papers. The course was organized to cover the following topics:

    I. Definitions of consultation
   II. Consultaton and other interpersonal modes
      A. Consultation and psychotherapy or counseling
      B. Consultation and administrative decision making
      C. Consultation and supervision
  III. Phases and processes in consultation
      A. The appraisal
      B. Initial forces for change
      C. Emergent change forces
      D. Communication barriers
      E. The relationship
  IV. Consultee motivation
      A. Resistance
      B. Dependency
      C. Competition
   V. Organizational and situational variables

    VI. Consultee systems
        A. The community (consultation as carried out by sociologists and psychologists)
        B. Operational patterns or agencies
        C. Administrators or executives
        D. Individuals
    VII. Areas of focus for consultation
        A. Case consultation
        B. Program consultation
    VIII. Areas for research
        A. Consultant behavior
        B. Consultee behavior
        C. Organizational and situational variables

As the program evolved, practicum experiences were developed to provide opportunities for enhancement of student skills in consultation, administration, supervision, and research. In the 1957–1963 phase of the program, the practicum experiences emphasized consultation, supervision, and administration. For the consultation experience each student was placed in a field agency with the explicit objective of developing a consulting relationship with the administrator and his staff. Although a number of different agencies were used for placements, most of the students faced a similar task—that of defining with the staff the nature of his consulting role. The following list of agencies used will illustrate the variety of field resources developed during this phase of the program.

> The detention center of the juvenile court
> A social group work program in a public housing project
> A neighborhood community center in a low income neighborhood
> A nursery school program
> A private school
> The welfare department

Prior to taking the community psychology courses and engaging in the consulting experiences, the students had gained experience in clinical administration and supervision. Within the clinical program, practicum experience at all year levels was organized in a "vertical team" arrangement. Each vertical team consisted of four to six students representing all levels of training and functioned as a self-contained clinical staff with service responsibilities at the Peabody Child Study Center. The third-year student, as part of his general clinical psychology training, took both administrative and supervisory responsibility for the team under the guidance of a clinical faculty member. The student assumed as much responsibility as he could in keeping the team organized and functioning. He also worked with the less advanced members of the group in an instructional capacity. At any one time there were usually three vertical teams in operation. Their tasks having a training focus for them, the three student administrators (team captains) met weekly as a group with a faculty member to help them conceptualize and carry out the administrative and teaching functions.

It is interesting to speculate about the processes by which some ideas have no consequences, while others catch hold and lead to change. In 1963, two events with important consequences occurred. They were both to have significant impact on the Peabody community psychology program, yet neither had the slightest immediate effect. The first was Rhodes' development of an extensive community psychology curriculum, "A Proposal for Comprehensive Training in Community Psychology." This proposal had two unique characteristics. First, it envisioned multiple levels of functioning in community psychology: an advanced specialist level, a general doctoral level, and a subdoctoral level. Second, it envisioned community psychology not merely as an arm of clinical psychology but as a differentiated specialty coordinate with other specialties within psychology. At that time the discrepancy between these proposals and the current program was so great that there was no immediate effect. The rest of the staff had not thought about community psychology except as an advanced offering within clinical psychology. Community psychology had not been exclusive to the clinical domain, and had been extended, as supplementary experience, to the doctoral curriculum in school psychology.[3] Nevertheless, the courses were organizationally part of the clinical program, and it was not until the 1966/67 school year that this began to change. More will be said on this under Phase III.

The second event in 1963 with delayed effect was a regional conference of psychology department chairmen convened by the Southern Regional Education Board to consider innovations in training for psychological services. Among the participants were Thomas Andrews, Chairman of the Psychology Department at the University of Maryland, and Julius Seeman, then Acting Chairman of the Psychology Department at Peabody. As the conference progressed, it became strikingly evident to these two participants that if the newly forming programs in community psychology were to reach fruition, they would need to build a conceptual structure and to develop research laboratories in the same way that psychologists since Wundt had done. Accordingly, Andrews and Seeman put forth an idea for the development of an entity which they called a "Center for Community Studies." The idea was that such a center would become the research arm of university training programs in community psychology, and that it would carry out research and evaluation projects as service to communities and as the basic part of its research training mis-

[3] The senior faculty members in school psychology, Raymond C. Norris and Susan Gray, had made consultation practice part of the training of their students and provided welcome support to the community psychology program. Their conception of the school psychologist is very similar to the community psychologist (Gray, 1963).

sion. The conference was not an action conference, and having many other items on its agenda, it did not take up the proposal specifically. Nevertheless, the idea persisted and later had visible effects upon the Peabody program.

PHASE II, 1964–1966

During the period of 1964–1966, Rhodes was on leave with the National Institute of Mental Health, returning to Peabody on a part-time basis to teach and to develop a research project. The research project took shape under Rhodes' leadership and was structured so as to have an interdisciplinary advisory group drawn from the Nashville University Center.[4] The project, entitled "Discordant Behavior and Community Response," had the purposes of (1) describing a high-pathology neighborhood in terms of the patterns of discordant behavior, and (2) studying the ways in which the community responded to this discordant behavior, as reflected through the action of its agencies (church, courts, welfare, school, etc.). In carrying out the study, Seeman assumed the responsibility of coordinating the project while Rhodes was on leave. Charles Spielberger, then at Vanderbilt University, consulted on the development of the research design and helped to establish liaison relationships with a number of community agencies, including the Nashville Community Council, the health department, and the public schools. Field work was carried out by Richard Spong under the supervision of Robert Stepbach, staff clinical psychologist with the Nashville Mental Health Center.

This study yielded a number of benefits which went beyond its specific research purposes. One effect was to increase communication among the agencies which had participated in the study. Another was the creation of a Neighborhood Counseling Center, an extension of the Nashville Mental Health Center. It was Stepbach's work with the local professionals and community leaders that led to the recognition of the need for a regular service agency and the desire to have it established with Stepbach as director.

[4] The members of the group were William Rhodes and Julius Seeman, codirectors (Psychology Department, Peabody College), Ernest Campbell (Sociology Department, Vanderbilt University), Lloyd Elam (Psychiatry Department, Meharry Medical College), Maurice Hyman (Psychiatrist and Director, Nashville Mental Health Center), Charles Spielberger (Psychology Department, Vanderbilt University), Richard Spong (graduate student in Psychology, Peabody College), and Robert Stepbach (Psychologist, Nashville Mental Health Center). The project was supported by the Maurice Falk Memorial Medical Fund.

Two other effects were involved, both of which were pertinent to the community psychology program. One result was to provide a resource for students for training in community research. The other was to be more far reaching. This study brought into being the kind of interdisciplinary group which had been conceptualized by Seeman and Andrews. Although the discordant behavior study was only a one-year project, there was no disposition to disband the group when it was completed. On the contrary, it formed the nucleus for the eventual formation of a Center for Community Studies, the establishment of which occurred in 1966/67, when J. R. Newbrough joined the Peabody faculty.

The years from 1964 to 1966 saw other extensions of the community psychology program. Charles Spielberger had just come to Vanderbilt University from Duke University with recent experience in the development of a community consultation program in a small urban community with limited professional mental health resources. He soon developed a consultation program in Columbia, Tennessee, a small city some 40 miles away from Nashville. The program was carried out through the newly established mental health clinic in collaboration with its director, James Cooper, and was directed toward public health nurses, members of the local ministerial association, staff members of the local welfare department, and public school teachers, principals, and administrators. Graduate students in clinical psychology from Peabody College and Vanderbilt University accompanied Spielberger and assisted in the development of a study of demographic and economic factors contributing to achievement of bright Negro junior high school students.

In 1965, when Spielberger left Vanderbilt to join the Training Branch, National Institute of Mental Health, Seeman assumed major responsibility for the consultation program. He focused his efforts on the school system as a potential training laboratory and involved a number of students in this experience. One student served as a consultant to the principal and faculty of a single school. Another student held weekly meetings with a group of high school teachers who were working with students who had learning problems. A third student worked with a group of first-grade teachers who came from different schools in the system. Other students sat in on meetings which Seeman held biweekly with the superintendent and all school principals in the system. James Cooper took over the consultation with the welfare department; he along with other clinic staff members worked collaboratively with Seeman in the work with the ministers, public health nurses, and school staff. When Newbrough arrived, he assumed the responsibility for consultation with the nurses and the ministers, with Seeman continuing the work in the schools. Each carried on the use of this experience as a training placement in community consultation.

PHASE III, 1966–

J. R. Newbrough arrived at Peabody College in the fall of 1966 from a six-year period at the Mental Health Study Center, National Institute of Mental Health, to serve as director of the community psychology program. His background included experience in project research, community consultation, and program development in community mental health. Newbrough's arrival prompted a fresh look at the organization and scope of the community psychology program. With regard to its organization, the program followed the historical tendency of institutions and became increasingly differentiated. Opinion developed in the clinical training program that the community psychology program could develop best as a separately defined area coordinate with the other specialty curricula within psychology. Organized in this way, the program could remain fully available to students in the other departmental programs (e.g., clinical, counseling, school, educational, mental retardation), and could also develop its own unique character.

With regard to the content of the program, efforts almost immediately began to be devoted to the development of three interrelated aspects of the community oriented program which will serve to broaden the scope of it. There was (1) the program of community psychology within the Department of Psychology, Peabody College, (2) a Center for Community Studies and (3) a University Center Program for Training in Community Science.

Community psychology training at Peabody has been continued as an integral part of the clinical psychology program. It provides supplementary experiences to students in the other programs in the department and serves students from the Department of Special Education and the Division of Education. The training program includes two seminars (each on an alternate year) and a series of three to four field placement semesters structured to the experience level of the student. The seminars are presented under the titles "An Introduction to Community Mental Health" and "Community Action and Community Development." Field placement courses are each a semester in length and are described in the order intended for the student new to community psychology:

1. Analysis of Nashville as a community along structural lines, using Roland Warren's *Studying Your Community* (1955). Each student is assigned a chapter and spends most of his semester in the field, often helped by a community volunteer (for example, one from the Junior League), collecting information for a report.

2. Consultation to an agency or a program under supervision of someone in the agency—often not a psychologist.

3. Participation on a program evaluation or community research project.

Format for the field placements provides for four to six hours a week in the setting and two hours weekly in a seminar where the experience of each student is reviewed and discussed by the group. Specialty training in community psychology beyond the two courses and the practica described above will be developed as a part of the University Center program in community science, using a wider variety of field placements including the Center for Community Studies as a primary research site.

The Center for Community Studies was formally organized in the fall of 1966 with the purpose of providing common ground for several disciplines and organizations to come together around their interest in community research. It originally included faculty from the departments of sociology, psychology, and psychiatry at Meharry Medical College, George Peabody College, and Vanderbilt University and a senior psychologist from the Nashville Mental Health Center. During the year the center became affiliated with the John F. Kennedy Center for Research on Education and Human Development at Peabody College and expanded its board of directors to include faculty from Fisk University, Tennessee State University, University of Tennessee School of Social Work, and the executive director of the Council of Community Services. The organizational representation now includes nearly all the major relevant departments and institutions in the University Center and has two community organization representatives to keep channels of communication open between the academic community and the community service system.

The work of the center during 1966/67 was descriptive research on a high-poverty population which was to be provided with a Neighborhood Health Center Program. A five-year evaluation of the impact of the health center on the level of illness and the use of health services on a sample of the residents is planned. Other programs of the center include an evaluation of a suicide prevention center, a long-term project studying the delivery of mental health services to residents of the metropolitan area, and work with the Mayors Office in the planning for a Model Neighborhood Project to be financed by the U. S. Department of Housing and Urban Development. These projects will provide field placements for students enrolled in practicum courses or serving as paid research assistants. Through this process of research and training, the aim of the center to advance knowledge of individual and group behavior in the community will be served.

The University Center Program for Training in Community Science is being designed to serve the needs of training programs in psychology, psychiatry, and sociology. It is planned that social work, nursing, urban planning, and religion will become part of the program as it develops. The program will be organized to provide jointly taught seminars and a wide variety of field placements—with a central purpose of providing interdisciplinary collaboration at the faculty and student levels for the participating departments. The talent in the several departments with community expertise can be pooled into a broad program from which each department can selectively fashion a curriculum for its students. The program has been termed "community science" to indicate that it is attempting to serve disciplines with two different orientations—those concerned about solutions of individual practical problems, and those concerned with substantive scientific problems. Since both types of disciplines often find themselves together working on community problems, it was thought wise to begin the acquaintanceship process during training.

EPILOGUE

The development of community psychology at Peabody College has progressed from a single course to a small curriculum within the department of psychology; it stands at the beginning of an interdisciplinary venture which will provide the experiences necessary to have an area of specialization within psychology. The Peabody tradition has been one of teaching an operational orientation (directed toward research), of using extensive field placements, and of involving the student in the contemporary process of social difficulties and social change.

As currently planned, community psychology is being developed as part of a larger program in community science—encompassing several academic disciplines. Since community problems and processes have always overlapped many areas of training, it was broadly designed in the belief that interdisciplinary training will lead to productive interdisciplinary collaboration in the world of work.

The issue of continual concern is whether the community represents more than the choice of the natural environment as the place to observe, study, and attempt to change the problems of man. We tend to think of it as less an area of application of proven psychological knowledge and expertness, and more as an area of inquiry in which one joins the social change process as researcher.[5] Research tends to mean both observation and experimentation; we are intrigued, and somewhat awed, by the potential for experimentation and development of knowledge in this area of overlap between sociology, psychology, anthropology, economics, and political science.

[5] It is clear that community psychology is well along with the process of differentiation into a specialty area, yet what the substantive area is is not clear (Newbrough, in press).

REFERENCES

Gray, Susan W. *The psychologist in the schools*. New York: Holt, Rinehart & Winston, 1963.

Hobbs, Nicholas. Mental health's third revolution. *The American Journal of Orthopsychiatry*, 1964, 34, 822–833.

Newbrough, J. R. Community psychology: A new specialty in psychology? In Adelson, D. & Kalis, Betty L. (Eds.) *Community psychology perspectives on community mental health*. San Francisco: Chandler, in press.

Seeman, Julius. Toward a concept of personality integration. *American Psychologist*, 1959, 14, 633–637.

Warren, Roland L. *Studying your community*. New York: Russell Sage Foundation, 1955.

7

Training Clinical Psychologists for Community Mental Health Functions: Description of a Practicum Experience

Emory L. Cowen

In 1967, the author, commenting on the current status of training in community mental health (CMH), suggested that such training was still very limited (Cowen, 1967). The nature of ferment and the rapidity of change in this emergent field have been so considerable that that statement is already well along the road to obsolescence.

The rapid jelling of the CMH movement has been far less a result of changes in curricula or training programs and far more a function of the activities of professionals who, perceiving insufficiencies in habitual modes of approaching mental health problems, have experimented with new orientations and types of interventions. With the seeming effectiveness of these new ways—they appear to bring us closer in approach and resolution to significant but heretofore refractory problems in the mental health fields—the importance of CMH training is coming more and more to be accepted. We are, therefore, more aware of the need to codify and transmit underlying assumptions and guiding theory, and of the requirement for further, more systematic articulation of training principles and practices in this area.

We should keep in mind, however, that the very process of crystallization of the field and the fact that much innovative and exploratory activity is pragmatically governed necessarily act as limitations upon the pronouncement of training guidelines. This may rather be the moment for sharing training experiences—both successes and heartaches—than for trying to establish immutable training ground rules. Since the terrain of CMH operations is itself in a process of delineation, the term, as presently used, means quite different things to different people. How we go about training must surely relate to a particular blind man's view of a particular elephant!

The development of most of the programs reported in this chapter has been made possible through an NIMH grant (MH 1500-01-02-03-04) on Early Detection and Prevention of Emotional Disorder. We gratefully acknowledge this support.

Early approaches to CMH training have followed disparate pathways in substance, form, and timing. Comprehensive or part-training has been undertaken both at the predoctoral and postdoctoral levels, as well as both within and across disciplines. By any conceivable standard CMH training, as it has existed for the past several years at the University of Rochester, has been a modest undertaking. In essence, such training has been limited to a single year-long practicum experience in which fourth-year clinical psychology trainees participate in one of several on-going community projects. Occasionally, students become involved in such work earlier, but this occurs in a largely *ad hoc* way, where special interest in the area is high. The primary purpose of this chapter is to describe the objectives and *modus operandi* of our advanced training experience practicum. Before doing so, however, it might be appropriate to make public certain viewpoints (perhaps biases is the better word) that have helped to shape this training experience.

CONCEPTUAL BIASES UNDERLYING TRAINING

More and more, in recent years, members of the mental health professions have become aware of inadequacies in existing "helping" structures. (Cowen, Gardner, & Zax, 1967). Problems are manifest at many levels, as has been suggested in a more detailed review elsewhere (Cowen & Zax, 1967). One central, very pressing concern is that the need for helping services far exceeds existing resources as well as any realistic extrapolation of our potential for developing such resources in the foreseeable future (Albee, 1959, 1963, 1967). A second difficulty is that time-honored, widely used modes of clinical intervention (e.g., psychotherapy) have, by and large, failed to reach certain classes of disorder, such as schizophrenia, and have proved to be less promising than earlier hoped, even where circumstances favor positive outcomes (Scholfield, 1964; Cowen & Zax, 1967; Turner & Cumming, 1967). Existing mental health helping operations are sharply limited in their social scope in ways that short-change many in need of help as a function of racial membership, socioeconomic status, place of habitation, and educational background. Seemingly, groups which are most in need of helping services find it least available. This problem, however, is more complex than the matter of sheer availability of services in that existing services and their modes of delivery appear to be disharmonious with styles of life and ways of interacting of potential recipients (Riessman, Cohen, & Pearl, 1964; Gardner, 1967; Klein, 1967; Reiff, 1967; Riessman, 1967).

Collectively these difficulties add up to a considerable sum. Notwithstanding steady and generous increases in mental health expenditures over many years, one would be hard-pressed to defend the thesis that there has been commensurate reduction in the mental health problems of modern society. Whatever the valiance of prior effort, its net impact may largely be that of "holding the dike."

The evident insufficiencies of our helping operations suggest several logical first approximations in any search for alternative pathways with seeming promise. One of these is the need to develop new sources of mental health manpower (nonprofessional) to help reduce existing lacunae in service. The second, and more basic, is the need for alternative conceptualizations about "cause and cure" and for the development of new ways—hopefully, more meaningful and parsimonious ones—of approaching mental health problems. Speaking to the latter objective, it may be of value to examine existing models and to hazard opinions as to where these have faltered.

To a considerable degree, practice in the mental health fields has evolved in the image of physical medicine. In particular, there has been a primary focus on the arrest and modification of manifest pathology, often in the context of an intimate one-to-one clinical relationship involving patient and a presumed professional expert. The technology of the mental health expert differs from that of the medical expert, but there is a striking similarity in the structure and timing of encounters between specialists in these two areas and their patients. Indeed, in one sense, the mental health specialist may better exemplify the medical model than do many physicians. Perhaps due to personnel shortages or to the prevailing ethos, the mental health professional is sought out primarily in instances of dire emergency, whereas in physical medicine such things as preventive check-ups, routine exams, etc. are far more commonplace.

The barriers inhibiting solicitation of help for emotional difficulties are formidable and run the gamut from economic to stylistic to psychological to geographic. In the main, people seek to resolve problems short of the "extreme recourse" of the professional mental health specialist. First lines of defense for one's emotional problems include family, friends, neighbors, and available others. In many instances these outlets are entirely effective. When they are inadequate many individuals, as Gurin, Veroff, and Feld (1960) have reported, turn to professionals in the community who are known and trusted (but whose training is not primarily in the mental health fields). Such individuals are described by Caplan (1964) as community caregivers and the category is well exemplified by clergymen, family physicians, and teachers. Contacts with caregivers concerning mental health problems are often voluntary and, fortunately, in many instances, have satisfactory outcomes. A person's emotional problems may also be brought, voluntarily or otherwise, to "urban agents" (Kelley, 1964)—people in society who, by the very nature of their roles, are likely to have high-frequency contacts with those in distress. Thus, our social structure is such that it not only is possible but also is easiest and most natural for many people to try to work out personal difficulties short of the formal network of mental health helping operations.

Characteristically, when the professional mental health specialist is contacted, the individual is either in acute discomfort or his symptomatology has become relatively extreme and well entrenched. At such moments the professional is perceived (and, indeed, often responds) as an authoritative expert who prescribes (typically, the prescription is a verbal one) and seeks to cure in a manner which, structurally, resembles that of the physician dealing with a virus or bacteria. In brief, then, the mental health professional finds himself in the position of struggling heroically to repair dysfunction when it comes to his attention. He is thus charged primarily with the responsibility of keeping things from getting worse. Though such a function is neither trivial nor undesirable, it is questionable that it is sufficient for resolving the complex mental health problems of modern society.

The argument can be developed that we have, historically, over-emphasized pathology and its cure and have failed to direct sufficient attention to understanding the origins and flow of disorder and its prevention. In this sense, the implicit analogy between psychological and physical disorder, that has provided a basis for day-to-day clinical operations, has probably been intrinsically limiting. Whereas physical disorder characteristically bespeaks invasion by virus, bacterium, or pathogenic agent, emotional dysfunction is more likely to mirror complex, long-standing determinants including important others in the person's life and highly influential, primary social institutions.

A more balanced portfolio for the helping professions requires greater conceptual emphasis on early detection and prevention of disorder (both terms easier to espouse than to implement) and on the development of technology better suited to the achievement of these ends. More effort needs to be directed toward building for psychological strength and competence as opposed to after-the-fact patchwork. This implies a sharper focus on the young child and his development and on influential primary institutions. We require further knowledge about key social institutions—how they operate, how they affect human development, how they may be modified, and how their change relates to the psychological development of the individual. All this is a tall order, doubtless implicating skills and knowhow far beyond what psychology can presently offer. Yet they are issues in which the psychologist should have a vital stake, and the psychologist may be able to contribute meaningfully both in framing relevant questions and in providing technology for seeking answers.

Recognition of the shortcomings, both in scope and effectiveness, of existing clinical operations affirms the necessity of finding judicious, impactful ways for allocating limited professional resources. Our need, more nearly geometric than arithmetic, is to reach more people and in more effective ways than has heretofore been possible. Mental health consultation (Caplan, 1964), crisis intervention (Caplan, 1964), and the development of new modes of delivery of services for the poor (Riessman, Cohen, & Pearl, 1964) exemplify potentially promising pathways to these objectives.

In very recent years there has been a pronounced tendency by professionals to rally around the concept of community mental health as if, in so doing, it would automatically solve mental health problems. Nothing could be further from the truth. Cautious but constructive critics of this development (Dunham, 1965; Glidewell, 1966; Romano, 1967) have observed, evangelistic fervor notwithstanding, that the term remains an ill-defined and nebulous one. Its rapid acceptance into the vocabulary and its superimposition on the coat-of-arms of the mental health professional mirrors less the demonstrated effectiveness of programs or supporting empirical data and more the availability of funds and a generalized sense of discomfort about prior achievements.

The CMH movement cannot be justified in geographic terms. If, in the successful tradition of American industry, we merely set up more shops doing essentially the same types of things we have always done, we will have failed to engage our most pressing mental health problems. The real utility of a shift in orientation from hospital, clinic, and consulting room to the community and its primary institutions must be justified at a functional rather than a structural level. In that sense, such a change in focus may provide opportunities for generating preventively oriented programs, for constructive modification of impactful social systems, and for effective and meaningful extension of the scope of mental health activities to the multitudes of the heretofore unreached.

It is already clear, primarily through Albee's work (1959, 1963, 1967), that the mental health fields are grossly lacking in qualified professional personnel. Moreover, extrapolations based on estimates of future demand and future training potential indicate that the present unhappy situation will become more acute in time. These facts suggest that two sets of developments be expedited: (1) exploration of new ways for meaningful utilization of nonprofessionals in the mental health fields and (2) recasting a substantial portion of the function of mental health professionals in directions described elsewhere (Cowen, 1967) as those of the "mental health quarterback" and the "social engineer." The first of these roles calls for a much greater emphasis on recruitment, training, and consultative and resource functions. It implies closer contact with community agencies and institutions and with the less well-trained members of an expanded, redefined clinical team. Necessarily, the furtherance of these activities will encroach upon the clinician's more traditional, one-to-one service activities. Doubtless, the psychologist does not, among mental health professionals, have unique credentials for fulfillment of the quarterback role. However, the bulk of the experience that has been acquired by psychologists in the community field, in recent years, related more closely to quarterback than to engineering functions.

The social engineer role is more difficult; it is one for which, at the present time, the psychologist is not well equipped. In the broadest sense this role is directed to issues of primary prevention and to the extraordinarily complex question of what can be done to modify social structures and institutions in ways that will ultimately produce a healthier society. This question obviously transcends psychology and the helping professions; one can readily perceive strands implicating disciplines ranging from political science to economics to urban planning to education on one side, and to biology, physiology, and neurochemistry on the other. The psychologist has neither an exclusive stake in this profound question nor an exclusive contribution to make to its multiple resolutions. Hopefully, however, the training of the psychologist (and other helping professionals) can help him to grasp relevant issues, propose more pertinent questions for study, offer technology that will help to answer these questions, and work more effectively and in fuller understanding with members of other disciplines in pursuing common objectives. All this, however, does not obscure the fact that the demands of primary prevention and for execution of the social engineer function are such that they will continually require significant involvement of many specialty groups other than mental health professionals. To date, training in psychology has not been primarily targeted to the mental health quarterback or social engineer functions (Sarason, Levine, Goldenberg, Bennett, & Cherlin, 1966). To the extent that these objectives are accepted as desirable "values" there will be a corresponding need to modify conceptions and implementations of graduate training in psychology and other helping professions.

The preceding views have influenced the initiation and shaping of the Rochester practicum training experience. The remainder of the chapter describes the latter in terms both of its general *modus operandi* and its specific subprograms.

THE TRAINING EXPERIENCE

GENERAL BACKGROUND

The vehicle through which practicum experience is obtained is a year-long psychology course, "Practicum in Early Detection, Prevention, and Community Mental Health." This is a required course in our doctoral curriculum in clinical psychology and is the only course taken by students in their final year. Even so, it is no more than a limited-time activity since the student is simultaneously fulfilling other obligations, notably those of the thesis and other assigned clinical practicum work. Though the time given by the student to this "community" experience varies somewhat from one subprogram to another, and at different steps of the sequence, students devote, on the average, about eight hours a week to it.

The pattern of operation we have favored establishes in parallel a series of subprograms each broadly relevant to the CMH field. Students are assigned in pairs to one of these programs, insofar as possible according to interests and preferences. Their participation varies with the specifics of a program: its setting, target population, and newness. Since there are typically six to eight students enrolled in the course, three or four programs are underway at any one time. While each student has a basic responsibility to his own assigned program, there are two ways (beyond normal channels of informal intercommunication) in which familiarity with the operations and problems of peer programs is fostered.

First, wherever possible and natural (i.e., screening of nonprofessionals, aspects of training), students other than those with prime responsibility are also asked to participate. Second, there is a weekly meeting of the entire group of students and the instructor for exchange of information and consideration of current "problems." These meetings are issue centered and problem-solving in their orientation. They may help students to perceive some of the communalities in seemingly diverse experiences and to grapple with a variety of the always plentiful problems, both concrete and conceptual, attached to development and implementation of the field programs.

A genuine effort is made to provide the student with a broad range of relevant experience. In one or another of our programs this has run the gamut from program conceptualization to consultation with responsible mental health planning groups in the community, consultation with specific agencies, recruitment and selection of nonprofessionals, training nonprofessionals, program implementation, serving in a consultative-resource-supervisory capacity for a variety of nonprofessional mental health workers, and program evaluation. It is by no means assured that each of these activities will be available to all students each year. The operational rule is that new programs invite broader trainee participation. As a program becomes more "institutionalized," the trainee's activities are restricted more to refinement of mechanics and day-to-day operations and he has fewer opportunities to share in the conceptual, creative, problem-solving aspects of the process. Experience suggests that the more removed a program is from prior experience, the more work will it be for the student, the more "headaches" and moments of uncertainty will it cause, but the greater will be its potential for learning and the more stimulating will it be for the group as a whole.

Were program selection to be decided strictly on grounds of training potential there would be good reason to establish a complete set of new programs each year. Other factors, however, render this possibility either impractical or unwise. First, all of our programs have been "live" ones anchored in the real world, and with potential for modifying existing ways of doing things in an on-going social system. In undertaking a program, we must therefore maintain continuing recognition that it is not in a vacuum and that several years of demonstration and evaluation may be required to get it off the ground. A related point is that we ourselves may not consider the program to be sufficiently "de-bugged" in a single year's run and may wish to learn more about it and to try to improve it.

Finally, it is necessary to yield to the one major artificial constraint to which we are subject—that all of our programs are essentially time-limited by the start and finish of the academic year (roughly from September 15 to May 15). We must be reasonably sure in starting a program that some appreciable progress can be achieved, with respect both to training and program objectives, in that period of time. Hence, where administrative redtape is likely to be severe, knowing base-rate interferences caused by vacations, colds, snowstorms, complicated and busy schedules, cautious approaches to new situations, etc., we sometimes have to forego a potentially exciting new program in favor of a somewhat more institutionalized one to assure achievement of some meaningful training goals.

In practice, then, complete annual turnover in programs is not feasible. We have, however, succeeded in introducing at least one entirely new program each year, and this has proven to be very useful. A rich experience may thus be gained by the students with direct involvement in that program, at the same time permitting the entire group, through common discussion meetings, to be informed at all steps in the cycle, to participate whenever possible, and to share in the significant problem-solving processes.

There is another (perhaps less obvious but nevertheless very important) factor which underscores the merit of developing new programs. Our concern in a CMH practicum is not only at the how-to-do-it level. We are also interested in fostering a way of looking at social problems in the mental health sphere—a way of conceptualizing. The virtue of such conceptualization is that it provides a framework which helps to transcend the specifics of a given situation. We, in Rochester, as in any other community, are bound by certain institutional styles and preferred ways of doing things. One high-value potential derivative of the present training situation is that of acquiring general problem-solving skills which may allow for flexible adaptation to the new and different demands of new situations, elsewhere called training for versatility or innovation (Reiff, 1966). This process may best be catalyzed by the challenges involved in coming to grips with pressing social problems in the mental health fields and in working through and living with new programs designed to solve these problems. In any case, the more generalized aim of training for adaptability and innovation should be seen as a salient training objective.

SPECIFIC PRACTICUM ASSIGNMENTS

The foregoing generalized overview of the training experience provides a backdrop for considering the specific practicum exercises of students in this course. This will be done concretely by describing the three practicum arrangements utilized during the 1966/67 academic year, and reporting briefly on changes in plans and new activities.

(a) *After-School Day Care Program.* A natural corollary of a focus on the community and its primary institutions is the view that the elementary school is among the most important potential targets for future mental health efforts. The school exercises a vital influence on the development of virtually all members of society during their early, formative years. As a highly impactful social system, its constructive modification, in diverse ways, could contribute meaningfully to building psychological strengths and resources in children. Moreover, as a social system which systematically affects the very young it presents a unique opportunity for early detection and prevention of disorder.

Quite apart from issues of CMH training, our convictions about the importance of the elementary schools prompted a series of research investigations beginning nearly a decade ago. The foci of this work involved establishment and evaluation of a preventively oriented mental health program in the primary grades of a single elementary school and the development of techniques for early identification of dysfunction in young school children (Cowen, Izzo, Miles, Telschow, Trost, & Zax, 1963; Zax, Cowen, Izzo, & Trost, 1964; Cowen, Zax, Izzo, & Trost, 1966). These studies demonstrated salutary effects of the experimental prevention program by the time children reached third grade. They also showed that within the first three school years children with early-detected dysfunction were performing significantly more poorly than their nonaffected peers on a broad spectrum of criterion measures spanning achievement, behavioral, personality, school record, and sociometric measures. More recently, we found, through follow-up at the seventh-grade level, that difficulties evident at third grade, left unattended, tended to persist over time (Zax, Cowen, Rappaport, Beach, & Laird, 1968).

This earlier research was indeed directed largely to the problems of detection of emotional disorder and to a determination of its correlates and stability. Our specific findings gave rise to the further question of what could be done to curtail the seemingly serious sequelae of early dysfunction (i.e., the problem of ontogenetically early secondary prevention). We therefore sought to develop several models of interventive programs designed to help the child with early-detected dysfunction in the school setting. Two such programs have been developed and field-tested. Each involves a focus on the very young child (primary grader), utilization of nonprofessionals as mental health aides, and deployment of the professional (or professional-in-training) in an essentially consultative, resource capacity. In one program, during school hours, housewives have been trained and employed as child-aides; in the other, college under-graduates have functioned as companions and "big brothers" to children experiencing difficulties in the schools. Each of these projects has been described elsewhere (Zax, Cowen, Izzo, Madonia, Merenda, & Trost, 1966; Cowen, Zax, & Laird, 1966; Zax & Cowen, 1967), though the focus in these reports was more on program substance than on issues of graduate training.

As interest evolved in the development of new interventive models for the schools, it became apparent that the roles we were seeking to carve out for the mental health professional were entirely relevant to graduate training, and that involvement in such activities could potentially constitute a meaningful training experience for clinical psychologists. The area in which we were working came to be perceived as one in which efforts to develop and research community mental health programs and to explore new ways of graduate training in the helping professions could be mutually supportive.

This gave rise to the development of our first systematic practicum training experience for graduate students in connection with the then-evolving after-school day care program. This training exercise is now in its fourth consecutive year of operation.[1] As such it is the "graybeard" of our new family of training experiences and it is also the most automatic of our programs.

When the program was conceived, it seemed on logical grounds to be potentially useful for undergraduate elementary education majors—people who would, shortly, be working closely with youngsters in a school setting. For such individuals an impactful practicum experience not only might provide help for the children with whom they worked, but also might make a primary contribution to their awareness of and effectiveness in an area in which relevant actions on their part would soon be called for many times daily.

[1] The following participated, as students, in this training experience: Phillip A. Miller, Ph.D.; Robert A. Pierce, Ph.D.; James D. Laird, Ph.D.; Dennis Carney, Ph.D.; Gail Frankel; Water Wild, Ph.D.; Peter O. Heinemann, Ph.D.; Carol Spencer; Robert L. Carlisle; and Gershen Kaufman, Ph.D.; Susan Horton; Myra Fougerousse.

Following preliminary discussion of the profile of the projected program and its approval by responsible administration in the School of Education, solicitation of education, and some psychology, volunteers was undertaken. Members of the graduate practicum group interviewed all candidates to screen out the few who seemed grossly unsuitable. Although pretraining of undergraduates has varied somewhat from year to year, it has been shared by instructor and graduate students and has been neither lengthy nor intensive at any time. The training agenda, ordinarily accomplished in several sessions, included discussion of the mental health problems of modern society, shortages in professional manpower, early detection and prevention of dysfunction, and the philosophy and objectives of the program. The graduate student leaders also visited at the school to meet and talk with the principal and mental health personnel and to discuss children for whom the program might be relevant. A system for referral and for obtaining background information was established that was feasible within the school framework. When information became available on potential candidates, graduate student leaders and relevant school personnel went over these data to make joint decisions about inclusion of children in the program and their assignments.

Graduate students in this program worked with groups of six to eight undergraduates, each of whom was assigned to a single child. Occasionally, with shy, asocialized children, one volunteer worked with two children. Twice a week the graduate student leader met at the university with the undergraduate volunteers at about 3:00 P.M. and they proceeded, as a group, to the schools. The volunteers arrived at about 3:20 P.M., when the children were dismissed for the day. Children, together with their volunteers, had the facilities of the school building and playground available to them and engaged in a variety of activities, either in dyads or larger groups, between 3:30 and 4:30 P.M. These activities ranged broadly from running around, to competitive or cooperative games, to musical, artistic, and food-making pursuits, to relatively sedentary talking and conversation. The graduate student himself did not work directly with the children. Rather, he observed the children, got to know them better over a period of time, and became more familiar with patterns of volunteer-child interaction. He was perceived as the person in responsible charge and used some of his time talking with the principal, teachers, and particularly the mental health clinical services personnel about the children or aspects of the program. In this way communication lines were kept open and a bridge between the clinical program and the host institution was built.

At the end of each day's activity program volunteers and the graduate student leader returned to the University and, for about an hour, discussed aspects of the clinical-contact experience that seemed most salient to them. Such meetings were broad-ranging and dealt with matters such as trying better to understand the behavior of a particular child, evaluating critical incidents, talking over possible strategies of interaction and intervention and, occasionally, discussing anxieties or concerns that the volunteers themselves may have. The initial stance of the leader toward his group was often based on the role model of the therapist. This is understandable, since it is a model with which the student had prior experience and in which he is likely to have felt relatively secure. However, it was not an optimally appropriate one since there had been no prior "therapeutic contract" and the focus of the experience was on a partnership between leader and volunteers in trying to provide help for young children. The preferable role model of the group leader seems rather to be that of an effective consultant, capable of drawing issues of general relevance to the surface and of providing opportunities for volunteers to sharpen problem-solving skills. During this process, the group leader-consultant might profitably contribute pertinent factual information or points of view (Cowen et al., 1966; Zax & Cowen, 1967).

Recordings of group meetings were taken occasionally and these were brought to our weekly seminar for playback and discussion. This enabled the group at large to discuss program and consultative-role issues periodically and allowed group members assigned to other projects to maintain continuing contact with developments in this program.

From a training standpoint, some of the prime potential of the after-school program resides in its opportunities (1) for first-hand contact with a key community institution and its relevant personnel, (2) to participate in selection and training of nonprofessionals (college students) for mental health-relevant roles, and (3) to function in an on-going liaison capacity with the school and in a consultative-resource capacity with the undergraduate volunteers.

(b) *Settlement House Program.* In our second year of operation a new program was introduced, involving selection, training, and utilization of 14- to 17-year-old indigenous Negro youth as counselors, in relation to 6- to 8-year-old neighborhood children, agency-referred for a companionship program. Although underlying assumptions and objectives of this program were not dissimilar from those of the school program, its implementation certainly witnessed sharp changes from prior practice.

This program began with a series of meetings between psychology personnel from the university, including the course instructor and participating graduate students,[2] and staff members of an "inner-city" Rochester

[2] The following participated as students in this training experience: Janice Porter, Ph.D.; James D. Laird, Ph.D.; Earl Dworkin, Ph. D.; and Louis Jacobson. In both years G. Ramsey Liem, Ph.D., affiliated with this program, on a volunteer basis, and made important contributions to its development.

settlement house. These meetings were designed to provide us with a fuller understanding of agency organization and facilities, as well as the problems of neighborhood children, and to acquaint agency staff with the types of potentially relevant programs that we had been developing. A joint decision was made to explore the utility of the after-school model in this setting, using indigenous Negro adolescents from the immediate neighborhood as "workers" with young children known to, and referred by, agency staff. The form and specific details of this program varied in its first two years of operation.

Neighborhood adolescents who had had some prior contact with the agency were informed of the projected new program, either directly by agency staff or through posted announcement. Arrangements were made to interview those interested in the program. Though the majority of these interviews were conducted by students with primary assignment to the project, each member of the practicum group was provided the experience of doing at least one or two interviews. Interviews were designed to acquaint the youngsters with the program, to find out a little bit about their current status with respect to school and/or job, to determine if the program hours were open ones for them, to learn a little about their backgrounds and family structure, and to get some idea of their future plans. The interviews were, in the main, brief and difficult. They were often characterized by monosyllabic answers, obvious signs of discomfort, and a tendency to respond in a pared-to-the-bone fashion. The most attractive part of the project for the would-be counselors was the prospect of being paid five dollars a week for two two-hour after-school sessions. This, however, did not obscure the understandable uncertainty and mistrust that many of them seemed to be experiencing during the initial contact.

In the second year, after the individual interviews, several small group discussion-screening meetings were set up. These used brief filmclips of young children experiencing interpersonal difficulty as a basis for observation and discussion by candidates of what they thought was going on and what might be done. This proved to be a relatively effective and more comfortable technique for eliciting comment and interaction.

Counselor selection, undertaken jointly with agency staff, sought to identify youngsters who fell somewhere between the twentieth and eightieth percentiles in overall desirability. Since from the start we were concerned with the potential of the program for the development of the counselor (as well as the child to whom he might be assigned), we sought to rule out those at the top end who already seemed to "have it made." Though, in principle, we would have liked to include the bottom 20 percent, we did not have the potential to work intensively with these youngsters—as, for example, in a core-group approach as described by Klein (1967). Referrals of young children, ages six to eight, were made by agency staff on the basis of direct knowledge of these youngsters and their families through other agency activities. With agency staff, decisions were made about counselor-child pairings before the program got under way, largely on the basis of personality and stylistic data, as well as knowledge about extent of neighborhood interaction between the two (often fairly high in this small-world setting).

Structurally, the pattern of operation of this group was similar to that established for our after-school groups. Counselors were assigned to children on a one-to-one basis. Meetings were held twice a week from the time school let out, about 3:30 to 4:45 P.M., ending in a brief refreshment period for the entire group. Counselors stayed on after the children left for a 45-minute discussion meeting. Some of these meetings, particularly at the beginning, were devoted to skill training, as for example, in games and crafts. However, their major purpose was to discuss what was going on, difficulties with the children, counselors own feelings, and the like.

The agency assigned a small, three-room basement suite, including kitchen facilities, to the program. Though not sumptuous, these quarters had the advantage of being perceived as "our turf," were relatively private, and were, in general, quite satisfactory. Graduate student leaders stocked the facility with an initial supply of materials and games which, on the basis of counselor recommendations, was periodically augmented during the approximate six-month course of the program each year.

Though the external structural trappings of this program were similar to those of the school project, the resemblance ended at that point. The nature of on-going activities, the way in which children and counselors spent their time, the relationship between counselors and children, the discussion meetings, and, particularly, the demands upon and challenges to the graduate student leaders, were quite different from any prior experience. More concrete illustrations of these differences are presented in the paragraphs that follow; many reflect the fact that this group did not seem to profit from the traditional middle-class "amenities of interaction" that seemed effective in other settings.

For example, activities involving children and counselors were, in the main, much more anarchistic than those in the school setting. While there were several counselors who "stuck" very close to their youngsters, such was not typical. More often, especially at the beginning, counselors remained disengaged from their assigned child and either "horsed around" with each other or got involved in their own games and activities. They did not particularly see themselves as responsible for "amusing" the children and, if the child wanted to be on his own or did not insist on doing something, the counselor's attitude was largely one of "that's fine by me."

Attendance by the children was quite spotty. Several youngsters discontinued after a very few sessions; these were replaced. Others showed up only on a limited and somewhat erratic basis. This created several problems. The counselors whose youngsters did not show up were without assignment during a given session and this tended to increase chicanery. They were also reluctant to try to track down their youngsters (some of whom would be at other on-going settlement house activities), in effect saying: "If he doesn't want to come here himself, nuts to him." Indeed, one of the key functions of the supervisor was to get the counselor to assume this responsibility. Moreover, attendance, particularly the problem of limit-testing through late arrival, was one which the counselors presented, as well as the children. As a function of these collective difficulties, the sheer problems of management and keeping the operation moving smoothly were continually in sharp focus for the graduate student leaders.

The postactivity discussion groups represented another area of some difficulty. The counselors were not spontaneously comfortable in these meetings and their uneasiness reflected itself in inattention, restlessness, fooling around, and direct expression of resentment to the group leaders. Much discussion time, certainly in the earlier phases, was spent in challenging authority, trying to tear down the meetings, arguing with each other, and testing limits. Discussion of children tended to be at the level of berating them or expressing anger with them. Whenever the behavior of specific children was introduced, it seemed to elicit spinal-cord defensiveness in the counselors. The group leaders invested much energy in trying to maintain an orderly setting as a precondition for discussion. In general our experience suggested that the failure to adopt a firm stance and a nonvacillative position multiplied chaos. The establishment of clear limits concerning attendance and functional utilization of the discussion period was typically followed by a greater feeling of comfort for everyone and a more effective expenditure of time.

The foregoing description conveys some of the flavor of the situation and points up some recurrent problems. There were, in addition, some encouraging signs of progress and sources of gratification. For one thing, over a period of time each of our counselor groups did indeed become a better welded, integrated unit. Counselors were able to assume responsibility for planning activities for a particular meeting as well as for outside trips. The latter included visits to a bowling alley and skating rink, and several picnics, which proved to be very gratifying both for children and counselors. Moreover, although the discussion meetings, in general, were not easy, after the concept of such meetings had been established some very good meetings took place. Sometimes these pertained to the counselors—the way they perceived and resented the authority of the leaders; sometimes it was a matter of rebelling against limits, or consideration of what it meant to be black in a white world, etc. And on several occasions there were highly useful meetings concerning children. For example, the presence of one white child in the group, who was continually isolated and rejected, served as the stimulus for a very fruitful discussion of how counselors reacted to this youngster and why. Nor was this entirely abstract, since following this discussion counselors tried, with some success, to engage this child and better integrate him in the group. Some counselor-child pairings proved to be very close and effective, and some of the counselors were able to come to a reasonably clear perception of the effects of their own interest and behavior on the child's reactions.

It is evident that investment in this program existed at two levels— the counselors and the children. Implicit in its very structure is the belief that the counselors themselves stand to profit from activities involved in being genuinely helpful to another person. Indeed, it is probably most accurate to say that the involvement of those running the program was at least as great, if not greater, with the counselors than it was with the children. At the end of the experience individual interviews were undertaken with each of the counselors to get a clearer understanding of their reactions to the program. Such reactions were by no means uniform. In all likelihood there were more than a few counselors who gained very little, save perhaps for financial recompense. There were others, however, for whom it was a much more meaningful experience in learning that they could help others, in cooperative group functioning, and, indeed, in helping them better to see career directions, albeit in limited ways.

From the point of view of graduate training, this has certainly been a frustrating and difficult experience but, perhaps, also a moderately rewarding one. It has served to bring student leaders closer to the problems of the poor, their very different styles of interacting, their ways of viewing human problems and the very environment in which they live. Lecturing, reflections of feeling, promoting intellectualized discussion—all valid currency of middle-class interaction and education—do not seem to have an entirely promising destiny in this setting. For us they have been far less fruitful than having five dollars ready in an envelope when it is supposed to be, backing up promises and plans, and the ability to be firm about limits and implicit contracts even when the immediate consequence of such a stance may be to alienate and to provoke unbridled hostility.

Though we can claim no overwhelming success for this program, it has helped us to a better understanding of a social milieu which must necessarily be an important arena for mental health-relevant operations in the future. Perhaps participation in such a program may provide students with a greater interest and sensitivity for the area and a bit more know-how and feel for potentially meaningful mental health interventions. These are ingredients which will eventually help students to do a more meaningful job than have their mentors. Moreover, through the use of playback of tape-recorded sessions and continued opportunity for program discussion and review at the weekly practicum group meeting, there is a salutary spillover of the learning experience for group members not directly assigned to the program.

(c) *A Program for Retired People.* The third and last program undertaken by the 1966/67 practicum group [3] was an entirely new one, designed to select and train retired people as mental health aides in the schools. Experience in the settlement house project led us to believe that one potentially important benefit to accrue from utilization of certain nonprofessional workers would be the value deriving to them from the process of being helpful to other people. This is the essence of what Riessman (1965) described as the "helper-therapy" principle. Retired people are one group that is systematically ignored despite its substantial potential in human service roles. Many retired people are rich in experience and the wisdom of living, but society rarely offers them a meaningful role. On logical grounds, we felt that such individuals could be trained to render extremely self-gratifying and useful service to people needing help. The details of the development of this program have been reported in a fuller account elsewhere (Cowen, Leibowitz, & Leibowitz, 1968). Here we shall be concerned primarily with the training aspects of the experience.

Because this program was an entirely new one, it provided a rich training experience (not to mention a very heavy work load) for the participating students. Their activities ran the gamut from initial conceptualization, through agency consultation, selection, recruitment and training, program implementation, liaison and supervisory functions in the schools, and, finally, to research evaluation. Since we were able to plan somewhat ahead for this program, the span of its activities more nearly covered the full calendar year, not just the eight-month academic year.

The starting point for the experience consisted of a series of planning meetings, attended also by appropriate community representatives, concerning the feasibility of the prospective project. Several meetings were held with members of the local Mental Health Council, and with representatives of community programs for retired people. Initial reactions were entirely receptive and further implementing steps were undertaken. We next met with representatives of several social and club organizations for retired people and outlined the plan. Reactions from those groups suggested that there was substantial interest in participation by retired people themselves. A series of meetings was then held with representatives of other local institutions (i.e., the Rochester City School District, several county school districts, Catholic Charities) to explore the ways in which these agencies felt retired people might be useful. Once again there was no difficulty in envisioning roles. Since we did not wish to spread limited resources too thinly, and because of prior experience in schools, two schools in the Rochester City School District were selected as the theater of operation for the pilot project. At this time we also selected a Golden Age club in the immediate geographic vicinity of these schools, under sponsorship of a neighborhood church. The church was pleased to see the project

[3] Gerald Leibowitz and Ellen Leibowitz were the students initially attached to this program. Later Mrs. Ann Yellott Laska and Mr. Gerald Specter were associated with it.

develop and was generous in making its facilities available for interviewing and training.

A meeting was held with club members to outline the program and those interested in participating were invited for a personal interview. All students in the practicum participated in these interviews, once again providing exposure for each to programs other than that of their primary assignment. These interviews were quite different from ones conducted with college students or indigenous youth. The interviewees, understandably, used them to reduce anxiety, to seek structure, and to ask many questions. A group of six retired people (four women and two men) was ultimately selected for the program.

The graduate student leaders were active agents both in planning and conducting training which included eleven 1½-hour meetings over a two-month period. Although there was some formal coverage at a rudimentary level of principles of personality development, parent-child relations, and behavior problems of young children, the emphasis was on catalyzing thinking in the mental health area and on fostering discussion and a point of view. Basically, however, we went along with the spontaneous styles and cumulated wisdom of the trainees and with the assumption that, given interest and commitment, each trainee would find a natural way for meaningful interaction with young children. Film presentations were utilized effectively. Contrary to popular stereotype, group members were characterized by their enthusiastic participation and willingness to consider new ways.

As training progressed, several additional meetings were held with the host schools to explore ways in which the program might best be implemented and to set up specific mechanisms for this. Mental health professionals in the schools were helped to appreciate how their own effectiveness might be extended through utilization of a portion of their time in resource and consultative activities with nonprofessionals. In the later phases of training visits to the schools were arranged to allow school personnel and the retired people to get to know each other and to acquaint the latter with school facilities, personnel, and programs. Brief classroom visits and observation of children were followed by discussion of these experiences with the graduate student leader and school mental health personnel.

These final meetings provided a natural bridge to the beginnings of the actual work situation. Each retiree worked three half days a week, for which he was paid fifteen dollars. Three aides and one graduate student leader were assigned to each of the two participating schools. The schools provided office space which was equipped with a variety of educational, play, and expressive media. Teachers were acquainted with the prospective program and were invited to refer youngsters who might profit from contact with an interested adult. Within the three-month course 25 primary-grade youngsters were seen. The pattern of activities varied from aide to aide and from school to school, and included some school work, play activities, reading, and conversation. Aides were adept in introducing special activities in their own areas of expertise.

Graduate student leaders maintained close contact with aides and with the program. They participated in supervision and maintained a continuing liaison and consultative role with school mental health and administrative personnel. Since there were, in fact, two separate programs in operation, monthly meetings of all trainees, graduate student leaders, and the project supervisor were held to exchange views and progress notes and to keep all participants maximally informed.

Some objective data were collected as a supplement to the (subjectively positive) clinical impressions about the program gleaned from the various participants. A brief, four-item attitude scale given to all trainees provided information indicating that the experience was highly rewarding personally for all aides and that it was also a reasonably meaningful learning experience for them. Evaluative rating scales, completed independently by teachers and aides for all children referred to the program, indicated significant improvement in the youngsters as seen by both rater groups (Cowen *et al.,* 1968). These data, though far from unassailable, at least provided a way-station closure in evaluating the experience.

In many ways this program has been a valuable training exercise. It enabled participating students to grapple simultaneously with a pair of significant mental health problems which offered the potential of convergent and mutually reinforcing resolutions. The first of these was to extend the range of our nonprofessional mental health manpower pool in a way that would be helpful to young children in the school situation. The second was to create a mechanism for more effective utilization of a group of people in society heretofore largely ignored to everyone's detriment including their own. The program that was developed appears to have made simultaneous contributions to both of these objectives in a manner which, hopefully, also advances graduate education in needed ways.

A second important attribute of the training experience was that it provided an extremely broad-gauge exposure to many basic functions of the community mental health specialist—including mental health planning at the community level, agency consultation, selection and training of nonprofessional mental health workers, program implementation, supervisory, resource, and liaison activities, and formal research evaluation. Although this experience was a primary assignment for only two students, its problem-solving demands and crossroad decisions were shared by the entire practicum group, thereby augmenting its overall training impact.

As a brief footnote to our description of this program, it can be said that development of new CMH practicum training experiences will often have to transcend their specific training functions. It is at once characteristic of many such experiences that they will be innovative, take place in the "real" world, and address very live problems of social reality. To isolate the training experience, test tube style, from this context would be to deprive it of its essence. A continuing concern in the development of new programs, and indeed of the training experience *per se,* must be with the question of how, if effective, these experiences may contribute to constructive modification of institutionalized systems in which they are set. There is much to be gained in having this focus incorporated, both at the level of abstract discussion and of concrete behavior, into the training experience. Specifically, in our program for retired people we have been very much oriented to the possibility of its ultimate adoption by the host system and have taken steps in pursuit of this objective.[4]

LATER ACTIVITIES (1967/68)

The preceding sections have summarized our CMH practicum training experience. Consistent with the objective of introducing new activities each year, several major additions are now in process. For one, we have developed an undergraduate seminar practicum course in CMH as a major practicum assignment for several of our fourth-year clinical students.[5] This experience got underway, with full participation of graduate students, several months before the start of the 1967/68 academic year—at the levels of conception, planning, and organization. All junior and senior psychology majors were informed, in broad outline terms, of the projected sequence. Those interested were invited to report for a brief (gross negative) screening interview during the fall registration period.

The course, in essence, consists of two major components—a didactic discussion section occupying approximately the first nine weeks of the first semester and a clinical practicum experience for the rest of the academic year. The didactic portion of the curriculum includes a historical review of approaches to mental health problems, a delineation of the major mental health problems currently facing modern society, consideration of basic conceptual models for approaching mental health problems, and detailed articulation of three basic areas both from the points of view of

[4] Continuation and expansion of this work was made possible by research grants from the John F. Wegman Foundation of Rochester, N. Y., and the Maurice Falk Medical Foundation, Pittsburgh, Pa. This support is gratefully acknowledged.

[5] Jack Chinsky, Ph.D., Julian Rappaport, Ph.D., and Paul Goldring, Ph.D., participated in the planning and implementation of this program.

what our problems have been in the past and what types of resolutions seem to be emerging. These are the areas of demand, need, and resources in the mental health fields, the effectiveness of existing helping approaches, and mental health problems of the poor. Graduate students have participated in teaching the course. In consultation with the author each has assumed responsibility for development of reading assignments, formal presentation of lectures, and leading discussion in several of the areas closest to his interest.

Concurrent with the conduct of the didactic portions of this course, graduate students have been involved in the development of practicum assignments for the undergraduates in several community settings. These include a large nearby state hospital and several local inner-city schools. Arrangements have been completed for 32 undergraduates to function as group leaders with chronic schizophrenic patients in the state hospital. Their role will be that of seeking to encourage verbal and nonverbal interaction with patients, each working with separate groups of about eight patients. A model for this type of program has been described by Poser (1966).

The remaining 16 students will be assigned to one of several after-school programs, each working individually or in small groups with primary grade children referred by teachers and other school personnel because of problems of adjustment or underachievement. The model for the after-school program will be similar to the one described in an earlier section of this chapter; however, by branching out to inner-city schools we hope to gain experience with a new population and with the utilization of alternate mechanisms for implementing a program of this type. Assignment to one of these two programs will remain as the undergraduates' primary responsibility for the entire year. We hope, in addition, to be able to develop a broad range of community-relevant activities for which students may volunteer, as an additional activity, if they wish. Examples of this category might include participation in interviews with inner-city Negro adolescents, working in reading programs with Head Start children—each such activity to be developed and monitored by a supervising graduate student.

It is expected that the undergraduates will see their assigned child, children, or patients approximately twice a week for about 1 to 1½ hours over a six-month period. The undergraduates will be divided into subgroups of eight, with a graduate trainee in charge of each. It will be the responsibility of the graduate student to take part in meetings establishing the program, to make the necessary arrangements for its proper conduct, to maintain a liaison relationship with relevant administrative and professional personnel in the host agency, and to serve in a resource-consultative-supervisory capacity vis-à-vis the undergraduate "workers." The last objective will be served by regular weekly discussion meetings, conducted by the graduate student leaders and attended by the eight undergraduates in their task force. The purpose of this meeting will be to talk about the types of ongoing activities, problems encountered during the experience and, quite probably, anxieties that may develop for some undergraduates as a function of their participation.

Though it is still too early to assess the impact of this program upon undergraduates or as a graduate training experience, it is already amply clear that it will raise a number of interesting issues and problem-solving challenges, particularly in its practicum phases, which will merit careful review and discussion by participating graduate students. To the fullest extent possible formal research evaluation of this experience was undertaken.[6]

A second independent effort, still being developed, seeks to develop a program for utilizing poor, minimally educated, inner-city Negro housewives as aides in inner-city schools.[7] This has involved working with representatives of the local antipoverty agency Action for a Better Community (ABC) and with city school district representatives to gain acceptance of the program itself and to establish a workable, mutually agreed upon set of guidelines for its operation. The types of roles to be assumed by these aides (whose life circumstances require full-time employment) include working directly with children in the classroom and schools as child aides, in addition to visiting otherwise inaccessible families of troubled children as social work aides. The graduate students will be charged with further training and supervising the aides, rooting the program in specific schools, and maintaining a consultative-liaison relationship with responsible school personnel.

Several months have gone into the exploration of program possibilities and role definition with potentially interested parties—school district administration, ABC administration, representatives of specific schools, and the aides themselves. These discussions have by no means been easy, and it is not clear at the time of writing that a viable program can be floated. In this sense, there is a calculated risk to the training commitment in this area which, at least for the moment, must be justified at the level of establishing contact and coming to know the problems of key community

6 The principal evaluation comes from two comprehensive Ph.D. dissertations. The first of these, by Julian Rappaport, evaluated the effects of the undergraduate participation program on chronic schizophrenic patients exposed to it for a six-month period. The second, by Jack Chinsky, studied the relationship of personality, attitudinal, and behavioral factors in undergraduates to their effectiveness as group leaders. A third study by Douglas Mace, Ph.D., affiliated with this program in its second year of operation, has also been carried out.

7 Alan Rockway, Ph.D., and Thomas Wolff, Ph.D., were involved in the development of this program.

agencies, rather than in terms of airtight assurances of actually being able to conduct a meaningful program in action.[8]

CONCLUDING REMARKS

The final section is directed, at a somewhat more general level, to several aspects of CMH training not yet considered. Our task at the present time is largely that of carving out viable programs and training models in areas where they have not, generally, been developed before. Certainty about the rights and wrongs of training is hazardous in any area, but is even more true here since we as yet have only a limited classification of the very field itself. Ambiguity may have as one consequence the generation of a variety of different approaches. This is desirable, since we are hardly in a position to foreclose on models. Open exploration should be seen as a first step in long-range efforts to separate wheat from chaff. While this involves the risk of committing errors and following blind alleys, it also offers the promise of exciting discovery.

Notwithstanding a growing interest by clinical psychology in CMH training, there is little reason to suppose that the pathway of clinical psychology is the only (or even a preferred) route to such training. If one emphasizes the mental health quarterback components of community function, clinical psychology, along with psychiatry and social work, may have something to offer. However, when the social engineer function of the CMH specialist is the salient training objective, new types of training experiences involving new organizations of professional specialists and areas of inquiry will need to be developed (Cowen, 1967; Sarason *et al.*, 1966).

In the light of recent developments one may hazard the guess that knowledge of the CMH field and practicum exposure to the area will become increasingly necessary in attempting to solve problems that helping-professionals must engage. Training institutions, already plagued by

[8] Since the time this chapter was written, several additional programs have been conceived and implemented within the practicum framework. In the first of these, conducted by G. Ramsey Liem, Ph.D., 4th grade children in the schools were utilized as helping-persons with 1st graders, referred by teachers because of reading disabilities. A second program, run by Mark Frankel, established a store-front setting on the college campus, using advanced undergraduates trained by him as counselors and referral agents for other undergraduates seeking immediate assistance with their problems. A third program, under the leadership of Gerald Specter, was housed in an inner-city settlement house, and was targeted to 10–22 month ghetto children evidencing, on routine well-baby examination, sharp slow-down in verbal, social, and emotional development. Undergraduates met three times weekly with these children seeking to provide stimulation, language-modeling, environmental enrichment and encouragement of prosocial behavior.

overstretched curricula, will be forced to exercise important value judgments concerning modifications in curriculum and practicum experiences for their products. In the helping professions we have reached the point where adding something new to training almost inevitably means giving up something old. Unfortunately, because they may be familiar and comfortable for us, old ways have the tendency to survive on a functionally autonomous basis. Thus, there are problems of tradition and inertia which need to be overcome (Sarason *et al.,* 1966; Cowen, 1967). Moreover, realistically, the present case for CMH development rests more on a base of logic plus dissatisfaction with the efficacy of prior approaches than it does on a foundation of supporting empirical data. If and when the latter become available, they will constitute a profound stimulus for changes in training regimens.

It may be possible to anticipate some of the preconditions that favor effective CMH training. The first of these is an active involvement by respected mentors—identification models during the still moderately impressionable training period—in the development of viable and challenging field programs in the community. A second is an atmosphere which, accepting the present limited clarity of the field, values openness, curiosity, and willingness to explore new ways even at risk of frustration and error. And a third is the need to approach training at a level beyond technique—to help develop a conceptual framework which enhances the ability of the student to assess problems, to utilize analytic skills, and to create new solutions which take cognizance both of the demands and the realities of new situations.

Our experience suggests there is a highly desirable compatibility amongst the objectives of graduate CMH training, the development of new models and programs for mental health activities in the community, and research. Undergraduate education may also be added to this list. Not only can these activities exist alongside each other, but also advances in one area seem almost logically and automatically to "pull" potential advances in others. We are coming around to the belief that the simultaneous furtherance of training, research, and service goals is more likely to be achieved in the CMH domain than has heretofore been possible in the training of helping professionals.

REFERENCES

Albee, G. W. *Mental health manpower trends.* New York: Basic Books, 1959.
Albee, G. W. American psychology in the sixties. *American Psychologist,* 1963, 18, 90–95.
Albee, G. W. The relation of conceptual models to manpower needs. In E. L.

Cowen, E. A. Gardner, & M. Zax, *Emergent approaches to mental health problems.* New York: Appleton-Century-Crofts, 1967. Pp. 63–73.

Caplan, G. *Principles of preventive psychiatry.* New York: Basic Books, 1964.

Cowen, E. L. Emergent approaches to mental health problems: An overview and directions for future work. In E. L. Cowen, E. A. Gardner, M. Zax, *Emergent approaches to mental health problems. Op. cit.,* 1967. Pp. 389–455.

Cowen, E. L., Gardner, E. A., & Zax, M. *Emergent approaches to mental health problems.* New York: Appleton-Century-Crofts, 1967. Pp. 474 ff.

Cowen, E. L., Izzo, L. D., Miles, H. C., Telschow, E. F., Trost, M. A., & Zax, M. A preventive mental health program in the school setting: Description and evaluation. *Journal of Psychology,* 1963 (part 2), 307–356.

Cowen, E. L., Leibowitz, E., & Leibowitz, G. The utilization of retired people as mental health aides in the schools. *American Journal of Orthopsychiatry,* 1968, 38, 900–909.

Cowen, E. L., & Zax, M. The mental health fields today: Issues and problems. In E. L. Cowen, E. A. Gardner, & M. Zax, *Emergent approaches to mental health problems. Op. cit.* Pp. 3–29.

Cowen, E. L., Zax, M., Izzo, L. D., & Trost, M. A. Prevention of emotional disorders in the school setting: A further investigation. *Journal of Consulting Psychology,* 1966, 30, 381–387.

Cowen, E. L., Zax, M., & Laird, J. D. A college student volunteer program in the elementary school setting. *Community Mental Health Journal,* 1966, 2, 319–328.

Dunham, H. W. Community psychiatry: The newest therapeutic bandwagon. *Archives of Genetic Psychiatry,* 1965, 12, 303–313.

Gardner, E. A. Psychological care for the poor: The need for new service patterns with a proposal for meeting this need. In E. L. Cowen, E. A. Gardner, & M. Zax, *Emergent approaches to mental health problems. Op. cit.* Pp. 185–213.

Glidewell, J. C. Perspectives in community health. In C. C. Bennett, L. S. Anderson, S. Cooper, L. Hassol, D. C. Klein, & G. Rosenblum (Eds.), *Community psychology: A report of the Boston conference on the education of psychologists for community mental health.* Boston: Boston University Press, 1966. Pp. 33–49.

Gurin, G., Veroff, J., & Feld, S. *Americans view their mental health: A nationwide interview survey.* New York: Basic Books, 1960.

Kelly, J. G. The mental health agent in the urban community. In *Urban America and the planning of mental health services.* New York: Group for Advancement of Psychiatry, 1964. Pp. 474–494.

Klein, W. L. The training of human service aides. In E. L. Cowen, E. A. Gardner, & M. Zax, *Emergent approaches to mental health problems. Op. cit.* Pp. 144–161.

Poser, E. G. The effect of therapist training on group therapeutic outcome. *Journal of Consulting Psychology,* 1966, 30, 283–289.

Reiff, R. The ideological and technological implications of clinical psychology. In C. C. Bennett, L. S. Anderson, S. Cooper, L. Hassol, D. C. Klein, & G. Rosenblum (Eds.), *Community psychology: A report of the Boston conference on the education of psychologists for community mental health. Op. cit.* Pp. 51–64.

Reiff, R. Mental health manpower and institutional change. In E. L. Cowen, E. A. Gardner, & M. Zax, *Emergent approaches to mental health problems. Op. cit.* Pp. 74–88.

Riessman, F. The "helper" therapy principle. *Social Work,* 1965, 10, 27–32.

Riessman, F. A neighborhood-based mental health approach. In E. L. Cowen, E. A. Gardner, & M. Zax, *Emergent approaches to mental health problems. Op. cit.* Pp. 162–184.

Riessman, F., Cohen, J., & Pearl, A. (Eds.). *Mental health of the poor.* New York: Free Press, 1964.

Romano, J. R. Psychiatry, the university and the community. In E. L. Cowen, E. A. Gardner, & M. Zax, *Emergent approaches to mental health problems. Op. cit.* Pp. 33–39.

Sarason, S. B., Levine, M., Goldenberg, I. I., Cherlin, D. L., & Bennett, E. M. *Psychology in community settings.* New York: Wiley, 1966.

Schofield, W. *Psychotherapy: The purchase of friendship.* Englewood Cliffs, N. J.: Prentice-Hall, 1964.

Turner, R. J., & Cumming, J. Theoretical malaise and community mental health. In E. L. Cowen, E. A. Gardner, & M. Zax, *Emergent approaches to mental health problems. Op. cit.* Pp. 40–62.

Zax, M., & Cowen, E. L. Early identification and prevention of emotional disturbance in a public school. In E. L. Cowen, E. A. Gardner, & M. Zax, *Emergent approaches to mental health problems. Op. cit.* Pp. 331–351.

Zax, M., Cowen, E. L., Izzo, M. D., Madonia, A., Merenda, J., & Trost, M. A. A teacher-aide program for preventing emotional disturbance in young school children. *Mental Hygiene*, 1966, 50, 406–415.

Zaz, M., Cowen, E. L., Izzo, L. D., & Trost, M. A. Identifying emotional disturbance in the school setting. *American Journal of Orthopsychiatry.* 1964, 34, 447–454.

Zax, M., Cowen, E. L., Rappaport, J., Beach, D. R., & Laird, J. D. A follow-up study of children identified early as emotionally disturbed. *Journal of Consulting and Clinical Psychology*, 1968, 32, 369–374.

8

The Psychological Foundations of a Community-Oriented Clinical Psychology Training Program

Jerome L. Singer and Morton Bard

Developing a graduate curriculum for clinical psychology students which includes community consultation as a major feature has proven a most exciting and deeply moving commitment. Many of us who went the route of the clinical training and shared the perception of the clinician's role which seemed so intriguing in the 1940s—the Boulder conference model, with its stress upon diagnostic and psychotherapeutic function and upon research in psychopathology within the medical settings of clinic and hospital—have become increasingly concerned with the issue of the most economic and socially meaningful application of our advanced psychological knowledge and methodology.

In our universities, set as they often are in the center of the urban sprawl, decay, and disorganization that now characterize so many American cities, we attempt to train clinical psychologists to work with individual neurotic and psychotic patients in the relatively controlled atmospheres of mental hospitals or in the middle-class "comfort" of the private consulting room. The challenge persists for us to develop methods for understanding and modifying the self-defeating patterns of thousands of hospitalized schizophrenics, as well as of the hundreds of thousands of maladjusted neurotics who know enough to seek the help of clinics or private practitioners. But our eyes have only too slowly been opened to look at the crowded streets around the university and to realize how desperate is the need of the millions in our cities for some types of psychological intervention that can begin to reverse the pattern of despair, hopelessness, violence, self-destruction, and ignorance in which they seem so hopelessly trapped.

When we can scarcely make a dent in meeting the need for individual attention of mental patients through our present training potentialities, what can we offer to the masses in our cities? Unless we choose to ignore the problem by a wonderfully rationalized denial mechanism—

that clinical practice is for an elite group—we must develop some new approaches to the prevention of a geometric multiplication of the built-in pathology of our urban ghettos. Community consultation represents a broad-gauged function that can at least begin to approach this problem, and it must be accorded an equal role with the more traditional functions of the clinical psychologist. In effect, we have to make a decision that in the limited time allotted for training doctoral level clinical psychologists special attention must be given to preparation for the consultative role.

ORIGINS OF THE PROGRAM—THE "FELT NEED" FOR CONSULTATION TRAINING

At the City College of the City University of New York a group of clinical psychologists has had an unusual opportunity to confront and attempt to meet the challenge to the graduate educator posed above. With the transition of the senior colleges in New York into a City University, it became possible to organize a new doctoral clinical program in a setting where no doctoral training had existed before. A combination of moral support from the Education and Training Board's Advisory Committee, financial support from the Graduate Division of the University and the City College, and a developmental Training Grant from NIMH led to the possibility of establishing a Psychological Center within the building that houses all psychology activities at City College. This combination of support coalesced around the expressed intention of the clinical faculty to establish an innovative program—indeed, it is doubtful if such support could have been forthcoming for the development of a more traditional type of clinical program.

In examining the nature of current clinical activity, as well as the social need expressed in the opening paragraph, it became clear that the clinical psychologist is, in actuality, increasingly involved in some type of community consultation. A very large percentage of psychologists and psychiatrists working in clinics or in private practice are being asked to serve as advisors to a variety of new agencies—for example, Head Start, store-front community groups, nursing homes, geriatric clinics, etc. Often enough the consultant appears on the scene, is greeted with great ceremony, pontificates on some theoretical issue or talks of his work with his private patients, and leaves the agency staff with a sense of emptiness. And why should it be otherwise? After all, relatively little in the clinician's training or early experience seems to have prepared him for this new role. It seemed clear to those of us examining the issue that some significant changes needed to be built into the fabric of clinical training to prepare the graduate psychologist for the reality of his role in the coming decades.

SOME DEFINITIONS

What should this training be? On what basis in psychological theory does the practice of consultation rest? What, indeed, is the nature of the process itself? How can it be fitted into the academic structure of a doctoral curriculum which is, after all, not primarily *professional* or *skill* training but essentially a broad education in a particular scholarly discipline? In describing the program in clinical psychology at City College, we hope to demonstrate some approaches to grappling with these basic questions—approaches that may lead, however, to hitherto unanticipated directions for clinical psychology.

But first, a few definitions. The program we shall describe is one in clinical psychology, not in community psychology. As we see it, the heart of the clinical approach is concern for the individual human being. For most clinical psychologists or persons who hope to go into clinical work, there is generally an intense interest in the unique personality. Our most valuable clinical knowledge has come from deep and prolonged diagnostic or psychotherapeutic study of the individual. The ameliorative impact of consultation upon individuals remains the focus of this program therefore. The focal point of training remains the understanding of the individual personality and of the nature of his motivation, cognitive capacities, defenses, and psychopathological tendencies. We stress this because consultation may take a variety of useful forms which are not equally concerned with the welfare of a given individual. Thus, a social psychologist might well consult with a group of mothers in a disadvantaged community to help them modify their attitudes toward nutrition or to assist them in the establishment of a workable parent group that can have some meaningful impact upon local school policy. The clinician's consultation activity is more likely to involve work with parent groups to assist them in direct work with children (their own or others') or to help them develop skills for providing child care training for other individual mothers. Without belaboring this point, we think it can be shown that most of the focus of consultation by the clinician ultimately comes down to an understanding of the subtleties of the individual personality, and it is this concern, sensitivity to nuances of defense, style, and transference distortion in the individual which make for the clinical psychologist's special contribution to community psychology.

The consultative training we describe is therefore very much within a clinical psychology framework. The students in the program must observe and interact in a variety of technical ways—for example, interviews of various types, observation and rating, psychodiagnostic testing, and counseling and psychotherapy with children and adults of diverse cultural backgrounds and degrees of normality and pathology. Some reasonably controlled interaction over time with an individual or a family group for whom some services may be performed seems to us an invaluable early training experience for any psychologist, but certainly for those persons who will ultimately be dealing with human welfare through a consultative medium. This experience should come early and should have some continuous aspects; too much of our psychological information comes from cross-sectional samplings by laboratory study or one-shot diagnostic batteries which fail to develop constructs to deal with fluctuations or persistence over time of many personality characteristics.

One of the great contributions of the psychoanalytic method has been the observation of individuals over long time periods with consequent discoveries of importance, such as transference phenomena, the persistence of infantile patterns in adult personality, the development of individual symbolism in fantasies and dreams or of individual defensive styles. The limitation of this method to the narrow confines of the office, while deepening intrapsychic sensitivity, hindered therapists' awareness of the complexities of role interactions and of social influences on behavior patterns in different settings. Preparation of the clinician for consultation ought to involve longitudinal observation and interaction but should also take place in a variety of settings, so that the important contributions of role theory and group atmosphere studies can be included in the awareness of the student.

Within the framework of this program consultation involves a contact with either an individual or a group and has as its function the preparation of the client for some more effective activity in the amelioration of difficulties in living for some other person or small group. This consultation is not ordinarily a matter of formal teaching, lecturing, or advice giving. It is essentially a clinical contact in which the client's emotional distresses, cognitive distortions, or other personal difficulties are dealt with, using the best knowledge of individual or group interaction techniques available. The consultation is thus not the situation of an expert doling out advice off the top of his head but of an intensive clinical investigation of a problem. It involves the application of some technical knowledge to a problem in which the ultimate client may never been seen by the clinician, but the psychological characteristics of the intermediary or group of intermediaries are what must be dealt with to enhance the eventual work with that client. Curiously enough, the case of Little Hans is one of the first cases of consultation, for Freud dealt with the boy's phobia through advice to the parent. But today we know far more than Freud did then about producing attitude change and about small group dynamics in consultation.

The community concept is another important focus of the training program. The notion of community mental health or psychological centers undoubtedly reflects an increasing awareness that our society has become so populous and complex with so much family mobility that subgroups and somewhat artificially created neighborhood centers may be more and more necessary to give individuals some sense of affiliation and community, in the deeper sense of the term. It is our expectation that more and more psychological or mental health centers will develop in delimited neighborhoods and that these centers will afford a variety of services to the surrounding community. We believe that, first of all, the centers should carry out regular ecological research using survey research methods, for example, to examine the characteristics of the community, focal points of stress or tension. Thus, one neighborhood may be characterized by a high density of narcotic traffic, another by racial tension, another by a sharply differentiated social class barrier at the borders of which there is tension.

The centers should also provide community leaders with other research and service functions—for example, participating in the planning of a new recreation center by combined consultation of psychologists, architects, urban planners, and community leaders. In addition to diagnostic and psychotherapeutic services, a variety of consultative services should be available particularly to those agencies or groups not otherwise likely to be tied in with mental health agencies—e.g., welfare agencies, the police, "poverty" offices, visiting nurses' associations, boys clubs, day-care centers, union locals, and, of course, the schools. The approach must be one not of specifically playing the mental health or public health role, in the sense of even a medical prevention model, but of providing a great variety of teaching and training services as well as other psychological guidance for the many kinds of interpersonal conflicts and distortions that arise in the functioning of such agencies in a community. When psychologists bring their techniques and analytic point of view to bear on many of these situations, new insights about critical issues in a community may be developed, opening the way to broader social change as well as providing some benefit to specific individuals.

The community focus of the clinical training program, therefore, involves exposing students early to the operation of a psychological center which serves a relatively delimited neighborhood. To the extent that, as in many center-city situations today where universities are located—City College, University of Pennsylvania, University of Chicago, and others— the neighborhoods represent relatively specialized ethnic or cultural minorities, the students obtain additional sensitivity to the problems of these groups, so long neglected by research and practice in psychology.

More important, however, is the fact that what is learned is not simply the best ways for middle-class graduate students to communicate with Negroes or Puerto Ricans. Rather, and ultimately generalizable to many other neighborhood settings, it is a deepened sensitivity to what must be learned about any community in which psychologists propose to offer their research, clinical, or consultative services. The clinician, whether working out of a small psychological center or out of a university-based urban facility, realizes that he cannot wait for the clients to come or withdraw into his consulting rooms. He perceives the degree to which his services call for his active communication at a variety of levels with the community members and their representatives, and he also has become more sensitive to the way in which personality structure in the individual clients he will eventually be studying or influencing directly or through intermediaries must be understood in the context of this specific community.

A DEVELOPMENTALLY-ORIENTED CLINICAL TRAINING PROGRAM IN A COMMUNITY SETTING

Let us now present a rather brief overview of the clinical program at City College, with particular emphasis on the community consultation features. We will omit discussion of the more general academic courses and examinations or the formal machinery of curriculum. The program is a general clinical program. It is felt that specializations—for example, child clinical—ought best to come at the postdoctoral level. Most clinical psychologists find themselves called on during their professional careers to serve in a great variety of situations, so that marked specialization during graduate training may be a disservice. Instead, as in a good liberal undergraduate education, the emphasis within the specialization of clinical psychology is to afford the foundations of technology, methodology, and theory in pyschology to maximize the flexibility of the graduate of this program. Many of our students, responsive to the prevailing group atmosphere of New York City, will undoubtedly go on to some type of postdoctoral psychotherapy or psychoanalytic training, but they will do so with a much firmer awareness of the nature of consultation and of the community structure and approach than any previous generation. And many more than ever before are clearly becoming challenged by the great social meaning of the issues they confront in our Psychological Center, so that they are likely to seek positions or undertake research addressed to dealing with urgent community needs.

The First Year

The program at City College is developmentally oriented. That means, for one thing, a greater emphasis in both course work and practicum training on the developmental cycle from childhood through old age. In the first year, for example, all clinical students take course work on normal and pathological development in childhood and adolescence and on cognitive development. They also work for eight to ten hours in the Psychological Center. They carry out systematic weekly observations on children, using rating scales or other techniques without benefit of case history material until much later in a semester.

The observations by the students provide them with an awareness of the range of a child's behavior in a variety of settings—classroom, lunchroom, free play with children, etc. Only after they have acquired skills in systematic scrutiny and description of this behavior do they proceed to a reading of case material, and their task then is to relate history to their own observations. They then formulate a description of the child, combining history and direct observation with any relevant research literature. This material is included in a report to the treatment center and to school authorities. The report is then included in each child's record.

The experience thus emphasizes careful behavioral observation freed from gross theoretical prejudice, as well as the development of skills, ability to integrate others' observations, and responsibility for formally communicating the material in report form. Thus, the intent is to develop a feeling on the part of the student that he is a working psychologist who can make a significant contribution even before he has learned the uses of those magical tools, the Rorschach and the Thematic Apperception Test.

There is still another facet to this developmental approach. Each student is assigned a three-generation family—a "normal" family with grandparents, parents, and children living in close proximity. The students perform advisory and consultative services for these families in return for the opportunity to meet with them regularly and observe them systematically for the balance of the three-year residence period in graduate school. The students thus obtain a first-hand view of the ongoing character of a family group from the local community. This procedure is embedded in a research as well as a clinical framework, for, as the number of families grows, a comparative study of father-present versus father-absent three-generation families is being carried out.

Indeed, in all ongoing center activities the research feature is stressed. Wherever feasible, each practical program of the center carries some research or evaluation aspect. One of the special gifts of psychology is its capacity to examine its own function and to ask scientific questions about the phenomena of human interaction. It is essential for students to realize the degree to which the psychologist's function is ever to formulate testable hypotheses and to demand increasingly precise information upon which to base practice. By involving the center in a variety of research activities, it is hoped that students will not only pick up some useful research ideas to pursue themselves, but also will grow into professional maturity with a sense that research and clinical practice are inextricable features of a psychological center.

Actually, the very first experience the student has during the required eight to ten hours a week of practicum time in the Psychological Center is participation as an interviewer in a continuous social psychological study of stress (the research directed by Barbara Dohrenwend) in the community. After training in research interviewing, students go into the homes in the area and carry out relatively structured interviews on life stresses with persons in their own homes. This experience, a bit traumatic at first to clinical students who count on their clients' coming to them, turns into a conversion experience when the students realize the tremendous meaning their visit has to the often isolated and psychologically alienated residents who are only too eager to discuss their experiences with an interested listener even in this relatively structured research setting.

During their first year, as clinical skills develop, students also begin cognitive function testing of normal and disturbed children. They also are exposed to the beginnings of consultative experience by participating in a controlled group experience midway between a T-group and group psychotherapy. The first-year class is divided into two groups which meet for 20 to 25 sessions with two experienced group leaders. In addition to providing some outlet for the anxieties of a heavily burdened first-year graduate group, this experience provides a model for later community consultation experiences which will be part of the students' work.

As suggested above, the focus in this presentation is upon the Psychological Center experiences of the student, with particular emphasis on community consultation. Formal academic course work goes on in both clinical and general psychology. In addition, students participate within the center in a lecture series on clinical psychiatry, neurology, and psychopharmacology offered by the center staff psychiatrist, as well as a series of presentations on social work and community resources presented by the staff social worker. Biweekly Psychological Center staff conferences and the regular graduate colloquia also provide enrichment of the students' experiences at all levels of training.

SECOND YEAR

In their second year the students' course work and practicum responsibilities involve diagnostic testing and personality assessment of adults and elderly persons. The students carry out intake interviews with persons referred by community agencies to the Psychological Center, and in the latter half of the year, in association with an introductory course in psychotherapy, they are introduced to counseling with community referrals and with local college students. Our experience has been that, despite the best of our intentions, counseling or psychotherapy with older adults or the aged from the disadvantaged, nonupwardly mobile portion of our community has proven beyond the capabilities of our student group.

In teaching psychotherapy and counseling through supervised practice, it has seemed more feasible to begin with clients closer in age and social background to the students. Gradually this range of clients is expanded so that in the third year, when more extensive psychotherapy is carried out, the clinical students (who tend, of course, to be white, native born, and middle class) work with Negro and Puerto Rican patients from the SEEK and College Discovery Programs, as well as with a variety of other patients closer to themselves in background.

In relation specifically to consultative functions, the second-year students are particularly involved in serving as advisors to undergraduate students from the college who have organized a tutorial program for local Negro and Puerto Rican school children. The clinical students' role is to help the undergraduates understand the nature of the cognitive capacities and limitations of the children, to provide technique hints for teaching, and to help the tutors confront their own doubts and frustrations about the particular difficulties they experience in their teaching efforts. Occasionally, referrals of tutorees who seem particularly disturbed may emerge from these contacts. The crucial feature here is the use of the tutor groups not simply as a mechanism for formal teaching or training, but as a medium by which the tutors can reexamine their own approaches and attitudes with respect to the children. Again, a research component —a study of small group dynamics—is built into this phase.

It may be mentioned that academic course work such as social psychopathology and lectures in the Psychological Center by the social worker are geared to helping the graduate students to feel more prepared for their consultative role. Work with the three-generation families is, of course, continued during this year. As special projects in consultation are undertaken by the center—for example, parent-education and training of child-care workers—second-year students are utilized as recorders, observers, or consultants, as appropriate.

Third Year

All advanced clinical students carry approximately three patients in psychotherapy for a year under supervision. These patients include both local college students and Negro and Puerto Rican students drawn from the College Discovery Program. The College Discovery Program is designed to move local disadvantaged but promising adolescents who lack the regular averages into some gradual college experience. The Psychological Center, through the third-year clinical students and a postinternship fifth-year student program, services the College Discovery Program, supplementing the counseling available with more extensive group and individual psychotherapy experiences. Supervision is carried out by faculty and supervisors selected for special background with these kinds of clients.

Consulting activity during the third year is more complex as well. A course in "Small Group Dynamics and Family Interaction Process" provides theory and research literature in the field. At the same time, students participate in three types of consultation groups. One involves a parent-education project, directed by Professor Herbert Nechin, in which mothers of children in day-care centers meet in groups with students and staff supervisors. The groups deal with the problems of child care, approaching them through the examination of the personal attitudes, level of knowledge, and environmental stresses upon the mothers. As groups progress, mothers who show particular leadership characteristics are identified and groomed as leaders of future mothers' groups.

A second consultant function for clinical students involves work with teachers' groups in a local school. Here the focus is on teachers' attitudes toward the disruptive behavior of the slum children, their cognitive characteristics, and their feelings about themselves in relation to the school, the administration, and the neighborhood.

Finally, the most interesting and novel of the consultant experiences, supported in part by a grant from the United States Department of Justice, involves work with a special unit of policemen. One of us (MB), Director of the Psychological Center, and Professor Bernard Berkowitz, after surveying relevant literature and statistics concerning the nature of various calls for police assistance locally and nationally, were struck by the fact that almost a majority of police calls, a great number of homicides, and, indeed, a high percentage of injuries to the police themselves are occasioned by family disputes. The police receive minimal training for intervening into domestic strife and generally merely try to keep order, often arresting the husband or other male figure without inquiring into what this may do to the psychological structure of the particular family.

The Psychological Center's program calls for training a special unit of police as Family Crisis Intervention Specialists on 24-hour call. This unit is available for every identifiable family quarrel reported to the central communications bureau or to the precinct headquarters, leaving the bulk of the force in that community free for other types of police activity. The initial training of the police has been carried out, and clinical students participate in T-groups with police in the unit and continue to serve as consultants to them. Participation in these groups not only provides support for the police in their new role by providing them with information and a psychological sensitivity to family attitudes, but also gives them a chance to express and examine their own attitudes toward the family crises they face. But the student's consultant activity goes beyond this. The students follow up the families involved and identify, where possible, potential sources of serious distress in the community by this means, offering, through the center or other local agencies, the opportunity for family or individual treatment. There is, in addition, a built-in research component—a further study of family interaction patterns and also (from the police reports already accumulating at an amazing rate) striking evidence of the pattern of family strife which shows a dramatic build-up as the weekend approaches and interpersonal tensions build to the point of maximum interaction between family members.

THE IMPLICATIONS OF CONSULTANT TRAINING

We have tried to skim quickly over the various Psychological Center activities, with emphasis on consultant roles. There are, in addition, consultations with HARYOU and VISTA group leaders, as well as the store-front Puerto Rican Guidance Center, located across the street from the college and directed by Dr. Reuben Mora, a member of the center supervisory staff. Perhaps most important from a training point of view is the exposure of the students on a daily basis to the various community involvements of the center.

What we are trying is to break down the gap between academia and the community all about it. This gap is not just a town-gown matter; it goes deeply into the issue of the nature of psychological research. Day after day we are forced to confront the degree to which our theoretical formulations, our studies with rodents or pigeons (however clever and illuminating in their special areas), and that kind of research so close to a clinician's own heart—experimental studies of daydreaming and night dreaming—remain unenlightening for the kinds of problems we encounter with the children and adults from our community: the disrupted family life, the patterns of distrust of authority, the motor hyperactivity of children modeling themselves on peers rather than on parents, etc. The whole question of reorienting our research, or at least attempting to muster the great improvements in our statistical and methodological technology in the service of urgent social issues, remains before us. Indeed, one of the critical functions, as we see it now, of the Psychological Center is to educate community leaders to the importance of systematic psychological research and program evaluation as a basis for important decisions about political action.

Here are some examples of implications for significant innovation and social action growing directly out of the clinical and consultative work of our students within the very short period of existence of our center. A student one of us (JLS) has been supervising is treating a young Puerto Rican girl. The girl, a College Discovery student, had been under great pressure from a very disturbed mother who placed insuperable obstacles in her way. Finally, with strength gained from her therapy experience, the girl moved out of her family's apartment into a room with another student—a great step for a young girl from this culture. Suddenly the Welfare Department entered the picture. The mother had been receiving welfare payments for the daughter. The therapist was consulted and recommended that Welfare consider separate support for the girl since her college training, if carried a bit further, would suit her for a good position and take her off welfare rolls. After investigating the home, the Welfare worker realized that the mother's hostility to the girl's college training might only lead to her dropping out and again becoming a dependent. The Welfare Agency agreed to support the girl independently. Out of this grew a plan for more extensive independent support of college students from families already receiving public assistance.

Somewhat related to this is a persistent experience that has emerged from various consultative contacts with Negro college students and from the mothers' groups. The urban student from a poor home where there has been no tradition of education and where overcrowded conditions prevail in the apartment has no opportunity to study. Typically, when a young girl returns home, the overburdened mother expects her to assist with housekeeping and child care chores. Her pleas for time to study are looked on as evasions of responsibility. Yet these same students are already disadvantaged educationally and are desperately trying to meet minimal college standards. Out of these experiences has grown an awareness on our part that special study hall and dormitory facilities are essential for the College Discovery and SEEK programs.

What form should these dormitory facilities take? Who will be the supervisory personnel? We see a role for clinical students in training local nonprofessional persons as advisors and caretakers for the dormitories. In addition, T-groups and other clinical contacts with student leaders may help them develop cooperative responsibility. In cooperation with social psychology students and faculty interested in environmental psychology, a blending of group structure and perceptual field organization, a plan is being considered to organize the physical characteristics as well as the social structure of these dormitories to maximize the potentialities of these eager young people who may be the community leaders in a few years. Thus, in both instances experience from clinical contacts has suggested significant institutional changes that may have important consequence in developing new concepts of social organization in urban areas—what Seymour Sarason has termed "the creation of new settings." We have also mentioned the research possibilities in studying family crises and the psychological consequences in the contrast of father-present and father-absent but otherwise intact three-generation families.

PSYCHOLOGICAL PRINCIPLES UNDERLYING CONSULTATIVE TRAINING

In describing the program, we have hinted at several points some of the foundations in psychological research and theory of the practice of clinical consultation. We believe that there is an increasing basis for psychologists to pin all types of clinical practice on the existent empirical knowledge or more sophisticated theory construction in the field, rather than look to theories such as the varieties of psychoanalysis for the bases of practice. The recent research on cognitive structures, information theory, communication, affect-systems, the social psychology of small group structure, attitude change, etc., provide considerable basis for practical efforts by psychologists. We do not propose to elaborate on this here but rather to deal specifically with the underpinnings of the consultation process.

First, the clinician is a psychologist. He should have a broad knowledge of substantive content in perception, learning, physiological psychology, etc. It is obviously impossible to sustain a detailed knowledge of current technical research in all these fields. What should be present is a point of view sensitive to the ways in which the perceptual situation may influence types of judgment or to the ways in which a particular approach to teaching used by parents or teachers may be ineffective and self-defeating. It is increasingly clear from our experience at the Psychological Center, in our work with disadvantaged adolescents and lower socioeconomic class parents, that many of the physical characteristics of environments which are ordinarily of minor importance in middle-class neuroses—for example, noise level of the neighborhood—turn out to be quite meaningful in understanding certain patterns of response. An important rule of thumb that must be stressed over and over with students is not unlike Lloyd Morgan's canon—before attributing a bit of unusual behavior to the operation of a complex layering of defensive structures, make sure that a simple cognitive principle such as primacy or recency effects, or figure-ground differentiation or some routine habit formation, cannot explain the behavior sufficiently.

Aside from substantive content, the general psychology background affords the student a way of thinking about phenomena that is one of the special gifts of psychology. It represents the scientific method, careful observation, and sensitivity to operations in a most deeply meaningful way. The psychologist ought not to jump into making pat judgments or accepting widely held stereotypes. He looks at each situation with an eye to establishing what types of replicable or communicable data are present. Where possible, he looks for research data or sets up a formal study. Take the case of a teacher who complains that Negro boys represent a disruptive influence in a particular school. The psychology consultant need not accept this at face value: he may carry out systematic interviews or behavior ratings under reasonably controlled conditions to pinpoint the problem, if indeed there is one.

The psychologist ought to be constantly on the lookout for situations that literally demand skillful psychological methodology or that make possible the test of important hypotheses. We mentioned earlier some problems that call for formal research answers—the physical environment and its impact on particular cognitive or affective patterns, the impact on the children of a fatherless family or of the relatively matrilineal family organization so often found in lower socioeconomic Negro families. What is the significance of sex differences in classroom responses for the intellectual development of Negro college or elementary school students? How do differences in sex or race of examiners or teachers or in the relative emphasis on praise or reproof affect male and female students from the urban ghetto areas? What types of family interaction are most likely to lead to crises in which police intervention becomes necessary? Some of these problems lend themselves to fairly neat factorially-designed studies. Others are in effect experiments in nature in which the critical data can be teased out by artful use of the newest multivariate analysis techniques. The point is that the psychological consultant should be trained not necessarily to know all the research techniques but rather to be alert to the fact that investigation is possible and that tools and procedures exist. In this sense a good foundation in experimental methods and in statistics is desirable but with a special sensitivity to the kinds of problems encountered in community settings.

In preparing students in this type of program some things have to give. In our program it is likely to be the kind of physiological knowledge and neurological diagnostic skills of which many clinicians have been justly proud. Beyond some fundamental courses in physiological psychology, the clinical student in a community-oriented program will simply get less of the experience (except possibly in his internship) working with brain pathology. There is also likely to be much less experience with rats or pigeons in Skinner boxes and not much knowledge of perceptual apparatus. Still, we have found that individual students, even with the heavy burdens of a community program, do indeed get into a number of such experiences—certainly some of our students have developed skills in dealing with EEG technology for sleep and dream studies.

As the program has unfolded over a four-year span, graduate students have become involved in a wide variety of doctoral dissertations—for example, studies of optokinetic nystogmus during fantasy activity, development of fantasy play in children, development of memory styles as a function of chronological age and social maturity, sex differences in Negro students' response to praise and reproof during cognitive functioning, studies of the effect of "double-bind" communication with normal groups, effects of stimulus uncertainty on daydreaming during a signal detection task, personality correlates of achievement in college students from low socioeconomic status backgrounds. The range as listed suggests that choice of thesis remains a complex one and that the community aspects of our graduate program have by no means dominated the research direction of the clinical students. On the other hand, it is clear that, as the built-in research components of the center activity go on, more and more students will be challenged to address themselves to the types of problems that grow out of the urgency of community work in an urban disadvantaged area. Indeed, it is our firm faith that the exposure of a group of bright students to the many problems presented will generate new developments in patterns and techniques of research in this area.

More central to the issue of consultation, however, are a number of other substantive fields. The essential contributions from personality theory, psychopathology, social psychology, and developmental psychology are the bulk of the consultant's apperceptive mass. The sensitivity to individual styles and defenses, to the distorting effects of anxiety or of longstanding unresolved conflict, to the problems of role repertory and of communication failure, and to the relative order of emergence in children of particular cognitive or affective patterns serves as an effective backdrop to the consultative modality. The consultant needs to be able to listen carefully to accounts of interactions, to descriptions of what is characterized by the clients as behavior disturbance or immaturity. He must be prepared to ask questions that elicit behavioral data, not merely clichés or judgmental comments, from the groups consulting him. He needs a point of view about personality, about the nature of class differences, and about subcultural group characteristics or value orientations. Academic courses of importance here include Social Psychopathology, Social Psychology, Small Group Dynamics and Family Interaction Processes, etc.

Course material provides theoretical information and relevant research literature on role theory, class and culture characteristics, studies of communication within family groups or other types of small groups, the ecology of mental disturbance, the relation of institutional structure to pathology in hospitals, etc. In addition, the courses are tied in with practicum experience in small-group interactions—the T-group, the consultation with tutorial volunteers, etc. In all instances the faculty supervisor's role is to demonstrate the nature of the communication process in small groups so that consultation is viewed not as simply lecturing but as a dynamic process of planned change. The research on bargaining and trust, cognitive dissonance, the relative degree of structure of the group, the use of role-playing—all of these become the basis of the consultative process. The astute clinician will also look for indications within a group that one or two individuals show unusual distortion patterns or hostility and will have to find means for dealing with such disturbed persons within the group framework if possible or outside in individual sessions if necessary. There is by this time in the striking increase of our knowledge on attitude change, consistency, dogmatism, persuasive communication a good basis in the experimental social psychology literature which can be added to the clinical knowledge derived from group psychotherapy. While in some cases a consultation may develop into a therapeutic group, this is not the optimal use of the clinician in his consultative role. Community consultation should have a finite structure for a particular group, although the consultative process may continue indefinitely in various settings.

SUMMARY

We have tried to sketch out the fundamental experiences and academic bases for a community consultation orientation in a clinical psychology training program. The major features of such a program include:

1. A solid basis in general psychology with particular emphasis on development of methodological skills and sensitivity relevant to generating research on human problems of a more socially relevant nature.

2. A particular academic focus on the social aspects of psychopathology, upon normal development, and on the social psychology of small groups or family structures.

3. Continuous practicum experience in a Psychological Center, in which a variety of consultative as well as research, diagnostic, and

psychotherapeutic activities are called for with increasing responsibility and complexity over the three-year, full-time academic residence prior to an internship.

4. Small-group experience for students, as well as continued exposure (for their consultative work) to supervisors with special awareness of small group processes.

5. Encouragement to look for research problems in the very fabric of their ongoing consultative experiences and to be alert to opportunities for effecting social change as well as individual change as an outgrowth of such research or consultation.

6. Generating among students a spirit of excitement about innovation and the possibilities for meaningful intervention by clinical psychologists in a variety of urgent situations with mental health significance in nonmedical settings and in agencies or institutions often neglected by traditional health services. Of particular importance is the mutual help and interaction among students as they work together in the center and confront problems new to their own faculty. Given the orientation of healthy inquiry and the basic methodological and substantive foundations, we have every reason to suspect that our students will forge new paths for clinical psychology and leave us behind. That's as it should be!

9

Graduate Education and the Yale Psycho-Educational Clinic

Seymour B. Sarason and Murray Levine

The origins of, rationale for, and the clinical and research activities of the Yale Psycho-Educational Clinic have been described elsewhere (Sarason, Levine, Goldenberg, Cherlin, & Bennett, 1966; Kaplan & Sarason, 1969). It is not possible here to summarize in concrete, descriptive detail the total clinic program, but we shall attempt to present some generalizations which may convey characteristics of our activities and serve as a basis of discussion of the aims and problems of training.

GENERAL CHARACTERISTICS OF THE CLINIC

The Psycho-Educational Clinic is an integral part of the Department of Psychology. On the graduate level it is used as a practicum setting for certain courses, and it also serves as an internship setting for those of our students having an interest in community psychology. The clinic is also used in conjunction with undergraduate senior seminars.

Six faculty members comprise the core staff and, in addition, there are three part-time psychologists who are not teaching members of the faculty but who are regarded as members of the clinic staff. In no instance is any faculty member's participation a precondition either for hiring or continuance in the department—i.e., each faculty member can opt in or out, and this is primarily his decision. The fact is that each faculty member gives at least a minimum of three full days to the clinic, and in several instances far more than that. The classroom teaching load in the department is light and supervision of students in clinical activity is

Although the authors are completely responsible for this paper, we believe we are reflecting views about which there is consensus by all faculty and students at the clinic. This paper was seen in various drafts by everyone at the clinic and discussed at special meetings for faculty and for students.

counted as part of one's teaching obligations. The clinic as a full-time, busy center is possible only because those who participate in it willingly give time far beyond that required by departmental or university criteria. And now to attempt to characterize the clinic.

1. The orientation of the clinic requires that we spend most of our time away from the clinic—we work almost exclusively in other people's settings: elementary schools, junior high schools, various parts of the local community action program, regional centers for the mentally retarded. There are times when individuals, families, or groups from these settings will be seen at the clinic—we are not open to the general public.

2. There are at least ten discrete settings in which some member of the clinic spends time, usually one and a half to two days per week. Regardless of the specific problems on which we focus or which are presented to us in the setting, our ever-present task is to understand the setting in its terms. We view our approach as one that phenotypically appears "clinical" but is genotypically an outgrowth of a social psychological or cultural anthropological point of view. For most, if not all of us, identification is more with a way of thinking than with techniques or conventional labels—for example, clinical, school, social, etc.

3. Since our commitment is to a setting and any individual or problem in it (that is presented to us), we work with people varying considerably in age, experience, and status. (In schools, for example, we work primarily with teachers, principals, parents, and supervisory help, and secondarily with children.) Consequently, we are not a children's clinic, although we work with children, or an adult clinic, although we work with adults, nor an adolescent clinic, although we work with them. Ours is a clinic that works in and with educational and helping settings.

4. On the procedural or technical side we are engaged in sustained individual and group work. By individual work we do not mean psychotherapy but rather a sustained relationship which is oriented both toward the problems of referrer (e.g., teacher) and the one being referred (e.g., child) even though we may never engage the referred individual in a face-to-face contact but will observe him in the setting over periods of time. Clearly, how and when to observe is the third technique we rely on heavily. Increasingly, we are doing more and more group work in each of the settings.

5. Leaving aside the question of the degree of consistency between intentions and theory, on the one hand, and activities and practices, on the other hand, there is little question that one of our major interests is how to learn to prevent problems—that is, we try to look at whatever we do from the standpoint of how the problems brought to us could have been prevented. To some of us the most important, intriguing, and unstudied question is how to create settings which have a low rate of orga-

nizational, self-defeating craziness. This question, of course, arises only if one truly understands that within a setting the problems of individuals to an undetermined extent reflect characteristics of the settings.

6. The clinic is justified on a number of grounds, but one of the most important is that it is a vehicle whereby a number of faculty members, having similar but by no means identical interests, can confront theory with practice and personal opinion with research and scholarship. We each do this in differing degrees and styles. While we have grown up together and tend to have a rather fierce loyalty to and identification with the clinic, we have each just as fiercely maintained our individuality—a heartening result which is not without its problems. Most, if not all of us, contend that to the extent that each of us experiences the processes of learning and unlearning, the necessity and excitement of no-holds-barred discussion and inquiry, and the need to be committed and tentative at the same time, we will be doing a major service to our students. These are, admittedly, virtuous intentions. Anything we could say about the realization would and should be held suspect. We state them here only to emphasize that we try to face and avoid the twin dangers of parochialism: to view what one does as the only way one can justify one's existence, and to view what colleagues do in other settings as misguided and unhelpful. Psychology has not been without its religious sects. We are not, by temperament or design, eclectics. We may have a sense of mission but we try not to confuse mission with mandate.

THE PRE-INTERNSHIP YEARS: PROBLEMS

In any new development within a field (e.g., community psychology) two major problems can be anticipated. The first is the struggle to develop and state a set of theoretical conceptualizations which serve both to order and justify one's activities and experiences. Put another way, the dominant theories in a field are not likely to be perceived as adequate to the task of integrating the new with the old—that is, they are likely to be perceived as incomplete in varying degrees or simply not relevant to the new developments. This perception is made more likely when, as in our case, the new venture is seen as being related not only to one field (psychology) but to several: sociology, cultural anthropology, education, and social history. It is not surprising, therefore, that we should feel that the dominant theories of learning, personality, and development seem to be inadequate as cognitive maps steering us through unfamiliar terrain. In short, the theory courses which graduate students take simply are not as relevant to "our problems"—both in a theoretical and technical-applied sense—as they are to the problems around which these theories were developed. Operationally, most psychological theory courses concern either the individual human being and/or a small group like the family. This emphasis, which has been and will continue to be productive for many important problems in psychology, has not been very helpful to us in our thinking with our problems and to students who choose to work with us. This state of affairs obviously presents students and us (and a department) with many problems, but it is with the intent neither to mollify nor to gloss over that we maintain that this state of affairs is much to be preferred to one in which the academic boat is unrocked, at anchor, and untested in stormy seas.

The theory problem is not made any easier by the fact that we at the clinic are, to an undetermined extent, prisoners of our own psychological training. It is not only that we have to reorient our thinking, to attempt to avoid the mistakes of overreaction, but also that we have to become familiar with other disciplines which would seem to have much to offer us—a scholarly effort which requires considerable time for reading and reflection (the latter being far more difficult). The more one reads the more one has to read and this is not easy when one is part of a full-time clinic devoted to research, teaching, and service. The point here is not what this means to us but what it means to our students who are trying to understand how and why we think as we do. When they inevitably learn that we are confronted with numerous problems centering on the contents and processes of our learning—that we feel ourselves to be students as they are—whatever satisfaction they may get by a feeling of community is counterbalanced by their awareness that whatever maps we can provide them are far from detailed.

That the model first-year graduate student is unfamiliar with the nature and activities of the clinic would not in itself present any undue difficulties were it not for the additional fact that he tends to come with certain expectations about what he will learn—that is, diagnosis and therapy, with the latter clearly being the status activity. He learns that this is not that kind of clinic, but he has difficulty comprehending just what kind of clinic it is. He is exposed in the first year to various kinds of active, stimulating, clinical settings with which he usually has some familiarity, but this seems to make our setting even more of a puzzle. This no longer surprises us (it bothers us) because this is a reaction we have gotten from many people, even after having read the book describing the clinic. Our own inadequacies in written description are undoubtedly a contributing factor, but beyond this we feel we are seeing the consequences of conflict. That is to say, the student has an idea of why he came into clinical psychology, what a clinical psychologist is supposed to do, where he does it (in his office in a clinic or hospital), and the personality theories he is supposed to know. The Psycho-Educational Clinic simply does not fit into his preconceptions. We think and practice differently and most of the time we are away from our office! When we think of our own struggles, personal and intellectual, to get where we are, we have much sympathy for the first year student.

There are usually some students who come to clinical psychology with the view that therapy (psychoanalytic, behavior, etc.) is the mental aspirin of the mental health professions, and these students are so wedded to this belief as to make them relatively impervious to what we have to offer. Although we understand their point of view, and the over-all clinical program allows for their pursuing such interests, they do not and cannot understand us. Most students, however, struggle with, for, and against us, a state of affairs which we, at least, consider healthy.

What perhaps deserves special emphasis as a problem is that community psychology, if it is to be properly understood as a body of knowledge, procedures, and theories, requires familiarity not only with social history but also with a variety of disciplines and traditions not ordinarily contained in graduate programs in psychology. However amorphous and shifting community psychology may be (and will be for some time), it is firmly rooted in the social history of our country, although we are only beginning to understand the social-historical forces which set the stage of its emergence (for example, Levine & Levine, 1970; Gladwin, 1967). The sense of identity, for an individual or a field, is not obtained from current ideas and practices but rather from a truly dynamic relationship between ideas and individuals, on the one hand, and social forces and contexts, on the other hand. This kind of history in relation to community psychology has yet to be written, but when it is, there is every reason to believe that much that we are now thinking and doing will not be found to be new and innovative. The settlement houses, the early juvenile courts, the visiting teacher movement, the explicit but forgotten initial rationale for the early child guidance clinics—these are but some of the early developments in the history of community psychology which those of us of today will have to rediscover (Levine and Levine, 1970).[1]

THE IDENTITY PROBLEM

What we have said so far will have occasioned no surprise in anyone who is knowledgeable about the history of clinical psychology and, in addition, is sensitive to the dynamics of identity formation particularly in an era of great social unrest and change. Without

[1] We are not partisans for the term "community psychology" if only because the concept of community, and preventive and remedial programs in relation to it, are not in the province of psychology or any other single field.

such knowledge and sensitivity—and this characterizes many psychologists and new students—the clash between the new and the old will tend to be viewed only in terms of individual dynamics, or the idiosyncrasies of small groups, or the ever-present gulf between generations. What will tend to be overlooked are those social forces and historical traditions which directly and indirectly give shape and direction to a field and thereby help determine the contents of the identity problem. This point need not be elaborated upon for those who after World War II lived through the forging of the identity of the clinical psychologist. It was the forging of this identity together with the accelerating rate of social change that set the stage for the new problem of identity we have been describing and confronting in ourselves and our students.

A sense of professional and personal identity is not easy to come by and once achieved it is understandable why it would be very resistant to change. It is probably clear to the reader that we are emphasizing the identity problem because it was our problem as part of a teaching faculty in clinical psychology. We realized early that the problem of training students was secondary to our own struggles and development. And struggle we did and struggling we are. We are not as concerned as we once were that this creates problems for students.[2] Our major concern is whether we are presenting ourselves honestly to our students and communicating to them our own sense of direction, excitement, growth, and uncertainty. Not surprisingly, the forging of the sense of identity occurs with great rapidity in the internship year if only because words, talk, argument, expectations, attitudes, and theories are inevitably changed in the crucible of experience.

THE INTERNSHIP

It is the intent of the internship experience to help students gain perspective on the social nature of human problems and to understand the contribution of settings to their manifestation. We are as interested that students come to understand the "craziness of settings" as we are that they understand the "craziness of people." An intern, except in rare instances, cannot be expected to be able to take full responsibility for changes in larger settings, but it is necessary that students come to appreciate the possibilities of change in settings as a goal of clinical practice. Moreover, since it is a goal of the internship to prepare students to understand the nature of settings, it is essential that students

2 Those of our students who have completed the doctorate and who have sought positions elsewhere tell us they become more aware of the identity issue when they try to describe their training and experiences to clinicians in other settings.

become exposed to more than one setting, concurrently, in order that they be able to experience the similarities and differences between settings. We are also interested in having students obtain appropriate experience with a variety of helping modalities including consultation, tutoring, group, individual and family therapy, supervision of nonprofessionals, program development, and participation in organizational decision-making processes. While not all students gain experience in all modalities, the hallmark of the internship is its emphasis on diversity of experience and on the unifying themes that run through diverse settings and forms of helping. As we shall see, we also have a continuing concern about our own setting as a training, a research, and a clinical center.

THE STUDENTS' EXPERIENCES

From the point of view of the students, initially at least, our good intentions as faculty seem to pave the road to chaos. Students come to their internships with a variety of attitudes and expectations. They come eager to accept responsibility because many feel that the earlier experience in undergraduate and graduate school is infantalizing, but they also experience the discontinuity from graduate school to the internship as a rather sharp one. The internship is the first professional experience, one in which the student fantasies he will exhibit his psychological virtuosity, and expects he will learn how to be a professional, whatever that means to him. He wants to win the approbation of those who are the embodiment of his ego ideal, and is concerned with how he will win his spurs. On the one hand, then, students are keenly aware of their own inexperience but, on the other hand, they feel the situation requires them to be expert. They not only feel responsible in an ethical sense, but because they are out in the world they feel responsible as representatives of the University and of the Clinic. Given this heavy burden of responsibility, given the acute change in their own life situation, and given that graduate study rarely provides directly relevant preparation for what the students will actually do and feel, the students' experience of considerable anxiety seems inevitable. (Those who have had the opportunity to observe in various settings without having to accept specific responsibility, report that such preinternship experiences were helpful.)

Anxiety is compounded by the confusion inherent in meeting many new people in several physical settings all at once, and in trying to make sense out of the varied reception in different settings, and from different individuals in the same setting. To be greeted as an honored, high status person, to be the recipient of cries of relief that you are finally here and will magically solve problems, to be ignored or to be met with a perfunctory nod, to feel yourself the cause of another person's discomfort and anxiety, or to be met with poorly disguised hostility when you have had no conceivable hand in creating that hostility, all within a few days, and sometimes within the same day, are a set of experiences guaranteed to create uncertainty even in one whose role and identity are fairly well developed. For the student who is in the midst of a change in identity, the varied environmental feedback can only contribute to a sense of a blooming, buzzing, amorphous world without firm guidelines. While it is true that any psychotherapist is the recipient and target of a similar variety of emotions, he is in his office, on his territory so to speak. Even though the rules of the game are clearer that situation is still difficult, for students as well as experienced personnel. It is little wonder that those in a Psycho-Educational Clinic internship have much to integrate in their first few months.

Initially, the student's problems take several forms. In some situations, where one is experiencing the ghetto with all of its vigor, strangeness, and implicit threat of violence, particularly in this day and age, one comes face to face with one's deepest emotions and gut level values. It is one thing to maintain an idealistic attitude toward dirt, child neglect, extramarital sex, apparent apathy and indifference, hostility toward learning, sadistic and explosive relationships, and a "primary process" orientation, and it is another thing to witness it and to work with it. Women students report uneasy moments when entering unfamiliar, poorly lit apartment buildings, or when they must walk down unfamiliar streets where groups of young men loiter, openly drinking even in daylight hours. We have not had any untoward incidents, but we must give our female students and staff credit for their courage and good will.

It is one thing to maintain an idealistic, therapeutic acceptance of all of mankind, and then to come face to face with archaic, lower middle-class operated institutions, with more than occasional petty officials, with small-minded, more or less openly prejudiced teachers who vainly try to impose rigid standards upon unwilling resistant children, or with inadequate people operating with inadequate resources and hamstrung by interminable lists of real and fancied regulations. It is not uncommon for students to react with a sick feeling that the whole system ought to be junked, and that any effort at help is hopeless. The clinical need to contain such extreme expressions, and to attempt to work with and to relate to people whom they do not understand or respect, make some feel hypocritical. At the same time, some students also observe the real competence and devotion of many teachers and principals and the natural therapeutic sense of many nonprofessionals (and the ability to act), which characterize many who function successfully in difficult interpersonal situations. Most students come to have feelings of guilt about their own relatively protected positions and about their right to offer counsel to those who are on the firing line daily.

All three sets of experiences (anxiety and the assault on personal values, the sense of hopelessness, and the greater competence of others) feed into the student's sense of helplessness and incompetence. Together they provide a powerful stimulus toward seeking the safety of the familiar and toward obtaining experiences in which their own competence can be validated by some form of quick feedback. Although such experiences tend to arise more acutely later on in the internship than at the beginning, they are the basis for a variety of defenses. It is very tempting to engage in therapeutic interviews with a receptive child, to give a familiar psychological test, to write a careful and thorough report, or to engage in meetings with likeminded professionals who speak one's own language and who thereby help to validate one's preexisting beliefs. There are many times when students (and faculty) report a distinct disinclination to get up and to go to work in the morning, not necessarily because things are not going well, but because of the continued emotional bombardment from within and without. A sense of being tired, hopeless, inept, and unwilling to withstand another day of emotional strain can lead one to overlook real accomplishment and to shrink from the hard, slow, day to day work, and the frequent frustrations and crises which arise in work in community settings.[3] The existence of a group of interns who support each other and of a staff who can support morale through difficult periods are quite essential.

The anxiety and confusion are balanced by the heady excitement of being out in the world, testing one's self and finding successes, and learning a great deal about the world and how it works. Because they are where the action is, the students can think and talk about phenomena based upon first-hand experience, and they experience rapid learning and the sense of discovery. Although students feel totally unprepared for the specific experiences and the specific responsibilities, in peculiar and unpredictable ways students find connections between the apperceptive mass, the residue of long years of formal and informal learning, and ongoing events. The discovery of the relevance of their general intellectual preparation, and the relevance of their indeed superior ability to conceptualize, is exciting and tends to offset the anxiety of clinical responsibility. The "mind-expanding" quality of the experience is itself a potent motivational force, as is the desire to master difficult challenges.

[3] It is our opinion that the intellectual and affective turbulence we are describing is in a basic sense identical with what many researchers, theoreticians, and writers experience in dealing with difficult and seemingly intractable problems. Many writers agree that writing is torture, and many researchers agree that thinking and doing research are by no means characterized by pleasantness and tranquility. It is asking too much of beginning interns to have a perspective which would allow them to view the *Sturm und Drang* as perhaps having beneficial consequences.

The total internship experience, for some, opens an interest in clinical and field research, and opens an interest in tackling larger problems than they might ordinarily take on if experience and research training were restricted to the laboratory. During the internship the student becomes aware of research problems in several ways. The most obvious way is by the formal and informal means whereby he becomes acquainted with the research of staff members. The research of most, if not all, staff members directly or indirectly has emerged from their clinic activities—an initial goal of the clinic, which has been achieved. An equally obvious way is the student's own questions which derive from his clinic activities, questions which come up in supervisory sessions and clinic meetings and which we encourage the student to pursue. Around the fourth or fifth month of the internship the student is expected to start thinking seriously about his thesis area, choose a major advisor, and begin the review of the literature. It is expected that by the end of the internship the thesis problem will have been formulated, the thesis committee appointed by the director of graduate studies, at least one meeting of this committee held, and the extent of pilot work or studies determined.

In the early months of the internship it is probably fair to say that he is equally at sea in regard to research problems and activities as he is in regard to his clinical tasks, and for much the same reasons. That is to say, his research courses and previous research experiences do not have any obvious or immediate transfer value to what he is thinking about or seeing in the complicated settings in which he works. The clinical demands on student (and faculty) time, energy, and attention are great, but such demands are not the primary issue. What tends to overwhelm the student is the feeling that the questions which intrigue him involve a host of complex variables he cannot control in the setting in which the questions arise and in which he wishes to study them. With increasing frequency, however, a number of students have undertaken difficult field studies involving data collected in the natural setting.

The discussion has been weighted in the direction of the dysphoric, but it is our impression that the excitement and the challenge of the total enterprise far outweighs the distress for most students. Although students voice a large number of concerns about being plunged into several different settings all at once, when asked later on most indicated they were better off for having been exposed to multiple settings. The varied experiences, the varied paces, and the differential satisfactions and frustrations did indeed seem to have provided perspective and did seem to enhance learning.

For some, the concepts of community psychology, particularly thinking about broad social processes and the possibility of influencing relatively large scale events, are far removed from any conception they held about clinical practice. Students become concerned that they are not learning to be clinical psychologists as they understand that term, that there will be no positions for them, and that there are bodies of knowledge and disciplines (e.g., sociology, political science, economics, anthropology) more directly pertinent to community psychology than anything they or their faculty have studied and mastered. For some, a whole new world opens up, however. It may be that the internship, just as any educational experience ought to be, is a time of decision. A legitimate goal of any training program ought to be one of helping students find themselves. That some do grow with new experiences, and that others become confirmed in other ways of thinking or believe they should seek something else, is expected and to be hoped for. This, of course, places on faculty and clinical supervisors additional responsibility to recognize student needs for development and to provide for the proper guidance of students.

SUPERVISION

As with any interpersonal situation in which one party is subject to an unexpected degree of anxiety, the other party, the person held responsible for the anxiety, is the target of hostility. In this instance, faculty sometimes are the recipients of intern hostility. The hostility takes the form of overt and covert attacks upon the competence, qualifications, and ethical responsibility of their mentors. That the interns and students sometimes touch on sore spots, on issues which give the faculty cause for self-doubt and introspective concern, does not help in maintaining an air of open interchange. We shall return to the techniques for maintaining openness within the clinic setting itself, but for the moment let it suffice that one of the problems faculty face is absorbing the anxiety and hostility coming from the very uncertainty of the new enterprise in which all are engaged. As the leaders, and the "experts" in the community psychology business, the faculty are the natural target for feelings stemming from real or apparent failures. It is necessary for faculty to recognize the hostility, to meet the challenges implicit and explicit in student concerns, to respond appropriately and realistically to the issues which are raised, and still to hold forth a vision of the future.

Senior faculty who have proven themselves in one arena, and who have as the core of their own identities a sense of themselves as social scientists, or as contributors to knowledge, or who view their experiences as intellectual nutriment for the development of their own research, may have a somewhat easier time of it. Junior faculty who are still finding their way, and who are competing in the academic jungles, may be in a somewhat more tenuous position in dealing with the uncertainties of an uncharted course. However, there are gross individual differences here, both on the junior and the senior faculty sides, and generalization along this dimension is hazardous at best.

Community psychology presents some unique teaching problems. In many situations it is extremely difficult to arrange either for the student to observe the faculty in action or for the faculty to observe the student. It is difficult, if not impossible, to disguise the relationship between student and faculty when both function together in some situation. There is a natural inclination for the client to turn toward the faculty member. Similarly, when the faculty member takes leadership, the student has an opportunity to observe, but the potential for the student to interact in a fully responsible way is reduced.

In group situations the problem of observation is somewhat less pronounced, but in individual consultations or in the observation of natural situations it is difficult to arrange for a meaningful observational position. In the standard clinical situation, where the client comes to your setting, it is possible to arrange for one-way observation rooms and tape recordings of interviews. In the natural setting one-way rooms are rarely available, and we have not yet found it feasible to try and record consultation sessions. In that part of the work that depends upon hurried snatches of conversation in the hallways, bits of business intermingled with small talk at lunch or on a coffee break, telephone conversations and the like, recording is simply unfeasible, and in any event would spoil the spontaneity of the interaction, an important quality of the kind of relationship certain kinds of consultative relationships require.

The lack of opportunity for direct observation of the clinical interaction makes for several problems. With regard to faculty responsibility to evaluate students, the supervisor is forced to rely largely on the student's report of events for evidence. He can inquire of the student's progress of people in the situation itself, but the data which come back are necessarily limited. If the student achieves some level of acceptance in the situation, others may wish to protect him by saying he is doing well. Those with whom the student works may feel they are in the position of informants and will be inclined to adopt the same standards of in-group protection they use for others in the setting. The student's acceptance in the setting may not be based upon any demonstrable competence in a helping role, but simply because the student is appealing as a person.

On the other side, a student with a great deal of potential competence may become the victim of the anxiety and ire of those in the situation by virtue of his propensity for taking action. It is very difficult to know when complaints about a student reflect important personal inaptitude for the work, errors of a kind that anyone can be expected to make, or the consequence of realistic confrontations and demands for change. It is all too easy for the student to become a victim in a situation in which one's presence depends on the good will of the host, or for the university-based clinic to adopt a hard line in defense of its students and not take into account realistic complaints. The activity of the student in several different settings and his interaction with several different supervisors is something of a safeguard in this difficult situation.

One of the major ways in which a supervisor can gain perspective on what an intern is reporting stems from the fact that the supervisor, with rare exceptions, has himself worked in the very setting in which the student has been placed—that is, the supervisor knows the people and the problems of the setting.

The difficulty in providing for direct observation creates still another problem. The supervisor does not exhibit his own style, the standard of accomplishment he uses for his own work, or his own clay feet. His errors are automatically concealed from the student. The supervisor, who also has evaluative responsibility, is placed in a position which, on the one hand fosters fantasies of omnipotence (both in him and in the student), and on the other, does not readily permit the discussion of differences even when they arise in the student's mind. We are convinced that supervision is among the basic elements in making for the student's growth, but the supervisory relationship has both a growth-enhancing and a growth-retarding potential.

The first requisite of the supervisory situation is that the student feel free to discuss all aspects of a particular situation, especially those which make the student look bad. Both students and supervisors feel an attitude of open inquiry is critical for the learning situation. Both students and supervisors feel that a nonevaluative, issue-centered approach is desirable, but both groups also agree such an approach is difficult to achieve.

On the side of openness is the supervisor's attitude, the student's trust in the supervisor, and the student's commitment to the scientific ethic of trying to report events as honestly and as fully as possible. On the side of dissemblance is the student's desire to appear competent, the vagaries of the human memory, the student's lack of confidence in knowing what is important and what is not, and the supervisor's attitude or interpersonal style.

Most important, however, is the student's desire to operate independently and to test his own ideas and competence. If a supervisor insists on the student following his directions too closely, the student will engage in activities which never come to the supervisor's attention. Students sometimes are headstrong and will rebel against too close direction. Sometimes students will undertake interventions which the supervisor has suggested were inappropriate for a particular situation. Some-

times the student will resent supervisory direction and will carry it out
in ways calculated to defeat the intent of the suggestion. In other instances, the student feels intimidated by the supervisor and reports that
the spontaneity of various relationships is destroyed because the supervisor is experienced as an invisible third party.

The supervisor has the distinct problem of developing that kind of
relationship with a student in which his clear warnings of impending
error will be heeded, in which suggestions will be offered primarily
when the student is stymied, and in which student suggestions for approaches to given problems will be encouraged and considered seriously.
When difficult situations arise as a result of student action, it is essential
that the supervisor be supportive of the student and treat the difficult
situation as a learning opportunity. In a sense, one almost needs to make
a full commitment to the student at the time of selection, and then stick
with him through thick and thin, if a true learning situation is to be
developed.

Supervisor support of the student through praise is really insufficient
from the student's viewpoint. While students appreciate some degree of
positive feedback, many state a distinct preference that the supervision
be issue oriented, rather than evaluatively oriented. When supervision
focuses on their particular difficulties, students feel more comfortable
with specific details, with concrete suggestions for improving, and with
opportunities to master situations which had been difficult for them.
While students want to feel respect for their supervisor, some prefer a
relationship of greater equality, one more like that between junior and
senior colleague, than one between an authority and a subordinate.

From the student's viewpoint there is real concern that they obtain
some evidence that what they are doing is indeed correct. They worry,
quite naturally, about the welfare of their clients. On the other hand,
many recognize that it is necessary to live with ambiguity and uncertainty
over long periods of time. The problem is to learn how to judge, from
available evidence, the progress of all of the intermediate steps in an
intervention. If the supervision is issue oriented, hopefully supervisors
and students together can make the rules of evidence explicit so that
students learn how to observe and evaluate subtle signposts. If the supervision is evaluatively oriented, then the students learn to do and to report
that which will bring the supervisor's approbation. If the supervision is
issue oriented, hopefully a student will learn to detect and rely upon the
subtle pieces of evidence available in his own direct experience.

Supervision in clinical work presents a distinct problem because of
its authority orientation. A student is placed in a subordinate position to
a supervisor who is presumed to be expert in the given area. Since the
student rarely if ever gets an opportunity to observe the supervisor in
his clinical work, and since supervisors are not usually inclined to share

their own errors with students, there is an implication of supervisory omnipotence. If a student follows a supervisor's directions, and it is successful, his belief in the supervisor's omnipotence is reinforced. If he follows the advice and no obvious change results, his supervisor's approval of the style in which the student carried out the recommendation reinforces a tendency to believe in whatever theoretical system the supervisor says he used, independently of observable effects. If the student is told his approach is incorrect, from the point of view of the supervisor, and no clear empirical evidence is produced to support the supervisor's view, there is the implication that although what the student is doing is wrong, there is a right way which the supervisor knows and which the student might some day learn. Once again, the authority orientation of the supervisor leads the student away from a reliance on whatever empirical evidence is available to him.

Since it is an intention of the internship experience to produce professionals who are committed to the concept of experimental innovation in practice, it is vital that the supervisory experience be directed toward developing the student's confidence in his own ability to observe and to draw conclusions even when these conclusions challenge his theoretical, philosophical, or humanistic biases.

The availability of supervision and its limitations are also important. There are frequent "emergencies"—that is, situations in which the student is in the field and others turn to him for advice for action or decisions. Some students find these emergencies quite frightening. Since supervisors are also in the field, and not always immediately available, the student often enough is thrown on his own. To some extent the student can be prepared for such occurrences and warned that emergencies of a given kind will arise, but it is difficult to set up rules which cover every contingency.

Supervisors attempt to make themselves available as much as is necessary and as close to the point of decision as is feasible. However, in today's academic world the time of faculty members is in great demand, and most try to preserve time for their own research and study. Thus they are not as readily available as is ideally desirable. To some extent the presence of a number of faculty members compensates for the difficulty, particularly if students can be encouraged to seek out people who are available. However, the other staff may not know anything about the case and be less than helpful.

In other instances students, rightly or wrongly, believe there are rivalries, enmities, jurisdictional disputes, or other conflicts among clinic faculty, which limit their freedom to seek out faculty members for advice and direction. Some of this may reflect conditions that faculty members inadvertently create, and some of it may reflect faulty inferences on the part of the student to personal differences from theoretical differences expressed vigorously in seminars. Since there is an inevitable status, age, and life situation gulf between faculty and students, students frequently do not have the opportunity to observe the personal, as opposed to the professional, life of faculty. They may not have the evidence, and faculty may not think to provide it for them, that personal friendship and mutual respect can flourish despite open and sharp theoretical and professional differences.

More than parenthetically, we wish to point out that these examples show that the broader social system in which the clinic members live affects their very day-by-day operations in subtle and not so subtle ways. The principles that hold for the outer world (other people's settings), hold for the inner world of the university-based clinic as well (as our setting).

Group supervision appears to be an important technique in providing for the growth of a group of interns. In one such meeting only the interns, or people on an equivalent level of status and experience, participate. The meeting is conducted by the director of the clinic, and other supervisors either do not participate or participate irregularly. The meeting serves several functions for the members. First, the director may express opinions and offer suggestions which are not in agreement with those of the immediate supervisor. The director must be careful to see that such suggestions are viewed as theoretical alternatives and are not to be used as a form of resistance to supervision. When differences arise, they are treated as examples of theoretical differences which elucidate basic issues. From the point of view of the student, the notion of alternatives is presented and exemplified. The student obtains concrete evidence of honest differences among professionals, and he is thereby encouraged to think for himself. The meeting is a form of antidote to the poorer features of the authority structure of supervision, providing perspective and necessary thinking time.

Second, the students need to have a sense of belonging to a group in order to help them form some concept of themselves as developing professionals. They need to compare themselves with others, both in order to feel an identity with some group, and in order to differentiate themselves from others. Opportunities for informal exchange among students is limited when they are in physically diverse settings. Coffee breaks, lunches, broken appointments, or report writing time, the time people in space-bounded settings use for informal interchange, are times not as readily available in an unbounded community oriented clinic.

Third, if students are to participate in a clinical community, they have both a right to know and a right to the satisfaction of their curiosity about what others are actually doing in similar and in different settings. Group supervision helps in this respect in that students learn from each other what is happening in different settings. They also learn from each other about alternative technical solutions to recurrent problems, and are helped to see the underlying unity of principle which may be observed in diverse situations.

CLINIC MEETINGS AND SEMINARS AT THE YALE PSYCHO-EDUCATIONAL CLINIC

Because of the problem of diversity of approaches and physical dispersal of the settings in which faculty and students actually function, a distinct effort was made to keep one full day, Friday, free for (a) a clinic-wide seminar, (b) a faculty-level staff meeting, and (c) a meeting with an outside consultant on group process. This last meeting originally began as a didactic meeting to discuss groups members were leading, but from time to time it served the function of focusing on the interaction among members of the clinic group. Almost all attended, including the clinic director who subordinated a great deal of his position of leadership to the outside consultant for purposes of that meeting.

The clinic seminar is a general meeting, open to the number of people who can fit around the seminar table, usually no more than a maximum of twenty. At one point a decision was made to limit the size of the clinic to the number of people who could fit around the seminar table, in order to preserve the quality of personal cooperation and face-to-face interaction essential to maintain a sense of unity in a diverse operation. The topics in the seminar range broadly over a wide variety of areas of research and study. Guests from within and outside the university are invited. Anyone may suggest a guest or a topic, or anyone may preempt a meeting for any area of content which concerns or interests him. Faculty and students present their own work in the seminar, and occasionally meetings are left open for agendaless discussions. The clinic seminars have been supplemented by one- or two-day paperless marathon meetings in which two or three outside guests are invited to participate in a general discussion of work in which all have an interest. The meetings have covered as diverse topics as Community Mental Health programs, the Preparation of Teachers, and the Conceptualization of Social Systems.

It may not have been a fully conscious intent, but it quickly worked out that the spirit of the seminar was one of open interchange accompanied by a fair amount of wit and repartée. We now introduce guests by informing them they can expect the first ten minutes to be theirs without interruption, but from that point on they are to expect to fight for a place at the table. Because there are a number of verbally fluent people around the table, and because the seminar often deals with many ideas that are new, startling, and at the frontiers of social thought and clinical practice, the experience for many is both a heady one and sometimes a frustrating one. Interns, and sometimes junior faculty, report the meeting to be exciting, bewildering, productive of tension within them, and they are concerned about their opportunity to speak. Others find the meetings consistently stimulating intellectually and experience no barrier to participation.

It is in keeping with the spirit of inquiry in the clinic that a visiting clinical psychologist, on a postdoctoral fellowship in the Department of Sociology, was invited to sit in on the clinic seminar for a full year and was encouraged to study the seminar from the point of view of its group process. She reported her observations that the seminar did indeed have a high proportion of emotionally toned communications. It tended to function in a "wheel" arrangement, in that remarks from various members were as likely to be addressed to other seminar members as they were to the seminar leader.

However, despite the apparent openness and freedom of the meeting, there was also a clear-cut status hierarchy in that senior faculty spoke more often and earlier than junior faculty, and the junior faculty participated more than interns. Moreover, there was some evidence that it was more feasible for senior faculty to disagree with each other than it was for interns to disagree with senior faculty. Intern disagreement was sometimes put down, while the same issue could be raised by a faculty member without any apparent hazard.

Given the inevitable problems of a free discussion between people of different levels of status and experience, the seminar leader makes a distinct effort to encourage intern participation. It is a matter of policy that, whenever feasible, visiting dignitaries have lunch alone with the group of interns in order that students be able to have the benefit of personal contact with the visitors. The problems are far from solved, but in order to enhance the learning experience, for both faculty and interns, it is essential that one pay careful attention to just such issues.

The clinic staff meeting deals with policy issues, intern evaluation, local crises, and sometimes with the relationships among staff members. There was some discussion about including interns in the staff meeting, but it was decided not to include them because many of the staff felt discussion of important issues would be inhibited. The decision was an ambivalent one in that some felt it useful in the training of students for them to participate in such decisions and to become aware of the issues which determine practices.

The staff meeting has not served the function of keeping staff informed about each other's activities, and there is continual concern that all are not equally informed about various ongoing projects. The director of the clinic is the only person who is well informed about all ongoing activities because he tends to be the hub of the operation. Usually, his central position creates no difficulty, but from time to time, when issues concerning the direction of the clinic arise, staff members have raised questions about the degree to which they are party to important decisions.

While the director has laid out his areas of responsibility clearly, he has encouraged free discussion of the issues. The issues concerning the direction of development of the clinic have come up not only in staff, but also in the clinic seminar and in the meeting on group process which interns attend. The discussions have been unusually frank and have been open to visitors and other consultants who have been invited to such meetings. At times the consultants have raised such questions themselves, and their presence has contributed to an atmosphere of openness in the clinic, even though the discussion occasionally resulted in rather public and direct criticism of senior faculty.

The third meeting on Friday is devoted to a study of group process. It was originally established as a didactic seminar on the theory and management of therapy and discussion groups. An outside consultant, Dr. Walter Igersheimer, has led this seminar for the last two years. The director attended the seminar and participated as a member. He usually succeeded in subordinating his leadership role in that meeting, but from time to time group members reported feeling the tension which ensues when there is a conflict in leadership. Both faculty, including the director, and students have presented groups, opening themselves equally to criticism from the group and the consultant. The consultant has had the problem of skillfully maintaining a focus on the theory and management of groups, and balancing off pressures in the group to turn it into more of a self-study group and less of a seminar group. From time to time the group does pause and examine its own group processes. Within the group there are two clear factions. One is experienced with and oriented toward various forms of sensitivity training and T grouping. The other faction has some distinct concern that given the inevitable status differences, and given the evaluative relationship between those at different levels of status, a fully free sensitivity group cannot evolve. Moreover, there is some objection to the idea that experiences in such a group are necessarily generalizable to other groups operating in different settings or that self-study is necessarily the most effective means of learning. This difference in viewpoint is subject to discussion and unquestionably has contributed to making both staff and group members alert to how issues in the organization of the clinic and how areas of conflict influence the very nature of ongoing clinical activity. The fact that many such issues arise in open discussion help to maintain the spirit of inquiry within the clinic. The clinic attempts to study and to think about its own

organizational structure, and its relationship to the psychology department and the university, in the same way that it attempts to think about
characteristics of settings in which it works.

SUMMARY

We have attempted in this chapter to provide a picture
of the issues in training in community psychology, how students perceive
and experience various situations, how the faculty sees the issues, and the
attempts at solutions. A few of the issues were anticipated, and a few
of the solutions were rationally constructed. In most other instances we
reacted to problems as they arose, and hoped that we would be sufficiently guided by an attitude of open inquiry and by a belief in the
essential benevolence of the future to permit new solutions to evolve as
the need became evident. We feel that as long as we take seriously the
principle that we need to be at least as concerned about the nature of
our own setting as we are about the nature of the settings in which we
work elsewhere, we will stand a chance of continuing to evolve programs which are meaningful in relation to our changing understanding
of how people live in their social worlds.

REFERENCES

Gladwin, T. *Poverty, U.S.A.* Boston: Little, Brown, 1967.
Kaplan, F., & Sarason, S. B. *Collected papers of the Psycho-Educational Clinic.*
    Massachusetts State Department of Mental Health (Monograph Series), 1969.
Levine, M. & Levine, A. *A social history of helping services: Clinic, court, school,
    and community.* New York: Appleton-Century-Crofts, 1970.
Sarason, S. B., Levine, M., Goldenberg, I. I., Cherlin, D. L., & Bennett, E. M.
    *Psychology in community settings: Clinical, educational, vocational, social
    aspects.* New York: Wiley, 1966.

10

A Psychology Department Graduate Sequence in Community Mental Health

Bernard L. Bloom

Although the community mental health graduate sequence at the University of Colorado began as recently as September, 1965, three distinct phases in its development can already be identified. Since these phases form what may likely be a common natural history in many psychology departments that are exploring the possibilities of teaching in the field of community mental health, this chapter will be organized around these distinct phases and the issues which arose regarding each of them. An initial description of the psychology department as a whole has been prepared in order to orient the reader to the context within which these developments are occurring and a brief section on the possible future of the community mental health graduate sequence concludes the chapter.

THE UNIVERSITY OF COLORADO PSYCHOLOGY DEPARTMENT

During the 1962/63 academic year there were 17 members in the psychology department faculty. The department had been at this level for several years. A university decision during that year to develop a significantly strengthened psychology department resulted in the recruitment of two outstanding people (including a new departmental chairman) during 1963/64, a year of developmental planning during 1964/65, the addition of four new faculty in 1965/66, four additional faculty members in 1966/67, and eight new faculty members in 1967/68. Five positions remain to be filled, and it is a fair assumption that five additional positions will be created within the next few years. Completion of this recruitment effort will result in a departmental faculty of 45 by 1972 or 1973.

Graduate training is handled by area committees. There are currently four established graduate programs including clinical (dating from the early 1950s), social (dating from the mid-1950s), experimental, and quantitative. Two new specialty areas (behavioral genetics and developmental) have recently been established and are undergoing a period of rapid growth. The clinical, social, and experimental programs are supported by NIMH training grants. While there are department-wide regulations and requirements, there is also considerable area autonomy. Members of an area identify an area chairman and serve as members of committees to consider the curriculum and all aspects of their students' progress.

The social psychology program is attempting to integrate two major conflicting trends, namely, the study of socially significant field problems, on the one hand, and the maintenance of methodological laboratory-based rigor, on the other hand. While there is a strong emphasis on methodological sophistication, research methods are identified which can be taken into on-going organizational settings. The clinical program aims toward the development of the "scholar-clinician"—that is, toward the training of individuals intellectually committed to the furtherance of knowledge about human behavior while at the same time skilled in those special assessment and therapeutic activities which are part of the normal armamentarium of the clinical psychologist. The doctoral program can be completed in four years of postgraduate work, although in the case of the clinical specialty, an additional internship year is required. This internship usually occurs in the fourth year with the fifth year being devoted to the completion of the dissertation.

As the clinical program is presently constituted, the first year of graduate work includes courses in research methodology and statistics, personality theory and psychopathology, and introduction to clinical study of the individual, and self-directed study in general psychology in preparation for the preliminary examination held during the first week of the second academic year. During each of the first two years each student works with a faculty member in a research apprenticeship. Emphasis shifts in the second year toward the development of clinical skills (including intelligence and personality assessment and psychotherapy) and in the third year to the continuation of training in clinical skills and to the investigation of research literature. For this latter purpose the student is required to prepare an integrative specialty paper involving the critical review of some body of literature relevant to clinical pyschology as well as a dissertation proposal. During the first two years each student has prepared a paper based on each of his research apprenticeship experiences. The program just described is viewed as minimal. All students are encouraged to enroll in seminars and courses beyond this minimum in keeping with their interests. In practice, however, students do not often register for more than the minimum program requirement. As was previously mentioned, the fourth year of the clinical program is devoted to a block internship, and the fifth year to the completion of the dissertation.

PHASE ONE—THE ESTABLISHMENT OF A COMMUNITY MENTAL HEALTH COURSE SEQUENCE

To the author, who between 1962 and 1965 was a consultant in psychology with the National Institute of Mental Health in the Denver Regional Office of the United States Public Health Service, it was becoming increasingly obvious that a significant portion of graduates of clinical psychology training programs would be working in community mental health facilities after completion of their formal education. The total commitment of NIMH to a national program of community mental health centers was clear, and the implications of this program upon the general organization and characteristics of clinical practice were evident. New Ph.D.s in clinical psychology would work in such facilities, it was felt, whether or not they had received any training dealing with the field of community mental health. New professional activities were being undertaken by psychologists—crisis intervention, consultation, mental health education, to name but three—ordinarily without formal training, but more importantly, psychology students needed the opportunity to think through the issues in developing their optimal roles within the community mental health center philosophy if they were to avoid some of the problems which have characterized their clinical role of the past two decades.

With this point of view, discussions were begun during the early months of 1965 with the clinical area committee of the psychology department. If the sense of urgency could be communicated regarding the need to provide some training in community mental health, and if the department could create a position for a person who would have responsibility for developing an appropriate course sequence, then the department could count on at least one applicant for the position. By April, 1965, these discussions had been concluded, and after the normal recruitment procedure had been activated an offer was made by the department and accepted effective September, 1965. During these initial discussions it became clear that there was high readiness to introduce a new subject-matter specialty within the clinical area. Furthermore, the field of community mental health seemed appropriate although its dimensions were a little unclear. The clinical area committee recognized that the field of community mental health was in some ways broader than traditionally defined clinical psychology and that social psychology students, for example, might be interested in some of these new course offerings. While nonclinical students would be welcome in the courses, the course sequence was viewed, however, as part of the clinical program and would derive its support from the clinical psychology training grant, and the author would be assigned to the clinical area within the psychology department. This latter decision was motivated primarily, of course, by the fact that the author's professional and training background and professional identification was in clinical psychology.

Four new one-semester seminar courses were to be established within the department and would be given at the rate of one per semester for two years. While this course sequence constituted the total commitment of the department to the new subject-matter area, there was explicit readiness to discuss proposals for expansion of this commitment as soon as new proposals seemed desirable. The four-course sequence constituted the explicit first stage of a new teaching development whose future format could not yet be perceived. These four courses were so organized that none was a prerequisite for any other and any graduate student could register for one or more as he wished. These four courses were tentatively called Basic Issues in Community Mental Health, An Introduction to Community Mental Health Practice, Epidemiologic Methods in Community Mental Health, and Research Problems in Community Mental Health, and the courses were to be given in that order between September, 1965, and June, 1967.

The courses were given during the next four semesters and had an average enrollment of seven students each, of whom approximately half were clinical psychology graduate students. The balance consisted of students in the social psychology program and two students from outside of psychology—one student doing graduate work in education, and the other in personnel services. Three students (two in clinical psychology and one in social psychology) took all four courses.

As can be seen, the first two courses were oriented at the level of issues and practice and the last two courses dealt with empirical problems in undertaking community mental health research. In order to understand the subsequent modifications made in these courses, it would be appropriate to outline the topics covered in each of the weekly sessions in each course. The following lists present this information. Because so much of the reading material would have been difficult for students to obtain, and because some documents were prepared especially for these classes, a reasonably successful effort was made by the author to assemble readings in multiple copies. At each session where readings had been assigned for discussion the students had been given their own set at the end of the previous class period. After the readings were discussed they were returned by the students and a new set distributed for the next class period. All classes met one evening a week for two hours. Near the end of each semester the students were invited to discuss their evaluation of the seminar, although they had generally felt quite free to be both complimentary and critical about individual class sessions and individual readings.

In reviewing these four seminars the observations made by students appeared to converge at a number of points. First, students found the documents extremely difficult to understand during perhaps the first half of each semester. The readings during the first year were essentially political in nature rather than scientific and students were com-

Seminar Topics: Course I
(Basic Issues in Community Mental Health)

Session I	The Dimensions and Hopes of Community Mental Health
Session II	Some Cautions Regarding the Community Mental Health Philosophy
Session III	Historical Antecedents of the Community Mental Health Movement
Session IV	The Practices and Concepts of Public Health
Session V	Current Developments in the Organization of Health and Welfare Services: *A. Social Security*
Session VI	Current Developments in the Organization of Health and Welfare Services: *B. Medical and Mental Health Services*
Session VII	The Economics of Medical Care and Mental Health Services
Session VIII	Issues in the Provision of Local Mental Health Services: *A. The Voluntary Health and Welfare Agency*
Session IX	Issues in the Provision of Local Mental Health Services: *B. Problems in the Organization of Services*
Session X	The Role of the State in the Organization and Support of Community Mental Health Services: *A. Comprehensive Planning*
Session XI	The Role of the State in the Organization and Support of Community Mental Health Services: *B. The Community Mental Health Services Act*
Session XII	The Federal Role in the Support of Community Mental Health Services
Session XIII	The State Mental Health Facilities Construction Plan

Seminar Topics: Course II
(An Introduction to Community Mental Health Practice)

Session I	An Introduction to Primary Prevention
Session II	Examples of Primary Prevention Programs
Session III	Secondary Prevention: Alternatives to Hospitalization
Session IV	Secondary Prevention: Psychiatric Units in General Hospitals
Session V	Secondary Prevention: Psychiatric Units in General Hospitals—A Case Study

Session VI   An Introduction to Consultation
Session VII   Examples of Consultation Programs and Practices
Session VIII   Tertiary Prevention (Rehabilitation Programs)
Session IX   Problems in the Provision of Rural Mental Health Services
Session X   Community Mental Health Programs in Action: I—An
                  Analysis of Existing Models
Session XI   Community Mental Health Programs in Action: II—An
                  Analysis of Existing Models (concluded)
Session XII   Community Mental Health Programs Outside the United
                  States: I—General
Session XIII   Community Mental Health Programs Outside the United
                  States: II—Great Britain
Session XIV   Community Mental Health Programs Outside the United
                  States: III—Scotland, Netherlands, Denmark, and Sweden.
Session XV   Community Mental Health Programs Outside the United
                  States: IV—France, China, and the Soviet Union

Seminar Topics: Course III
(Epidemiologic Methods in Community Mental Health)

Session I   Introduction to Epidemiology: *Exercise A.* An epidemiologic
                  study of skiing injuries
Session II   Concepts of Cause; Classification of Disorders and Persons:
                  Exercise B. Problems in the interpretation of epidemi-
                  ologic findings
Session III   The Strategy of Epidemiology: *Exercise C.* Determination
                  of statistical association: tonsillectomy and poliomyelitis
Session IV   Case History Studies: *Exercise D.* The London fog
Session V   Cohort Studies: *Exercise E.* Chronic nephritis in Queensland
Session VI   Experimental Epidemiology: *Exercise F.* Psychiatric hos-
                  pitalization following hysterectomy
Session VII   Student Report: Snow, J. *Snow on cholera.* New York:
                  Hafner, 1936. *Exercise G.* Infectious hepatitis in Des
                  Moines
Session VIII   Student Report: Jaco, E. G. *The social epidemiology of
                  mental disorders.* New York: Russell Sage, 1960. *Exercise
                  H.* A field investigation of inactivated measles virus vac-
                  cine
Session IX   Student Report: Hollingshead, A. B., and Redlich, F. C.
                  Social class and mental illness. New York: Wiley, 1958.
                  Exercise I. Low-level radium 226 exposure
Session X   Student Report: Leighton, Dorothea, *et al. The character
                  of danger.* New York: Basic Books, 1963. *Exercise J.* In-
                  fantile diarrhea in Kuwait
Session XI   Student Report: Langner, T. S., and Michael, S. T. *Life
                  stress and mental health.* New York: Free Press, 1963.
                  Exercise K. Some studies on the epidemiology of tuber-
                  culosis
Session XII   Student Report: Taylor, L., and Chave, S. *Mental health
                  and environment.* Boston: Little, Brown, 1964. *Exercise
                  L.* A physician-related outbreak of hepatitis

Session XIII   Student Report: Dunham, H. W. *Community and schizophrenia*. Detroit: Wayne State University Press, 1965. *Exercise M*. Rubella and congenital malformations

Seminar Topics: Course IV
(Research Problems in Community Mental Health)

Session I   Biostatistics: Introduction
Session II   Biostatistics: Rates and Ratios *(Part I)*
Session III   Biostatistics: Rates and Ratios *(Part II)*
Session IV   Biostatistics: Life Table Methods
Session V   Methodological Problems in the Study of Whole Families
Session VI   Studies in the Field
Session VII   Problems in Case Identification
Session VIII   An Introduction to Mental Health Program Evaluation
Session IX   Examples of Mental Health Program Evaluations
Session X   Community Mental Health Center Record Systems
Session XI   Follow-up Studies
Session XII   Psychiatric Case Registers
Session XIII   Uses of Census Tract Data

pletely unaccustomed to reading such documents. During the second year the methodology and research orientations were equally unfamiliar to the students. When they appeared to understand the actual content of the documents they often did not understand the significance of what they read. By midsemester they were beginning to read the materials with a good deal of appreciation, and by the end of the semester were showing signs of being able to read between the lines as well as on the lines. Second, clinical psychology graduate students were much more poorly prepared for these seminars than were social psychology students. The latter group seemed, not surprisingly, much more aware of the community at large and of the issues which were community-wide in their importance. Clinical students had a lot of catching up to do in familiarizing themselves with the backgrounds for the various issues and programs discussed. Third, the students recognized the difficulty any individual faculty member would have in avoiding unnecessary repetition and at the same time ensuring an adequate foundation of information at the start of each course when he conducted a series of seminars. Some of the problem is related to the psychology department tradition of one-semester graduate seminars without specific course prerequisites. In addition, there is probably an upper limit in the number of courses one faculty member can give without repeating himself, and, in the case of the author at least, this upper limit is less than four. An effort was made to identify guest speakers whenever this was feasible and while these opportunities did not present themselves very often, they were generally a welcome change for both the students and the instructor. Fourth, students had been accustomed to having a more active role in graduate seminars than was provided for them in these courses. While students objected to graduate seminars organized exclusively around student reports, they also objected to having no opportunity to exercise individual initiative in the preparation of special assignments. Partly as a response to the interest of the students in making their own substantive contributions to course content, two related course projects were developed. During the first semester each student and the author worked independently on the task of developing a format which could be used in making a reasonably comprehensive analysis of any national mental health program. These independent efforts were integrated at the end of the first semester into a single format which could be used, it was hoped, for reviewing the mental health program of any nation (see Bloom *et al.*, 1969). During the second semester each of the six enrolled students selected one country and attempted to obtain the information included in the format. Both a written document as well as a class presentation were prepared. Three seminar sessions were devoted to these six class reports. The countries studied included Canada, Great Britain, the Soviet Union, Israel, Ireland, and Liberia.

In summary, the first phase of the community mental health sequence consisted of the creation of four one-semester courses and two associated special projects. It was clear that when the two-year sequence would start again several changes should be incorporated in the course content and organization, but in general, the courses served as a valuable and workable foundation upon which to build further elements of the sequence.

PHASE TWO: A COMMUNITY MENTAL HEALTH FIELD PLACEMENT

As the second year of the community mental health course sequence began, it had become clear that some kind of field placement was necessary to give students an opportunity to have first-hand experience of the issues and to engage in the kinds of professional practices they had been discussing. Students had yet to set foot in a county or state health department, had yet to attend a meeting of a health and welfare agency coordinating body, and with rare exceptions had not participated in any community mental health professional activities. At the same time as the need for field placement was becoming clear, it was equally clear that such a practicum could not be effectively organized without the addition of another faculty member in the community mental health subject-matter area. Accordingly, discussions were again

inaugurated within the clinical area. These discussions provided an opportunity for a review of the first year of the community mental health
course sequence and a reorientation of the clinical committee to the
general area of community mental health. It was suggested that the
term still was not clearly defined but that at least two overlapping do-
mains could be identified. These included, first, concepts, issues, and
practices in the organization and delivery of services for the prevention
and control of mental disorders, and second, community organization and
community characteristics and their impact on the emotional stability of
the individual.

Examples of the first domain were thought to include techniques
for the identification of high-risk groups, early case-finding procedures,
primary prevention, innovative techniques of secondary and tertiary
prevention with particular emphasis on alternatives to psychiatric
hospitalization, concepts of comprehensiveness of services and con-
tinuity of care, planning and administration of community-based mental
health services, and economics of mental health care. Examples of the
second domain were thought to include social system analysis, social
phenomenon and their relationships to human effectiveness, community
decision-making processes, professional and lay agency structure, interagency coordination and collaboration, the medical care and welfare
agency systems, and public health theory and practice. In keeping with
the general point of view within the clinical area for the training of re-
search-practitioners, it was thought that students interested in training
in community mental health would need to develop special research
orientation and skills in addition to their usual areas of research competence. These new areas of skill would include biostatistics, demography,
epidemiology, social system analysis, and research design problems associated with action programs, particularly as related to mental health program evaluation.

The field placement experience should be relevant to these subject-
matter considerations and should be open to all students enrolled in the
community mental health courses. At the least, the field placement
should not be restricted to clinical students, although some portions of
it might be more suitable for clinical students than for other gradute students. The relationship of the community mental health field placement
to the clinical practicum was discussed at length within the clinical area.
Requirements for the doctorate in clinical psychology included two years
of a clinical practicum. It was agreed that one year of clinical practicum should be a prerequisite for the field placement and that the community mental health field placement should serve as a substitute for
the second clinical practicum year for interested students. Students elect-
ing the field placement, however, would be allowed to take a second
year of clinical practicum if both they and their advisors thought it de-

sirable. Three types of facilities were thought to be eligible for consideration as the sites for such field placements. These included community-based action programs relevant to mental health, selected comprehensive community mental health centers, and total communities in which the power structure and decision-making processes could be studied and where it would be possible to explore the organization of both public and private sector health and welfare services.

Regarding the question of nonclinical students registered in the community mental health field placement, it was decided to try to arrange a broad range of field experiences for all students with the more clinical activities limited to clinical graduate students. These clinical activities would include anticipatory guidance techniques, crisis intervention, brief psychotherapy and mental health consultation. Additional experiences open to all would include such activities as community organization, community decision-making, work with interagency groups and other coordinating bodies, action research programs designed to reduce incidence or prevalence of emotional disorders by means of strengthening either social systems or the individual, and mental health education.

Finally, it was agreed that a second faculty position was required and that half of the new position responsibility would be in the community mental health subject-matter area. The sequence, at the completion of this second phase would involve two faculty members and would now include four one-semester courses and a one-year community mental health field placement. The field placement would require the equivalent to two half-days each week during the academic year. The clinical area agreed that the next position which would be established should have a major subject-matter specialty responsibility in community mental health sequence. Quite soon after these discussions were concluded, a new position became available and was successfully filled by an unusually well-qualified young psychologist with both experience and interest in the field of community mental health. With his successful recruitment and arrival in September, 1967, it was possible to develop specific plans for the field placement which was tentatively scheduled to begin in January, 1968, on a trial basis and in September, 1968, as a regular part of the university curriculum.

Due in part to the extensive participation of metropolitan Denver mental health facilities in the Federal legislation supporting the costs of construction and staffing of community mental health centers, a number of facilities were being developed which might serve as suitable field placement sites. The main tasks for the trial semester included selecting the facilities, allocating time among them, and choosing which kinds of professional activities within each of the chosen facilities to include. A number of program directors were interested in having their facilities serve as field placement sites. Some facilities had already been identified as sites for social work students, psychiatric residents, and occasional graduate nursing program students. Other organizations expressed interest in developing brief training experiences and it became clear that regardless of how stringently the standards would be established for eligibility as a community mental health field placement, the greater Denver area (including Boulder) offered an unusually rich array of appropriate facilities, each wishing to participate, each fully expecting the students to spend their two half-days per week with them and each petitioning for an increase in the amount of time students could spend at the field placement. This phenomenon, not dissimilar to experience during the early days of clinical field placements, required the judicious balancing of training needs, agency proposals, and students' interests.

It seemed inevitable that just as course content would be modified from year to year, so the nature of the field placement would require continual review and revision. At the present time, however, it is possible to suggest at least some of the elements which should be included in a community mental health field placement and the kinds of facilities where such elements might be found. First, a well-functioning community mental health center (defined for the present purposes as a coordinated array of agencies which are seeking to provide a comprehensive range of empirically monitored preventive and therapeutic services for a defined catchment area, working with an advisory board whose identification is with the emotional well-being of the catchment area population) can provide beginning training in consultation, crisis intervention, administration, mental health education, and a variety of research experiences including studies in demography, epidemiology, and program evaluation. Action programs—such as those working toward cultural enrichment of children, reduction of school dropouts, reduction of alcoholism or drug addiction or juvenile delinquency or other forms of social disequilibrium—can be particularly useful in developing an understanding of community structure and of the issues in working collaboratively with recipient group representatives, as well as the special problems of program evaluation in these settings. In a community at large it would be useful to develop some familiarity with the programs and interrelationships of a large variety of health and welfare agencies and with the functioning of interagency councils. It would be particularly important to learn about general hospitals, courts, law enforcement agencies and their value systems and problems, and the decision-making processes involved in the political, legislative, and financial aspects of city and state governments. As should have become clear, these field placements should not be used as sites for undertaking long-term individual or group psychotherapy or for developing increased skills in diagnostic psychological testing. Rather, the sites should offer the opportunity to develop awareness of the problems unique to community mental health practice and particularly regarding those problems which can be subjected to empirical study. Thus, the field placement should continue in the tradition of training scholar-clinicians, with the clinical emphasis on practices essentially unique to community mental health.

PHASE THREE: A COMMUNITY MENTAL HEALTH CURRICULUM

The major question now being considered has to do with the organization of the community mental health training sequence within the university psychology department set of course offerings and specialty areas. This kind of concern arises whenever any relatively new professional development seems to have some implication for training. What is the best way of presenting a training effort in community mental health? Should a formal, separately identifiable program within psychology be identified? Should there be a formal subspecialty curriculum within clinical psychology? Or should the set of courses and the field placement simply constitute departmental offerings available, in part or in whole, to any student upon demand? While the outcome of the third phase in the development of opportunities for training in community mental health may not be known for some time, the issues can be identified and described.

The concept of a subspecialty curriculum within the clinical psychology specialty area is not an easy one for many faculties to accept. It inevitably would result in a certain degree of separatism within an area that has heretofore been a unified program. It might result in the creation of new sources of devisiveness within an area that has traditionally worked with a high degree of collaboration. And it would raise serious questions about the enterprise called clinical psychology—questions regarding its viability as a general subject matter and set of concepts and professional practices. Yet with the large number of course requirements in the clinical area, logistic problems face anyone interested in adding to the course offerings. If these new offerings are to be realistically available to a significant proportion of students, only three alternatives are open to a faculty. Either the total number of courses required or urged must be increased, or the current specific list of required courses must be reduced, leaving more room for elective courses, or separate tracks must be established within the clinical area, each with its own set of course requirements. Each of these alternatives has its advocates, depending on positions on such questions as:

1. How much academic work constitutes an optimal load for the graduate student?

2. Is there a rich enough substance to the newly emerging field of community mental health theory and practice to justify a special curriculum?

3. Should the present list of course requirements in clinical psychology be reduced, and if so, what specific courses should be dropped?

4. Should the entire clinical psychology curriculum be redesigned, with present courses recombined and streamlined so as to retain the same essential content and yet leave room for more elective choices?

5. Can a new course in community mental health be developed which will have such general salience to the clinical program that it would be designated a required course?

6. How much importance should be assigned to the maintenance of a single curriculum in clinical psychology in contrast to a set of overlapping but conceptually separate subspecialty curricula?

7. Are there some special administrative virtues of having a community mental health program, in contrast to simply a group of courses?

8. Some of the required courses in the clinical psychology curriculum are general departmental requirements; other requirements are unique to clinical psychology. If course requirements are reduced, should those few courses where all psychology graduate students sit together be vulnerable?

9. While it might be possible to decide against the creation of a subspecialty curriculum in community mental health, with the increasing degree of specialization characterizing the clinical enterprise, is it only a matter of time before recognition will finally have to be given to training programs in group therapy, in childhood psychopathology, in mental health administration, in mental health consultation, or in the application of reinforcement principles to behavior modification?

10. If a special curriculum in community mental health is to be created, should it be defined as within the interest of clinical psychology or should it be broadened to the larger domain of community psychology and be separate from and parallel with all existing psychology programs?

11. Can a set of courses and field placements be effectively administered without knowing from semester to semester what the student demand will be for such training?

12. Should efforts be made to locate special internship settings for students interested in community mental health?

13. Should special provision be made for identifying field-setting, community-based research practicum, and dissertation topics for those students interested in community mental health?

These issues are not quickly resolved, and psychology departments may very well decide to try a variety of methods in response to the questions posed by the growing interest in community action and community mental health. Indeed, there should be considerable variation in these responses. The development of a set of standards for training in community psychology or in community mental health seems premature.

FUTURE DEVELOPMENTS IN THE COMMUNITY MENTAL HEALTH SEQUENCE

The field of community mental health is undergoing a period of rapid growth and change. Research papers, position statements, philosophical discussions are all emerging very quickly. One new journal specializes in community mental health. A new division of community psychology has been established. A second journal will undoubtedly be founded in the near future. Under these circumstances it should not be surprising that the content of all of the community mental health courses described here will be changing quite significantly each time the course is given. The first course in the sequence, Basic Issues in Community Mental Health, has already been given a second time. Three of the topics covered in the first course have been eliminated. Two new topics have been added. The sequence with which the topics are considered has been changed. New readings have been introduced for virtually every session. Some old readings have been discarded to make way for the new ones. In total, about 40 percent of the material now being used in the first course was not included when it was given two years ago. Major changes are planned for each of the other courses as well, and this is surely as it should be. The field placement will undoubtedly go through its annual evaluation and revision, as will the entire subspecialty curriculum, when it has been established.

One problem yet to be considered in sufficient detail has to do with dissertation research. If students who are identified with the community mental health program are to undertake community-based dissertations, a pool of community data must be developed and made available for their studies. Currently under preliminary consideration is the development of a household survey covering a 15 to 20 percent stratified sample of Boulder County. In the development of this survey, the active participation of Boulder health and welfare agencies will be sought, as well as that of the city council and mayor's office. If the survey can furnish information pertinent to the program needs of these various offices and agencies, the likelihood of its success will be considerably enhanced. Periodic resurveys will furnish additional information which can be equally useful.

Somewhat further in the future lies the development of discussions regarding the place of this curriculum in the university at large. The University of Colorado does not now have a School of Social Work although some discussions have been held regarding its establishment. Could any portion of this curriculum serve for such a school? The establishment of a School of Public Health also undergoes periodic consideration. Could the courses or field placement experience play any role in such a school? Perhaps more broadly, will there be any interest in the development of interdepartmental core programs in community health and social welfare, which might be available either as a whole or in part to students in psychology, sociology, economics, political science, social work, preventive medicine, or public health?

It should be clear that every aspect of the community mental health training sequence described in this paper is most tentative. A tentative and open attitude toward content and method of training in community mental health seems entirely appropriate (see Anderson *et al.*, 1966; Hoch *et al.*, 1966). The field, however narrowly defined, is still broad enough to allow for a great variety of training approaches. Some years from now, after the field begins to have some clearer dimensions and after many independently developed training programs have been established, it would seem timely to undertake their systematic study and evaluation. Perhaps then, a desirable training model could emerge. For the present, however, maximum freedom to develop community mental health training programs should be given. The program described here is in no sense a model. Rather, its description serves as a vehicle for discussing the major issues which have already emerged in its short history, issues which are likely to emerge wherever initial efforts are made to provide such community mental health training.

REFERENCES

Anderson, Luleen S., Cooper, S., Hassol, L., Klein, D. C., Rosenblum, G., & Bennett, C. C. (Eds.). *Community psychology: A report of the Boston conference on the education of psychologists for community mental health.* Boston: Boston University, 1966.

Bloom, B. L., Bartz, W. R., Brawley, Johanna M., Holmes, J. R., Jordan, D. L., Pomeroy, E. W., & Ziegler, M. A cross-cultural format for national mental health program analysis. *Community Mental Health Journal*, 1969, **5**, 227–232.

Hoch, E. L., Ross, A. O., & Winder, C. L. (Eds.). *Professional preparation of clinical psychologists.* Washington, D.C.: American Psychological Association, 1966.

IV

Multidisciplinary Training Programs
in Community Mental
Health and Community
Psychology

11

The Graduate Training Program in Community Mental Health at the University of Texas

Ira Iscoe

ORIGINS AND BACKGROUND OF THE PROGRAM

The importance of community cooperation as well as the possibilities for field experiences within the community are central to the planning of a mental health or community psychology training program. The acceptance of the program by various components of the community is essential to its growth. This acceptance is quite different from that which presently exists in most areas. Many social agencies, state institutions, and school systems have long accepted the "tester" role of the psychologists and have been willing to place a psychology trainee or two in their settings. A role that as yet is not a familiar one to most communities, however, is that of the community psychology or community mental health trainee, who offers no direct services and whose avowed purpose is learning about the community and its varied components. This role is somewhat unfamiliar to university departments as well.

At the beginning of a community mental health program there is need for much mutual trust and, as the town-gown dialogue expands and as sensitive areas are dealt with, there is need for a reexamination of this trust. Community representatives and agencies are understandably defensive and often a bit suspicious of the motivations of graduate students in mental health who, in the face of enormous demands, render no direct services. The community must eventually become convinced that the trainees, despite their academic orientation, are capable of recognizing and dealing with the "real world." There is need for tolerance and patience on both sides.

In recognition of the burgeoning community mental health movement and the increasing involvements of psychologists, the Department of Psychology, in 1965, approved the setting up of a community mental health training specialty. In 1966, support was granted by the Training Branch of the National Institute of Mental Health.[1]

In establishing the program, advantage was taken of a history of excellent cooperation between the university and the community. Because of these good relations, there was a willingness to accept the program. This acceptance is not taken for granted; it is maintained by constant communication with the community and a frank interchange of feelings and ideas with persons in the settings in which the trainees work.

The community setting is the capitol of Texas, situated in Travis County, with a population of over 200,000. Ethnically it is composed of approximately 15 percent Mexican-Americans, 15 percent Negroes, and 70 percent Anglos. To a large extent the economy is dependent upon the university and state government plus southwest centers for a varied group of national organizations. There is no heavy industry, but there is a rapidly developing electronics and "brain" industry.

PURPOSES OF THE PROGRAM

The goals of the program, as presently construed, are to provide graduate students from various disciplines with both course and field work experiences to develop their knowledge about the community and skills in dealing with its complexities. There is emphasis on the study of the methods by which mental health services are presently delivered and the ways in which these can be improved. The activist stress is tempered with the caution that the students must first gain acceptance into a community setting before helping various components conceptualize problems and devise more effective coping techniques. There is little or no emphasis on the rendering of traditional clinical services.

The general philosophy of the program is that a true community mental health orientation draws ultimately from three main sources of support and interest. There are (1) the professionals themselves; (2) the sources of funds, be they government, state, local, or any combination of these; and (3) the citizens of the community, including subprofessionals and community leaders as well as the recipients or eventual

---

[1] Support under Grant No. 10504, Training Branch, National Institute of Mental Health for the period 1966–71, provides for six traineeships, partial faculty support, travel, and consultants. Initial support for the beginning of the program was obtained from Hogg Foundation for Mental Health.

The program has an interdisciplinary Advisory Committee; there is also a Training Committee consisting of university and field training supervisors. The counsel and help of both committees has been most valuable.

targets of community services and planning. The manner in which these three sources interact ultimately determines the quality and scope of the community's mental health. The complex interrelationships among these sources are studied as are the sociopolitical realities that must be faced and dealt with in any community setting in which effective mental health and preventive services as well as the planning for effective problem-solving techniques are a main goal.

The program makes no pretense of turning out a polished specialist in community mental health or community psychology. Rather, it is hoped that the trainee will broaden his views about the human condition and will recognize the need for the creation of more relevant behavioral science research to be carried out within the context of the community.

ELIGIBILITY FOR THE PROGRAM

The program is open to graduate students from psychology, educational psychology, sociology, and anthropology. From within the psychology department trainees may enter the program from two sources: (1) clinical psychology students who have elected to specialize in community mental health either before or after predoctoral internship; and (2) students from other specialty areas, such as social or personality, who wish to receive didactic and field work experience.

Students must first satisfy entrance requirements and basic course work, including qualifying examinations and subspecialties in their own departments. These requirements usually take from 1½ to two years. Although some aspects of community mental health training can be started in a student's second year, it usually is not until the third year that the concentration of community mental health and community psychology begins. This concentration lasts a full year and, in the case of clinical psychology students is continued on in an internship setting in which there is a heavy community mental health orientation. For students from other areas within psychology a second year of experience is possible and encouraged, as it is also for students from educational psychology. To date, although graduate students from sociology and anthropology have taken seminars in mental health, none have formally elected to concentrate in this area. In the two years since the program started the majority of students have come from clinical psychology backgrounds, with two from social psychology and three from the counseling psychology program of the Department of Educational Psychology.

COURSE WORK

The emergent nature of the program and the varied backgrounds of the students requires flexibility in regard to both course and field work. Four courses currently are required: Mental Health Consultation, Seminar in Mental Health, Seminar in Community Mental Health, and Seminar in Community Organization (School of Social Work). Elective seminars and courses include Seminar in Human Ecology and Demography, Sociology of Health Services, Seminar on Cultural Deprivation and Poverty, Introduction to School Psychology, and Computer Techniques and Programming.

Crossing interdisciplinary lines in order to take courses in other departments has not been the barrier that was predicted. More important than departments has been the attitude of individual instructors who have been willing to recognize that students from other departments may not have the usual prerequisites. The assignment of a minimum of background reading and the willingness to let a psychology graduate student approach a course in Community Organization, for example, from the point of view of a psychologist rather than a social worker, has proved sufficient. It has, in some cases, resulted in a livening of the seminar itself.

FIELD TRAINING AND EXPERIENCES

The richness and variety of experiences afforded the trainees constitute the heart of a viable community mental health program. Therefore, the settings utilized were selected for their relevance to the goals of the program. In general the eagerness of the trainees to get involved plus their enthusiastic reception within the settings has been encouraging. With the exception of mental health consultation in school settings the supervision and monitoring of experiences is done by non-psychologists. The "letting go" of trainees serves to widen their horizons about the community and its subsystems. The opportunity to gain first-hand experience with the problems faced by administrators and decision-makers has proved valuable. Trainees are able to observe the rapid changes occurring within most communities, such as the emergence of new leadership, the melding of new and old sources of funding, and the formation of innovative mental health services.

As the community changes so will the nature and location of the field experiences afforded the trainees. For example, a county-wide mental health–mental retardation center has been started and is currently in operation. It is anticipated that trainees will participate in some of the activities of this center, especially in the areas of mental health consultation. For the present the following experiences are offered the trainees.

A. Mental Health Consultation to Public Schools: This is central to one of the main roles that will be played by the community mental health trainee later on in his career, namely that of the consultant. Training is embodied in a year-long seminar in mental health consultation. In the first three months the students' time is devoted to lectures, readings, and literature reviews on the consultation process. They also role play and view films on consultation as well as watch experienced consultants at work. The organization and administration of the school system is discussed. Trainees also attend school board meetings in order to learn something about the decision-making processes or perhaps about the decision makers of the school system. They study the city proper and the ethnic composition and problems of the schools in which they will be working. Before actually going into their assigned schools, they thoroughly explore the neighborhood which the school serves.

The entrance into the school itself can be considered as a baptism of fire for each trainee. In schools which have had previous consultants this is not too traumatic. In schools just entering the cooperative consultant relationship, the trainee, accompanied by the instructor, meets with the principal and his faculty and explains what mental health consultation is all about. The trainee also meets the faculty in a separate meeting or sometimes individually. It comes as somewhat of a shock to the trainee that no matter how carefully the consultation model has been explained, there is initially much complaining on the part of teachers that the consultant does not give tests or see students directly. These complaints subside rapidly, and the trainee quickly learns that if a teacher is determined that a child will be seen, chances are that the teacher or the principal will manipulate the situation to this effect.

The trainee spends one morning or one afternoon per week at his assigned school. He usually has lunch at the school and socializes with the teachers. He is encouraged to work out his own relationships, although advice and guidance are available to him at all times. Each school uses its consultant differently, and how the consultant is used and what problems he is referred constitute an important learning situation for him.

In terms of supervision, each trainee has time for individual meetings with his university supervisor, and additionally all consultants meet in a two-to-three-hour group session per week in which they review their consultative activities and trade off experiences. It is here that they can begin to recognize the individual problem-solving styles of various schools and how these styles contribute to the referral of certain problems and the ignoring of others.

In fostering the consultant attitude, the questions most frequently asked of the trainee by the supervisor focus around what problem-solving mechanisms are being used, what resources the teacher is using or avoiding, why one particular type of problem should be continually brought up, what the role of the principal is as administrator and as educational leader, and how this particular school relates to the central administration.

Toward the end of the school year each trainee is required to write up a detailed characterization of the school he has worked in, including the problems he has had referred to him and their outcome as far as he knows. The types of relationships between the principal and teachers are noted. Suggestions are asked for in terms of improving the overall mental health of the school, taking into account its resources, student population, and particular problems.

The principal and teachers are also asked to evaluate the consultant trainee. General reaction on the part of principals and teachers has been quite favorable. However, it would be folly not to recognize the large individual differences that exist amongst trainees. Some of them are almost born consultants; they adjust easily, they quickly become a part of the school, they get invited to school functions, and are called upon outside of the morning or afternoon they spend at the school. Others have more formal relationships. It appears that, just as in psychotherapy, there are personality and background variables which will have to be searched out in the training of consultants.

The role of the consultant as a systems analyst dealing with situational factors rather than the interpersonal dynamics of a child or children is brought home to trainees during the course of their consultant experience. For example, one mature consultant with previous teaching experience was assigned to an all-Negro school. The principal, although affable on the surface, was actually quite authoritarian and did not encourage the trainee's interacting with the teachers. It became obvious to the consultant that in this particular school there was great stress on achievement and that many of the children were being pushed beyond capacity. The consultant wanted to do something, but was encouraged by his supervisor to wait. This "stand-off" went on for about four months with the consultant becoming increasingly frustrated.

One morning the consultant received a phone call at his home. The principal wanted the consultant to deal with a nine-year-old boy who had become "violent" and attacked a teacher. Upon arrival at the school the consultant took advantage of this crisis situation and suggested a look at causes. In a meeting with the principal, his faculty, and administrative personnel, the consultant "wondered" whether there were certain pressures on the child and whether other children in the school might not also want to behave in this way. This led to a series of discussions about academic pressures with a subsequent lessening of these pressures and the breaking up of the classes into more realistic ability units with extra help provided to the teachers. This further led to solidifying of the relationship between the principal and the consultant in which the principal felt free to discuss for the first time some of the pressures put upon him by some parents and his frustration with what he perceived to be the lack of motivation and low learning ability of many of his students.

B. *Hogg Foundation for Mental Health*: Established some 25 years ago, the foundation operates as a private foundation within the administrative structure of the University of Texas. The foundation not only carries out an active program in mental health education, but also supports projects that have as their primary aim the translation of behavioral science and psychiatric findings into action projects and the evaluation of these projects. This orientation is ideally suited for community psychology trainees. Some 120 projects in different stages of progress are supported by the foundation. These range from the reshaping of curriculum materials for Mexican-American students to innovative approaches such as camping experiences for state hospital patients to assisting a child guidance center in the working out of new patterns of financial support from the community it serves. Students are assigned to specific projects and follow them from intake through review by the staff, resulting in acceptance, rejection, or consultation and recommendations to the applicant or agency.

Trainees gradually acquire sophistication as to the essential ingredients of a promising project, the key variables to be looked for and the ones to be avoided. They learn that it is not the elegance of the experimental design so much as the idea, and that the judicious use of a small amount of "risk" capital frequently results in tremendous returns to the community or agency.

Trainees also sit in on the semiannual meetings of the national advisory committee to the foundation. This affords them the opportunity to become acquainted with developments on the national scene as well as personally meeting prominent persons in community and mental health affairs.

C. *Juvenile Court and Probation Department, Austin and Travis County*: In this setting can be learned the goals, problems, and financial support of the Juvenile Probation Department. Here students become acquainted with the legal aspects of problems and the statutes as they refer to juveniles. They learn the duties and responsibilities of the chief probation officer, make visits with probation officers, sit in at citizens advisory committee meetings, and attend sessions of the Juvenile Court. In working with the chief probation officer, they become aware of the progress to date as well as the needs and possibilities for effective delinquency prevention programs. It is in this setting too that trainees can begin to appreciate the interrelationships among a school system, a police department, the employment picture, and the incidence of delinquency. Here too trainees gain respect for the efforts of probation officers and persons generally not formally trained in psychology.

D. *Human Opportunities Corporation of Austin and Travis County:* The corporation has the official responsibility for the administration and monitoring of all community action programs in the county. In accordance with recent OEO directives, its 36 members include 12 direct representatives of the culturally deprived. Membership also includes representatives of the university, the Council of Churches, labor, the city, the legal profession, business, and the school system. Under its jurisdiction come such projects as Day Care, Head Start, Upward Bound, information and referral centers, Neighborhood Youth Corps, and a variety of special programs. Trainees visit each of the projects, finding out some of the main problems that are faced, the relationships to the community, the mental health problems, and the manner in which community participation is encouraged or hindered. Additional time is spent at the information and referral centers where the students can observe and work with persons seeking all types of general and special help.

Trainees also are required to attend most of the monthly meetings of the corporation. Here they are afforded the opportunity of making direct contact with a variety of persons working for the betterment of the community. It is here also that trainees begin to gain an appreciation of the difficulties involved in beginning and carrying out constructive social action programs. During the past year they have witnessed decisions concerning funding of projects and cuts in appropriation, heard complaints from all sides of the community, and seen some signs of genuine progress.

REACTIONS, EVALUATION, AND PROBLEMS

The general reaction of the students to the four field experiences has been extreme enthusiasm. They feel that the experiences open new vistas to them with regard to the community as a whole plus the individuals within it. Understandably, some are a little critical and impatient. They have their own heroes and villains in the community and sometimes get so involved that other aspects of their graduate work begin to suffer. Their main complaints realistically concern lack of enough time. It is hoped that as the program develops, a better balance between relevant courses and field experiences will be worked out.

How the combination of courses and experiences will prepare the students for further active participation in the areas of community mental health and community psychology remains as yet to be determined.

Although the feedback from the students is encouraging, the newness of the program has not permitted any long-term follow-up of the trainees. One student went on to serve an internship in a center with a heavy community mental health and consultation orientation, stayed on to serve as a staff psychologist, and has now accepted a university position in which he will be centrally involved in the developing of a community psychology program. Another is now a staff psychologist in a crisis oriented mental health clinic; and still another has accepted a staff position in a comprehensive mental health center. One trainee who entered the program through the educational psychology route has accepted a position in a large university counseling center which is starting a program of mental health consultation to dormitory personnel and faculty. Other trainees are now at various intern settings. One of the problems that is beginning to emerge is the location of internship settings compatible with the community psychology orientation acquired by the trainees. For example, one of these trainees who performed excellently as a mental health consultant to the public schools and was well liked and respected in other field training settings served an internship in a setting which did not live up to its avowed community psychology orientation. His comparative lack of interest in "sick" people was a handicap in this particular setting. The importance of appropriate internships or advanced training placements will no doubt increase in this program as it will in others which have a strong community psychology emphasis.

Finally, there is the legitimate question of the effects of a community mental health training program on the regular graduate training within a department or departments concerned. Again the newness of the program precludes any firm data. An increasing interest in mental health has been noted. Students in social psychology particularly are becoming involved and have participated in some of the seminars and training experiences. This fostering of a community mental health attitude is viewed as a positive sign not detracting from the legitimate endeavors of other training subspecialities in psychology or educational psychology. On the contrary, the existence of the program affords all interested students the opportunity for training and research activities where much of the action is taking place, namely in the community itself.

12

Apprentice-Collaborator Field Training in Community Psychology: The Halifax County Program

John Altrocchi and Carl Eisdorfer

This chapter will describe field-placement training in which university faculty members and trainees are jointly involved in all aspects of community mental health consultation. The training occurs within the framework of an apprentice-collaborator training model in which trainees begin by observing experienced mental health consultants while gradually working toward relatively independent, supervised functioning.

SETTING AND HISTORY OF THE HALIFAX COUNTY MENTAL HEALTH PROGRAM

Halifax County is a farming region in northeastern North Carolina with a population of just under 60,000, of whom 55 percent are nonwhite. There is one city of 12,000 which has paper and textile industries and the county is considered a borderline poverty area with a mean income per family of slightly over $3,000 per year. Other data relevant to mental health in the county include 19 percent illegitimacy (Halifax County Commission on Community Health Services, 1964); over 20 percent net out-migration of all nonwhites and young adults; over 80 percent of nonwhite families with less than $3,000 income; 65 to 70 percent military rejectees, all causes; 66 percent nonwhite adults with six or less years of education; and more than 30 percent of nonwhite children under age 18 not living with both parents (North Carolina Mental Health Planning Staff, 1965).

We are indebted to Stuart Golann, Cynthia Ganung, and Derek Shows for critical reading of the manuscript, and especially to our former colleague in Halifax County, the late Robert F. Young, who concurred with our training model.

A history of the development of the Halifax County mental health program has been presented elsewhere (Eisdorfer, Altrocchi, & Young, 1968) so that only enough background data will be presented here to clarify the training features of the program. In 1958, the Health Director of Halifax County prepared the ground for the county commissioners' acceptance of a mental health program by collecting data on mental health problems and talking with key community leaders. The health director then worked out a liaison with a Duke faculty member for help in establishing a mental health program. Because the county is almost a hundred miles from the nearest major sources of trained mental health personnel (Durham and Chapel Hill, North Carolina, and Richmond, Virginia), it was agreed that a program organized around consultation with key care-givers would be most appropriate.

The consultant began to visit the county for two or three one-day visits every month in 1959. Because of the distance to Duke and the infrequency of the visits, Caplan's (1964) crisis intervention approach did not seem appropriate as the central feature of this program, particularly since the consultant was attempting to initiate mental health services for the entire county. At the outset the bulk of the consultant's efforts involved consultation with a few key individuals in the community and a number of professional groups such as principals, public health nurses, county welfare workers, and ministers. The program has grown steadily over the years so that now, in addition to the original consultant, five other staff members from Duke and ten trainees make regular visits. Group consultation (Altrocchi, Spielberger, & Eisdorfer, 1965) has been expanded to include other professional groups. Other major aspects of growth in the program have been the extension of mental health consultation to all of the schools in the county, the recent initiation of a 24-hour telephone suicide prevention service (Altrocchi & Batton, 1968), and regular consultation with all the physicians in general practice in the county. Support for the establishment of a full time Mental Health Center in the county was approved and the Halifax County Mental Health Center began operation in 1968.

BASIC PRINCIPLES OF TRAINING IN THE HALIFAX COUNTY PROGRAM

When the Halifax program was initiated, certain policies were part of the training *Zeitgeist* among psychologists at Duke (Spielberger, 1967). These policies have been elaborated with experience over the years (Eisdorfer *et al.*, 1968) and several have become guidelines for training in the Halifax County mental health program.

The inclusion of training in the development of new programs is an excellent way to assure continued enthusiasm, development of manpower, significant criticism, and the challenge of new ideas. A key feature of the Halifax County mental health program is that graduate students, psychology interns, psychiatry residents, and colleagues have been invited to accompany the consultants and to participate in virtually every aspect of the program from the beginning. Such visits and the discussions which followed were key factors in maintaining a pattern of continual growth and interest in community psychology at Duke. The training was also instrumental in providing a ready manpower pool to handle new community services when these were required by this program or by other communities in the state.

The traditional policy of stabilizing an operation over several years before initiating training has been purposely avoided. Given the growth of mental health programs in this country, it is likely that many of the professionals now being trained will start new programs during their careers. Some of the most useful experiences for trainees in this program have involved participation in the initial gropings by a consultant into a new area. The trainee's excitement, willingness to explore, and professional growth resulting from participating in these ventures have seemed evident. Quite evidently we have adopted an apprenticeship model of clinical training. While this is not unusual, the apprenticeship model is frequently not adopted in clinical training, especially in departments of psychology where the mentors of clinical graduate students often do not perform the functions for which they are training students and very rarely perform the functions with students watching them.

A significant element in training toward professional competence is the observation of an accomplished professional in action. It is instructive to note that this is identical to a principle which was made explicit for training in research by several of the most prominent investigators in psychology:

> Probably the most important part of education for research in psychology is what may be called apprenticeship. Apprenticeship here is broadly defined to include, not only a close working relation with a specific faculty member who himself is actively engaged in research, but also exposure to a more general atmosphere of productive and creative work. As we have emphasized, much that is important in research training cannot be taught in didactic courses. It can only be learned through participation in research itself. (Garner, Hunt, & Taylor, 1959, p. 176)

In order to put such a principle into effect the instructor has to maintain open communication and be willing to allow students and trainees to see his errors as well as his successes. This has resulted in some embarrassing but also some very gratifying experiences. In addition, the trainees' observations and criticisms of the day's activities, particularly during the two-hour drive back to Durham, have been most instructive to all concerned.

It is useful to note that it has been extremely rare for consultees to object to the presence of trainees. The degree to which consultees—such as community administrators, caregivers, and patients—accept the presence of professional trainees appears to be a direct function of the degree of comfort of the senior consultant involved. The extent to which the consultant's explanation of the trainee's presence is done matter-of-factly and indicates that the trainee is observing the consultant even more than the consultee probably determines the infrequency with which there are objections to the trainee's presence.

Although an occasional extroverted and self-confident trainee will begin to participate on the first day, most trainees in the early stages of apprenticeship are somewhat reticent about becoming involved in any interactions with consultees. Trainees are encouraged to participate when they feel comfortable, and most begin to do so within a few days. Needless to say, these and other individual differences need to be taken into account in any training program. Occasionally trainees' questions or interventions are at cross-purposes with those of the consultant, but much more often they are parallel and sometimes serve to elucidate a point that the consultant was underplaying or ignoring. After a while this becomes a pattern, and the trainee is less an apprentice and more of a collaborator working as a junior partner on a community psychology problem. Since there is usually a much greater demand for service than one person can handle at a given time, the consultant soon begins to turn some aspects of an ongoing problem or a new situation over to the trainee: for example, it might be suggested that the trainee see a problem student for brief assessment while the consultant collects other data about the student's behavior patterns, after which they may both return to the referring teacher for consultation. Thus the trainee moves through graded steps toward the semi-independent status of making many visits on his own to the particular school or other installation involved.

Moving from apprentice to collaborator to semi-independent functioning is a natural course of events in this training model. The trainee begins to perform relatively independent functions within a setting and a set of relationships already established by the senior professional. This feature of the apprentice-collaborator model of training seems essential enough to embody in the next guideline: Semi-autonomous functioning is most satisfactory for the trainee and the consultee system if the senior professional continues his relationships with all the personnel involved. When the consultant continues his relationships with the school personnel or other community people involved, the trainee who functions in the setting alone some of the time is much better accepted. He is more likely to be consulted about a wide range of problems and more likely to provide valued services, and therefore he will have a richer training experience. Many training programs seem to suffer from nonadherence to this principle.

It has been stated before (Eisdorfer *et al.*, 1968) that a long-standing set of relationships is most meaningful for training in consultation. Similarly, a consultant-in-training should spread his hours in one setting over the longest calendar time possible. Two days a month for a year makes a far more effective experience than every day for six weeks. For example, each of the several mental health consultants in the Halifax County program has noticed increased trust and depth in his consultation as he returned after a summer vacation or a leave of absence. As in intensive psychotherapy, it often takes time for trust to develop in a relationship. The same principle applies to trainees in their relationships with consultees. Thus, for example, in a few instances where a graduate student made two or three visits to a school in the late spring, this turned out to be most beneficial because in the fall he tended to be seen as a familiar rather than a new consultant-in-training. One of the most meaningful training experiences in Halifax County involved a graduate student who later became a psychology intern at Duke Medical Center. This trainee participated as a mental health consultant-in-training for three years in the same school system. Such in-depth experience cannot often be arranged, of course, but we are convinced that training in community psychology should be spread over a period of time rather than compressed.

Graduate students and psychology interns have, in our opinion, received considerably better training in the Halifax County program than psychiatric residents because the psychology trainees can be assigned for at least nine months of part-time training (approximately two full days a month) whereas the structure of the psychiatric residency usually restricts training in the Halifax County program to a six-month time block. A similar comparison between the experiences of psychologists and residents in the Halifax program has led us to the belief that it is better for a trainee to be involved in at least one consultation experience in depth than a number of superficial contacts. In most instances a trainee can generalize from one intensive community experience to other community experiences better than he can generalize from the superficial sampling of several kinds of experiences to later, intensive experiences. Needless to say, during supervisory sessions and in seminars the trainees learn about what their supervisors and fellow trainees have experienced in other settings.

The most appropriate attitude of the consultant and the consultant-in-training in a community is eagerness to learn from the community. This final basic principle, which we have stated before (Eisdorfer *et al.*, 1968), is at least as important for trainees as for senior mental health consultants. Many of the citizens of Halifax County, and presumably also of an urban ghetto, often manifest an exquisite understanding of the dynamics of their social structure, a kind of knowledge which can enormously expand a consultant's vision. Community psychologists, of course, have knowledge that they can teach to community caregivers but the reverse is also true. Those consultants (for example, Kiesler, 1965) and trainees who have adopted the attitude that they are eager to learn from as well as give to the community have usually been successful. Those who have not taken this attitude have usually achieved more varied results. When the consultant-in-training has taken a posture which inhibited two-way learning, problems have almost always developed (Berken & Eisdorfer, in press).

Running through these principles and, indeed, through this book is the assumption that a community can provide a most useful laboratory for research and training (Bennett, Anderson, Cooper, Hassol, Klein, & Rosenblum, 1966). While a number of training arrangements are possible, and examples of them are seen in other chapters of this book, the Halifax County program has involved a liaison between faculty members from a university and a community through one of its service agencies, in this case the county health department. This liaison has provided the community with a pool of highly trained talent not otherwise available because of its out-of-the-way location. It has provided the university with many training and research opportunities and has continually confronted faculty and trainees with issues of practical significance. Other advantages generated by such liaisons include the availability of trainees to perform supervised professional work at minimal expense to the community and the interest of well qualified job-seeking professionals when full time positions become available.

TRAINING: WHO AND WHEN

Most of the trainees in the Halifax County program have been graduate students in the Department of Psychology at Duke (and in one case the University of North Carolina) or psychology interns at Duke University Medical Center. Two psychiatric residents have taken a four-month elective in community mental health in this program, and their role has been differentiated from that of the residents who serve as clinicians in the program. Two undergraduate honors students carried out a special project on illegitimacy in the county and numerous students and colleagues from psychology, psychiatry, psychiatric nursing, sociology, pediatrics, and public health have accompanied the consultants.

Graduate students who were interested in the program have often started making trips with the consultants in the earliest stages of their graduate career. Thus they usually have a chance to see what the training is like before committing themselves to it. This approach differs from programs which accept only accomplished professionals for training. In the latter programs the trainees have often shown considerable resistance to learning the principles and approaches of community psychology. This contrasts with the high degree of interest in learning the principles of community psychology consistently noted in the Halifax County program. Community psychology, however, requires a high degree of skill and is fraught with many dangers (Cummings & Cummings, 1959; Eisdorfer *et al.*, 1968; Berken & Eisdorfer, in press). Consequently, trainees in this program do not function semi-independently until they have demonstrated their skills, and even then they are closely supervised. Since much of the community mental health activity in this program involves considerable clinical skill, it has been customary for the trainee to assume a semi-independent training status only when he has had a reasonable amount of traditional clinical experience. It is clear that this program has not emphasized epidemiology and community organization as prerequisites and it is clear that not all community psychologists in all programs must be clinicians, but we have found clinical training almost essential for this particular program to date (Eisdorfer *et al.*, 1968). As a result, the students who have been involved in the more advanced phases of consultation experience have always been at least third-year graduate students who have begun their training in psychotherapy.

It is apparent from other chapters in this book that many community psychology training programs involve extensive amounts of course work. This program has placed much more emphasis on field training experience than on academic course work. Nevertheless, there are community mental health seminars in the Departments of Psychology and Psychiatry at Duke. Since books, journal articles, and works in progress elsewhere are constantly being referred to by the staff and trainees, keeping up with the literature has become an implicit and necessary commitment on the part of all who are involved in this program. As one intern phrased it, there is a "commitment to competence" on the part of all concerned with the program.

Early in the development of interest in community psychology at Duke, a relationship was established with the South Shore Mental Health Center in Quincy, Massachusetts, whereby one or two students were sent to them each summer for training in community psychology. Thus many of the graduate students, though not the interns, who were involved in the Halifax program also had intensive training in the South Shore program.

Despite such planned training experiences, one of the most significant improvements in the training program developed spontaneously because a trainee had made some very subtle mistakes which resulted in a

number of significant negative repercussions from the community (Berken
& Eisdorfer, in press). The supervisor, who was also the program coordinator, felt that the issues involved were sufficiently important to justify as-
sembling all of the consultants and trainees for a special meeting to hold
a postmortem conference on this near-disastrous training experience. The
meeting, which was held at Duke on a Saturday morning, proved so useful that it has developed into an unstructured, twice-a-month seminar
for all those involved in the program ("the Halifaxers"). In addition to
presentations by trainees and staff and discussions of crises in the community or in the development of the program, theoretical or research issues often emerge. There is much brainstorming about novel situations
or interventions and the community's possible responses to them. This
seminar illustrates the considerable usefulness of discussion, openly and in
detail, of the failures, crises, and emerging issues in a community psychology training program. Repeated emphasis upon program critique,
guidelines for program development, and interstaff or professional rivalries has led to an appreciation for the enormous value of frank, open
communication between professionals.

WHAT TRAINEES ACTUALLY DO

            In the apprentice and collaborator stages trainees observe
and help the senior mental health consultants in their normal activities.
For one consultant these activities tend to focus largely upon group
consultation with nurses, police, and ministers, individual administrative
consultation with the health officer and the mental health nurse, and program development with new agencies. For a second consultant normal
activities involve consultation in the schools and training of and consultation with the suicide prevention counselors. A third consultant's work
involves consultation in the schools, with a heavy emphasis on work with
first-grade teachers concerning the results of testing of entering first-
graders and the development of ungraded primary-year experiences. A
fourth consultant works individually with physicians in general practice
and is developing an alcoholism program. For all of the consultants normal activities may also involve some direct clinical service—such as brief
assessment and very brief supportive therapy with a key community
person, brief assessment and therapeutic intervention with the family of
a child who is having problems in school, a brief therapeutic interview
with a high school student who has requested it, or an emergency interview with a person referred by the suicide prevention counselors.
    The apprentice and collaborator aspects of the training do not end
when the trainee assumes semi-independent consultant status in the pro-

gram. On every third or fourth visit the senior consultant accompanies the trainee. While they tend to function as collaborators on these visits, the trainee continues as an apprentice in some aspects of his work. For instance, we have rarely given trainees the task of independent ongoing consultation with groups of caretakers although this has occasionally happened fruitfully.

When a trainee begins to work as a relatively independent mental health consultant, usually in the schools, he may perform a wide range of functions, ranging from direct clinical service to consultee-centered mental health consultation to program or administrative consultation. It has been our experience in this rural area where there are few health services of any kind, and where there never have been any mental health services before, that when we enter a school (or any other agency), the school is likely to express demands for a considerable amount of direct clinical service. Furthermore, these demands will often involve their most serious and long-standing problems—for example, an eight-year-old Mongoloid child who is disrupting a first-grade class, a nine-year-old third-grade child who has to be helped even to blow her own nose, a twelve-year-old girl who is seeing "visions," a seventeen-year-old girl whose father has been taking advantage of her sexually for seven years, and so on.

The four senior mental health consultants in the Halifax County program have somewhat different approaches toward handling such requests for direct clinical service, but all four have had to compromise somewhat between staying strictly within the consultant role, which we think is the most efficient use of professional time in the county, and the schools' demands for direct help with their desperate problems (Altrocchi, 1968). The same is true for the trainees except that they probably perform direct clinical services a little more often than the senior consultants. Trainees often lack the experience to screen requests accurately and the authority necessary to resist the demands for service and to direct the interaction toward consultation. Also they are usually at a stage in their clinical training at which they are especially interested in demonstrating their ability to perform clinical services, which services fulfill a strong community need and may help establish the competence and trust necessary for productive consultation. Thus there are times when our trainees find themselves doing intelligence testing for placement in a special education class, or very brief individual, group, or family therapy. There are many other times, of course, when they are performing a straight consultation role with a principal, guidance counselor, speech therapist, or teacher. Sometimes consultation is administration centered, sometimes it is consultee centered, but more often it is client centered (Caplan, 1964).

Since we have encouraged trainees and school personnel to explore new ways of dealing with problems, the trainees have also found themselves conducting high school discussions of sex and marriage or helping teachers in discussions with such classes, aiding a special education teacher to meet with parents to encourage their cooperation, visiting a backwoods home with a teacher after school to help investigate charges of child beating, using rebellious high school boys as research assistants to explore the functioning and use of informal gatekeepers, going to a classroom and persuading the children to discuss what they can do about one of their classmate's problems (with the boy in question playing an active role in the discussion and with the expectation that the teacher can use the same techniques later if necessary), or helping the school personnel to deal with potential school riots. Thus, the problems the trainee faces are extremely heterogeneous.

It might be useful to describe briefly a rather dramatic situation in which one of the trainees became involved. It demonstrates the degree of confidence the community had in the competence of the trainee and illustrates many of the principles of community psychology training which are proposed in this chapter. The trainee, a fourth-year graduate student in his second year of community training in the same school system, had shown an unusual degree of maturity, clinical skill, and understanding of community problems. Normally, the senior mental health consultant would have been with him on this day, but the consultant was out of the state and the trainee could not even reach him by telephone. When the trainee arrived at the school, the superintendent and the supervisor of instruction expressed considerable anxiety about an emergency meeting of the school board which was called for that evening in order to hear complaints from Negro parents that their children were being mistreated in the high school which had recently moved slightly beyond token integration. The supervisor and the superintendent earnestly asked the trainee if he could stay over for the meeting and help them. The trainee agreed to stay. He was gratified that they trusted him enough to ask him to stay but was concerned and anxious about the request because he understood fully the enormous tensions that are involved in desegregation of a rural Southern school system. He also recognized that he was being asked to take sides in a divisive community problem.

Many factors were apparently operating in this request for help. It was probably very important that this was the second year of the trainee's association with the school system and that he had built up good relationships with the school personnel. The senior consultant had been working in this school system for several years and had gained the trust of the key people in the schools and, in addition, this trainee and the consultant together had discussed the tensions of desegregation with the superintendent and the supervisor many times, had met with community and student leaders and the faculty to help them discuss problems they would be facing when many Negro children entered their school, and had helped a new principal deal with a potentially incendiary fight between a Negro boy and white boy. Although the trainee and the consultant were seen as outsiders (and therefore probably integrationists), many persons had evidently become convinced that the consultant and the trainee were fairminded and understood the many complexities of the issue.

The superintendent and supervisor wanted the trainee to come to the evening meeting of the school board to provide evidence of their sincere efforts to be fair to both sides in the painful process of desegregation. The trainee indicated that he would be glad to do this but he was aware that he needed to be very careful to remain in the role of consultant and not be seen as an ally of the white "power structure" or the petitioner group. Thus, during the morning's discussion about the meeting the trainee stayed closely within the consultant role, with stances such as "I realize how difficult this is for you"; "What have you done before about situations like this?"; "What would you do in this situation if the race issue were not involved?" And he generally took the position: "This is your problem; how do you think it should be handled?" This particular kind of consultation role has been basic in the Halifax program. The responsibility for the solution of problems in the community has always resided in the community. The consultants never maintained that they would solve the community's problems but rather indicated that they would help the community to solve its own problems.

Late in the day the trainee was joined by another trainee who had driven to the county with him to work in another school during the day. The two trainees spent the dinner hour reviewing the situation and planning for the evening. In an effort to make clear their relatively neutral position, they decided that they would not sit at the front of the room with the school board or at the back of the room behind the audience, but in a middle, neutral corner of the room.

The meeting, as predicted, was very tense. The trainee was called upon to tell about his observations of the efforts of the school personnel to be fair and he did so as objectively as possible. After the public meeting the school board held an executive session and asked the trainee to stay and offer comments. The trainee was able to point out that the board had been rather unresponsive and evasive during the meeting. When the board asked him to meet with male high school students and point out to them the consequences of harassing Negro students, the trainee suggested that the school lawyer rather than an outsider do this. The attorney subsequently carried out this task with effective legal authority.

Thus the evening's meetings were successful to the extent that some progress resulted. The trainee performed several useful functions—that is, as a neutral observer and information giver, a supportive but also critical consultant for the harassed school officials, and a stimulator of some ideas for handling their difficult problems. Furthermore, he did not fall into any of a number of potential traps. The experience, needless to say, was maturing for the trainee. The apprentice-collaborator method of field training not infrequently leads to such training experiences.

RESULTS OF THE TRAINING PROGRAM

In addition to the many colleagues and students who have made occasional visits and the psychiatric residents who have spent six months or a year in the program performing somewhat more traditional clinical services, the following kinds of trainees have had intensive training experience in this program: (a) two undergraduate Duke students who spent a school year involved in a research project on illegitimacy during which they made several visits to the county; (b) an advanced psychiatric resident who started by spending most of his time in a more traditional clinical role in the health department but who worked into a consultation role with nurses, a school, and local physicians; (c) two third-year psychiatric residents who took a four-month elective in community psychiatry in the Halifax County program; and (d) 19 psychology graduate students or interns. In the early years of this program there were only one or two trainees at any one time; only since 1965 has there been a sizable number of trainees during any single year.

In an attempt to obtain some feedback from trainees about their training in Halifax County, all of them were sent a brief questionnaire asking them to rate their experience. The four questions and a tabulation of the results appear in Figure 12–1.

It is apparent that almost all of the trainees feel that the Halifax experience was at least a significant feature of their professional training and that more than 40 percent of them consider it very significant. The range is greater in the extent to which they think the training influenced them, but the greatest clustering again is at "significantly."[1] It is interesting to note that trainees who answered separately for different areas of endeavor indicated that their thinking and clinical work were affected rather than their research. This is probably because the program has not had a heavy research emphasis in the past. The current or anticipated proportion of work which involves community mental health covers the entire scale from 0 to 100 percent, with the median at 35 percent, which, it should be noted, is a higher percentage of time than any of the four

---

[1] Only one rating scale was provided for question 2. When someone made only one rating, it was assumed that this rating applied to thinking, research, clinical work, and teaching.

FIGURE 12–1

1. To what extent do you consider your experience in Halifax County to have been an important feature of your professional training?

		1	13	10
NOT AT ALL	SLIGHTLY	SOMEWHAT	SIGNIFICANTLY	VERY SIGNIFICANTLY

2. To what extent has this training influenced your thinking, your research, your clinical work, and/or your teaching?

Thinking

		2	13	5

Research

2	3		6	2

Clinical work

		2	1	13	5

Teaching

	1	2	8	1
NOT AT ALL	SLIGHTLY	SOMEWHAT	SIGNIFICANTLY	VERY SIGNIFICANTLY

3. What percent of your current work involves community mental health? (If you are still in training, interpret this question as "What percent of your future work do you expect will involve community mental health?")

```
3 1 1 3  2    1 3 1 1 1    2 1      1 1          1
•—•—•—•—•—•—•—•—•—•—•—•—•—•—•—•—•—•—•—•—•
0  5 10 15 20 25  30 35 40 45 50 55 60 65 70 75 80 85 90 95 100
```
PERCENT

4. How important do you feel this time is in the spectrum of your professional life?

		3	11	7
NOT AT ALL	SLIGHTLY	SOMEWHAT	SIGNIFICANTLY	VERY SIGNIFICANTLY

senior consultants spend. The trainees feel that their community mental health time is important in their professional life with most answering either "significantly" or "very significantly."

It is relevant to question whether these results might be influenced by current and past trainees' attempts to please us. While this possibility cannot be completely discounted, it is noteworthy that these trainees have often been openly critical of other aspects of their graduate or internship training, while consistently giving positive feedback about their community training, even though the same supervisors are involved in both. Furthermore, it is not likely that the reports of the percentage of time in which they are involved in community mental health would be extremely influenced by a need to please their former trainers.

One can summarize these results by saying that the program has consistently had a significant impact on trainees, especially influencing their thinking and clinical work. Most of them are investing or plan to devote a substantial portion of their time to this area. Two former trainees, whose only community training was in Halifax, are especially heavily involved in community work: one is working full-time in community mental health and the other has become a prominent contributor to the field.

Two especially positive and penetrating comments from the questionnaire are worth quoting:

> I now see emotional problems, or mental disorder if you will, in greater perspective. Previously, though cognitively aware this was not true, I would still conceptualize the problem at hand at the individual unit level. First-hand experience in the community has made me appreciate the larger social milieu as the unit which gives rise to the individual presenting complaint. Cultural factors assume more importance.

> It has changed my concept of my own eventual professional role and given me a different perspective on clinical work, broadening it to include social system change as well as help to individuals. My dissertation research grew directly out of consultation experience.

There are other criteria of the results of this training program. At the present time one doctoral dissertation is in progress and another is being planned within the context of this program. The program has developed from bimonthly consultation in 1959 to about 30 consultation days a month. Currently, five psychology interns and three psychology graduate students are involved in a full year of training in the program. Moreover, the Halifax County Mental Health Center began operation in 1968. This center will have several full-time professional personnel but it retains the part-time consultants. Finally, the training features of this program have significantly enriched our professional lives.

REFERENCES

Altrocchi, J. Consultation as a method of providing mental health services for school personnel. *North Carolina Journal of Mental Health,* 1968, in press.

Altrocchi, J., & Batton, Lois. Suicide prevention in an underpopulated area. Paper presented at the First Annual National Conference on Suicidology, Chicago, March, 1968.

Altrocchi, J., Spielberger, C. D., & Eisdorfer, C. Mental health consultation with groups. *Community Mental Health Journal,* 1965, 1, 127–134.

Bennett, C. C., Anderson, Luleen S., Cooper, S., Hassol, L., Klein, D. C., & Rosenblum, G. *Community psychology: A report of the Boston conference* on the education of psychologists for community mental health. Boston: Boston University Press, 1966.

Berken, G., & Eisdorfer, C. Closed ranks in microcosm: Pitfalls of a training experience in community consultation. *Community Mental Health Journal,* 4, 211–220.

Caplan, G. *Principles of preventive psychiatry.* New York: Basic Books, 1964.

Cummings, Elaine, & Cummings, J. *Closed ranks: An experiment in mental health education.* Cambridge, Mass.: Harvard University Press, 1957.

Eisdorfer, C., Altrocchi, J., & Young, R. F. Principles of community mental health in a rural setting: The Halifax County program. *Community Mental Health Journal,* 1968, in press.

Garner, W. R., Hunt, J. F., & Taylor, D. W. Education for research in psychology. *American Psychologist,* 1959, 14, 167–179.

Halifax County Commission on Community Health Services. A stereo report of the community. Halifax, N. C.: Halifax County Health Department, 1964.

Kiesler, F. Programming for prevention. *North Carolina Journal of Mental Health,* 1964, 1, No. 2, 3–17.

North Carolina Mental Health Planning Staff. *A comprehensive mental health plan for North Carolina.* Volume 1. Raleigh, North Carolina: State University Press, 1965.

Spielberger, C. D. A mental health consultation program in a small community with limited professional mental health resources. In E. L. Cowen, E. A. Gardner, & M. Zax (Eds.). *Emergent approaches to mental health problems.* New York: Appleton-Century-Crofts, 1967. Pp. 214–236.

13

Community Psychology Training in a Multidisciplinary Setting

Herbert Lipton and Donald Klein

In this paper we have two major goals. First, we will describe a new training program in community psychology that takes place to a large extent in a multidisciplinary setting. Second, we will attempt to assess the advantages and drawbacks of training in such a setting and, at the same time, raise issues that we believe derive from the newness of community psychology training itself.

THE BOSTON UNIVERSITY COMMUNITY PSYCHOLOGY PROGRAM

Training in community psychology at Boston University began in 1965, under the joint sponsorship of the Psychology Department and the Human Relations Center. This program has been supported in part by a training grant from the National Institute of Mental Health since its inception in 1965. The project trains clinical, counseling, and social and personality psychology graduate students in the study of the reciprocal effects of individual behavior and community, group, and institutional behavior. It also teaches methods of intervention in this interactional process. The training is integrated with the doctoral programs already mentioned and does not offer separate degrees. Rather, through interdisciplinary and interspecialty seminars and supervised field experiences students are helped to develop the competencies required for understanding psychosocial processes and for dealing with community research as a social process. Fellowships are provided at the advanced graduate level for one year, with an opportunity to continue for a second year. Field and research activities are selected from one of four areas of application: community mental health, intergroup relations, community development, and educational systems.

Training in community psychology at Boston University is conceived of as an orientation or an area of focus rather than as a formal program or specialty. The program was established in this manner in order to develop in students a general approach to community psychology that would not cut them off from already developed doctoral programs in psychology. The goal in community psychology training thus conceived has been to allow the generalist to capitalize on the rich contribution that the specialty programs make while at the same time enabling the generalist to stimulate the specialist with newly formed questions.

The decision to include three areas of application in addition to the area of community mental health was linked to critical questions raised by psychologists who already had experience in the community. The illness model, as a conceptual framework, did not seem to have applicability to a wide enough range of community circumstances. Psychologists and other professionals in the mental health field—for example, Szasz (1961)—have used the problems of living orientation rather than the illness model and have derived new intervention techniques as a consequence of this approach. Still others—among them Bennis, Benne, and Chin (1964)—have used the human relations model which they find has broad applicability in organizations and institutions. Freidenburg (1963) has suggested still another model, which he calls participant democracy, to guide the psychologist interested in the community into new areas of study and application. Thus, in order to activate fully the contribution of psychologists to community psychology, we felt that students should be trained in complex community settings where they could learn by working with colleagues from other disciplines and with citizen leaders, the manifold implications of diverse models. We also felt that the community psychologist needed to develop a scientific and professional outlook that placed value upon bridging the gap between basic research and its possible utilization by society.

The Human Relations Center of Boston University was established in 1953 with a mandate from the university to pursue the study of human relations and applied behavioral science in a multidisciplinary context. The center has provided an opportune setting for training in community psychology at Boston University. The Community Psychology Training Program has two unique characteristics: (1) it is multidisciplinary, and (2) it is based on a human relations model from which practice and research efforts derive. This model focuses centrally upon the ways in which values infuse and direct personal and professional behavior.

The center has been able to develop multidisciplinary interests and collaboration because of the broad appeal of its substantive interest in human relationships. We can define the study of human relations as the study of the effectiveness of people in their relation with each other. This study includes, of course, a person's awareness of himself and his personal impact on others. In general, the study of human relations overlaps the interests of a number of academic disciplines, from medicine and psychology to political science. In the history of the center there has been a differential response by different departments to the center's programs. Until recently, the traditional helping professions—nursing, education, and theology—tended toward greater participation. A detailed consideration of this history however is not germane here. Rather, we will sketch briefly how the center's program is implemented.

The heart of the center is its fellowship program for which graduate students in any of the university's schools or departments are eligible to apply. To date, students have come from a variety of fields, including philosophy, theology, law, business, psychology, sociology, social work, nursing, and several areas of education including continuing education. Fellows receive stipends or fellowships up to $3,000 per year for one or two years of study in the center. Depending upon funds available, between 15 and 20 students are accepted each year. This number includes eight community psychology fellows who are supported by NIMH stipends. The general training program includes course work, field work, research, and informal learning experiences. All fellows, including the community psychology fellows, are required to take a basic two-semester course sequence offered at the center. The first semester offering is a practicum in Human Relations. This course, through a laboratory training format (modified T-group), seeks to develop a greater awareness in the student for dealing with others as well as a deeper understanding of group phenomena. Topics covered include the development of mutual trust, setting of norms, inclusion-exclusion phenomena, communication processes, helping and collaborating, emergence of leadership, and coping with relationships with authority.

In the second semester a proseminar on Theories of Changing is offered. This seminar is always staffed by an interdisciplinary faculty. Conceptions of collaborative change as well as other strategies of change are discussed and evaluated through participation in action projects. In this seminar an attempt is made to keep in focus the person himself as a resource for initiating and implementing change as well as the multiple strategies and methods available to him.

Additional courses which fellows can elect include the following seminars: *evaluation research*, in which a critical review of applied and evaluation research methods and findings is conducted, along with an examination of the choice of criterion variables; *psychological consultation*, in which theories and principles of psychological consultation, viewed as a process of assisting professionals confronting problems in their work, are discussed and practiced; *advanced practicum in human relations*, in which different aspects of technique related to the dynamics of planned change and the work of the change agent are reviewed. In addition, summer residential workshops (two to four weeks in duration) are available in human relations, intergroup dynamics, and community relations and community development. In these workshops intensive group experience, lectures, skill sessions, and field experiences are available. Students as well as staff come from a variety of disciplines and professions.

In addition to multidisciplinary student participation in seminars and multidisciplinary faculty collaboration in teaching these seminars, students and faculty from different disciplines have an opportunity to collaborate in training, consultation, and research projects undertaken by the center or by center staff in conjunction with faculty in other departments. In the past few years these projects have included a multiuniversity, multidisciplinary approach to introducing self-renewal techniques in a number of school systems, an annual workshop in which behavioral science techniques and learning were introduced to metropolitan leaders from a variety of areas in the community, and a training program for antipoverty neighborhood workers and central office staff. Community psychology fellows have also had opportunities for field placements with mental health and geriatric facilities, a self-help organization, public schools, a state commission against discrimination, and with a leadership training and evaluation project that was coordinated by an inner city voluntary organization.

SOME ADVANTAGES AND DISADVANTAGES OF COMMUNITY PSYCHOLOGY TRAINING IN A MULTIDISCIPLINARY SETTING

We cannot trace systematically at this time all the implications of the human relations model for training in psychology. Nor can we deal in detail with the relation of the human relations model to a multidisciplinary approach to teaching. We will examine some of the effects of training bearing these two features on community psychology graduate students.

A first advantage that accrues from training in such a setting is that the range of contingent factors that play a role in determining an individual's behavior is much more forcibly brought to the student's awareness. His experiences are not limited to lecture and reading, but often include direct contact with the way in which values and attitudes affect individual and interpersonal behavior, the effect of institutional and organizational processes on personal and professional behavior, the range of change strategies available to a person in his environment, and the many conceptual frames of reference and definitions of community problems that may be considered. A disadvantage is found in this same experience when it is compared with the experiences of psychology graduate students trained traditionally within a department. The traditionally trained student receives more assurance, we believe, because of the more restricted range of concepts and subject matter he is asked to master. At the center the student initially finds it harder to develop a personal frame of reference.

There is another kind of hardship associated with training at the center. Not only does the student find it difficult to integrate his experience intellectually, but also he receives considerable emotional buffeting. This comes from students from other disciplines and also from students in other specialties in psychology. His professional language, in the multidisciplinary setting, may be met with blank looks, with shrugs, and sometimes even with amusement. One student may find that his scientific precision is looked at as being unrealistic or artificial, while another student may find that his free-wheeling, experiential approach is looked at askance by the conceptualizer. Still another may find that his unexamined values, bluntly expressed, are recoiled from by others.

On the other hand, the advantages of such an experience to the psychologist who wants to work in the community must be obvious. Often, with no malice intended, people and groups in the community expose professionals, experts, planners, and consultants to such experiences every day. The knowledge, and the acceptance of the knowledge, that much of this frankness of expression is sincere and legitimately motivated is a fundamental experience for which the community psychologist must be prepared.

There is still another potential difficulty that is worked on students and staff of the center. We are all familiar with problems involved in teaching and learning when a wide range of preparation is represented in any student group. This range is undoubtedly greater at the center than it would be in a psychology department, since the consistency of preparation varies so widely between schools and departments. For example, the sophistication of psychology and sociology students in research methods stands out when compared with this type of knowledge in students from other fields. The theoretical sophistication of students in the behavioral sciences also exceeds that of students from the professional schools.

On the other hand, we find that students from nursing, theology, and adult education are often older, have had considerable field experience, and are returning to school to develop a system of ideas that will help them organize the experiences they have had. They often bring personal involvements in organizations, field work, and community development into seminar discussions, and these experiences serve as extremely useful case material. The pedagogic challenge inherent in this problem is to extend the range of ways in which knowledge can be gained for students who come together at many levels of preparation. At times, the establishment of interest subgroupings within the seminars has proved a useful way in which to meet this problem. At other times, students have helped or tutored each other very effectively.

The training problems that face the community psychologist in working with other professionals include confrontation with differences in values and style and also differences in technical and conceptual sophistication. However, since teams of specialists are frequently called upon to collaborate in planning and implementing change in the community, experience with this type of collaboration in graduate training will certainly be put to good use.

The staff of the center, in addition to being concerned with the issues just discussed, are not without their own professional identity problems. Most staff members share some feeling of disaffection with the main stream of the specialties in which they are trained. Feelings of dissatisfaction with the methods and the academic requirements of their own field provides a major reason for their participation in the center. Students also share some of the identity problems. Many students who seek training in community psychology look on themselves as mavericks; others are caught up in the tensions they come to feel between the home sod of the department and the new culture of the center.

The problem of identity is gradually eased at the center because there is acceptance of the maverick and because this special tension is put to use in the service of "bridging"—that is, in serving as a link between disciplines and orientations. One student in social psychology did her field work in a neighborhood settlement house in the inner city. She brought with her a research interest in cognitive style in children. As part of her field work she visited and interviewed the parents of many neighborhood children in their homes and consequently came to have a much richer appreciation of the reality setting in which the children developed. Another student in social psychology attended a multidisciplinary summer workshop as a research member of the staff. Tensions between Negroes and whites played an important part in an intensive community simulation exercise developed in the workshop. As a result of his experience, the student was stimulated to choose a field placement for the next academic year with an antipoverty project in which his interest in small group phenomena could be put to use and adapted to the training programs that were being developed for neighborhood clients of the antipoverty agency. A student in clinical psychology, in a multiservice center setting, began work as coleader with a group of Negro women. In the course of several months a key issue developed in the area of role definition: were the women patients; were they to be worked with as the mothers of acting-out adolescent girls; or were they women in their middle years with all the attendant concerns and personal needs?

Apparently, the women themselves, through their actions, urged the last definition on the leaders. A staff person with clinical training had a similar experience recently in leading a group of women in an alcoholism clinic. For several months they discussed themselves almost entirely as alcoholics; in fact at times the meeting room figuratively reeked with their reminiscences. However, to their own surprise, they began talking about themselves as women rather than as alcoholics. They then explored a series of needs common to women like themselves, in their late thirties or early forties, with children either married or well on their way in school, with less than high school education, and with a mean life expectancy of about 30 years. Several of them were then able to become engaged in activities which began filling voids in their lives: one became active in an antipoverty neighborhood program; another led a Sunday school class; a third sought training from a rehabilitation agency so she could qualify for a more interesting job. From experiences such as these the clinical psychologist, for example, who has had experience in the community can begin to make systematic comparisons between community and organizational processes and a systems approach and the psychotherapy model that is advocated by the clinical psychology faculty. Thus, while the bridger may often be caught between two camps, his linking function can at times be extremely rewarding, and may make possible a new personal integration.

While there are many difficulties involved in the center's multidisciplinary and multimodal approach to training, the challenges and the experiences they provide seem to more than compensate the students from psychology who get involved in community training. In addition to its value as a training model, we believe that the center operation provides students interested in community psychology with a possible model of a facility for the delivery of services to the community, and for the utilization by the community of applied behavioral science knowledge.

However, we are continually made aware by students and colleagues that there are many questions and assumptions fundamental to our thinking that have not yet been clearly and effectively stated and few have been answered. For the many clinical psychologists who have recently turned to community work, community may sometimes connote all that exists outside of the traditional medical settings where we were trained and first practiced as professionals. Is this new horizon sufficiently charted and defined to create a new field or discipline, even a new specialty within psychology? There are several important issues that we believe must be faced and resolved. In doing so, it will become clearer whether we are psychologists in the community or community psychologists, and what special contributions to intervention and research we can make along with other behavioral scientists in the community.

First, the psychologist needs a model of community, a model that defines the special psychological quality of community we are personally seeking and will be professionally oriented toward studying. Second, we will need to specify how we will use terms like small group, organization, institution, neighborhood, community, and society, and we will need to begin examining the psychological implications of these different levels of organization. Third, we will need to develop a conception of a model community that psychologists and others can work positively toward creating. Otherwise, we will always find ourselves reacting to the multiple and compelling social problems that we find on all sides that betoken a failure of community. Fourth, we will have to reconcile our personal multiple community memberships—residential, professional, social—with the model community we develop to guide our professional activities. These are among the issues we believe should command our attention if we are to develop a psychology of the community which will in turn command the attention of a future generation of psychologists.

REFERENCES

Bennis, W., Benne, K., & Chin, R. *The planning of change.* New York: Holt, Rinehart, & Winston, 1964.

Freidenburg, E. *Coming of age in America.* New York: Random House, 1963.

Szasz, T. *The myth of mental illness.* New York: Hoeber, 1961.

14

Research Training in Community Mental Health

Kent S. Miller

The aim in this chapter is to discuss research in community mental health and to describe a specific research training program in which sociology students are trained in community mental health research at the doctoral level. The terms community mental health and community psychology have been discussed in detail elsewhere in this volume. But before describing a specific training program, some additional comments need to be made about the use of these terms in this chapter.

DEFINITIONAL AND CONCEPTUAL PROBLEMS

The field of mental health has been highly successful in obtaining support since the passage of the National Mental Health Act only 20 years ago. The National Institute of Mental Health, recently elevated to bureau status within the Public Health Service, employs 25,000 people and has an annual budget of over $340,000,000. In many of our large-population states the budget of the department of mental health is exceeded only by those of the departments of education and welfare. There has been extensive citizen activity in the planning of mental health programs and in the raising of funds for services at local levels. Public support of mental health activities has grown beyond the dreams of most people.

This growth has taken place in the face of the fact that there is very little agreement as to what the content of mental health programs should be. There seems to be no limit to the range of social problems seen as the proper concerns of mental health experts. This point is underscored by simply listing some of the areas in which the NIMH supports training and research programs: alcoholism, suicide, drug addiction, urban crowding, sexual deviations, the social problems of poverty, mass violence, the biochemical basis of behavior, etc. Not much is excluded and the range of focus extends from severe social problems to self-actualization. All of this supports Brewster Smith's statement that mental health is not a theoretical concept but a chapter heading under which a number of heterogeneous concepts are lumped together (Smith, 1961).

Community mental health is a topic that certainly would be emphasized in any discussion of mental health, although the discussion would undoubtedly reveal a lack of conceptual clarity. It is apparent that much of the activity under this banner reflects a social movement designed to bring about a significant change within the mental health field. This movement has its roots in the reaction of many mental health specialists to the heavy influence of Freudian psychology and its almost exclusive focus on internal processes in attempting to understand and modify human behavior. Additional impetus stems from a dissatisfaction with current treatment programs, particularly with respect to their questionable effectiveness. Other dimensions of community mental health have been described in this volume in the chapters by Golann and by Iscoe and Spielberger. One point that is clear is that members of the movement are articulate and passionate about their shared set of ideas despite the lack of evidence to support them (Baker & Schulberg, 1967).

It is difficult for me to distinguish community psychology from community mental health, although it has been suggested that the former is a more inclusive concept. Reiff (1966) has described community psychology as not so much a discipline or specialty as it is a point of view, an approach that cuts across many disciplines and specialties. Certain commonalities can be identified: the focus is on social systems, there is a concern with social problems and social competence, and there is the idea of involvement as change agents. The presence of an action orientation and a desire to innovate in program development could lead to agreement that community psychology represents a splinter movement within the larger community mental health movement as well as a protest against the traditional training of psychologists for clinical practice roles. But beyond this, the ambiguity is such that distinctions between community mental health and community psychology are difficult to draw and probably irrelevant at this time. This ambiguity is not necessarily bad. The major point of these remarks is to suggest that training programs should not be crystallized too early and that no two programs need look alike at this time.

One further comment about community psychology as a reflection of a social movement. Social movements are highly dynamic and have an uncertain life span: they lack institutional status and often meet with hostility and indifference. But as a movement gains increased support, its work is done and its active life, as a movement, is over. Contented people do not join social movements. It seems that community psychology may have achieved institutionalization quite early. It is already an "in" phrase and currently meets with very little hostility. Indeed, its claim to being a social movement may have died when Division 27 of the American Psychological Association was established. Let us hope that early institutionalization has not ruled out needed innovation in this field.

A FOCUS FOR RESEARCH IN COMMUNITY MENTAL HEALTH

Among those interested in community mental health, there is a heavy emphasis upon action and a concern with "not only understanding but changing the world." I have no objection to a role definition as an action-oriented-question-asker, but I am concerned that the question-asking part of the definition not be slighted. Universities generally shy away from applied and evaluative research, and there is some evidence that the professionals most strongly identified with community mental health devote relatively little time to research activities (Baker & Schulberg, 1967). Therefore, it seems more important than ever that the role of the psychologist and the sociologist in community mental health work should be that of the question asker, the skeptic. This is a rather conservative notion that has been voiced frequently, but we have failed to act as if we believed it. An estimated $20 billion is spent annually on mental health services in the U.S. but relatively little on planning and evaluation of these services. The research activities which hopefully were to be programmed into the community mental health centers already appear to have gone by the board. At the same time, the rapidly changing models of mental health and new methods for the delivery of services make it necessary to devote considerably more energy to critical evaluation than has been the case in the past.

The difficulties inherent in the evaluation of mental health programs are readily acknowledged and it is recognized that many programs will continue to operate for some time to come on the same kind of faith that backs national foreign policy. But our methodology is such that we are now able to quantify at least some aspects of our service programs, and attempts at evaluation must necessarily contribute to a clearer statement of program objectives.

In addition to the need for program evaluation, there is a related area in which research should be focused. This has to do with the processes by which social systems create and foster deviant behavior. The mental health field has been characterized by an almost total focus upon intrapsychic phenomena, as was noted by Levine (see Chapter 5). Even the behavioral modification approach within psychology has emphasized changing systems within the individual rather than environmental systems. Yet there is strong evidence that in many instances it is the societal response that defines the role for the deviant.

There is good reason to believe that deviant behaviors are much more common than we previously thought. With most people, in most situations, the deviance is transitory or denied. But from the larger general flow of persons experiencing transitory deviant behavior, certain individuals are singled out, labeled, and started on a career of deviance. Once such a career is established, the individual is rewarded for playing this role and punished when he tries to leave it. It is important that we come to understand the process by which all of this occurs for it has implications not only for the treatment of disturbed individuals but also for preventive mental health efforts. The significance of this kind of focus cannot be spelled out in detail here, but some organization of the basic propositions has been provided by Scheff (1966).

These two general areas of concern, program evaluation and social processes in the development of deviant behavior, can profitably serve as points of focus in a doctoral program concerned with research in community mental health.

SOME BASIC ASSUMPTIONS REGARDING TRAINING FOR RESEARCH IN COMMUNITY MENTAL HEALTH

Recent concern with manpower problems in mental health has lead to suggestions that students at all levels should be able to participate in some manner in research (Baler, 1967). We agree with this position, but the greatest need is for people with the most advanced training. The selection of criteria and the problems of conceptualization are of such complexity that in most instances, these kinds of problems can be successfully handled only at the doctoral level. We noted earlier that community mental health is not a theoretical construct but rather a particular perspective or approach to problems, and for this reason the researcher in this area should be trained in a given discipline such as psychology or sociology. Such training provides some assurance of basic competence in relevant social science theory and methodology, and a professional base from which to operate.

A second assumption which we make regarding training for research in community mental health is that the student will spend time in the community and that he will most likely function in the community in a split role. He will be there as a question asker, but he is also likely to be involved in other roles. The scientist-professional model described by Gelfand & Kelly (1960), or the participant-conceptualizer suggested by Reiff (1966) serve as guides to possible alternatives. The issue of whether research competency and action competency can be combined in a single person has been debated extensively and will not be dealt with here. But in our training we assume that there is not as much of a dichotomy as many have claimed. If students are expected to spend time in the field, the nature of the research they get involved in is such that action implications frequently follow.

A third assumption underlying a successful research training program in community mental health relates to the kinds of research activities which get reinforced within university settings. Psychology has been particularly vulnerable to the charge that it is preoccupied with the college sophomore, the white rat, and the brass instruments laboratory. According to Sarason's (1966) analysis of this charge, psychology has been preoccupied with molecular theories about molecular sized problems. The problems associated with community mental health are clearly of a different order. But I think that it is possible to attempt to quantify some of them without being any less of a scientist. Although the climate is such that a number of universities could come to value research in community mental health, this increased latitude in research topics and methodology will not be welcomed by all faculties. While many do not have the appropriate skills or interests reflected in their faculty, an increasing number do. Institutionalized resistance is certainly present, but I have a suspicion that it is not nearly as great as some of the complainers would have us believe. It is easier on the part of everyone to stick with the college sophomore and the laboratory, but we operate on the assumption that a much wider range of investigations is acceptable for degree requirements.

GOAL OF RESEARCH TRAINING IN COMMUNITY MENTAL HEALTH

We have already referred to the obvious need for knowledge of theory and research methodology and may now turn our attention to specific areas relating to mental health. What is it that a student preparing for research in community mental health should know?

1. He needs to be aware of the kinds of things that are being done under the name of mental health. This would include knowledge of the organization and financing of a variety of services: local, state, and Federal. He should have more than a passing acquaintance with treatment techniques (but not necessarily to the extent that he can apply them himself). There should be an exposure to the training and ideology of the various mental health professionals.

2. The student should be thoroughly acquainted with current re-

search definitions of mental health and aware of the need for multiple criteria. The possibilities and problems of program evaluation should be dealt with in detail.

3. He should have some knowledge of the public health model and of epidemiological techniques, not so much because of their uniqueness or intrinsic value, but rather so that he will know their limitations as applied to the subject matter of community mental health. In particular, he should come to realize that statistics regarding mental and social disorder have little or nothing to do with incidence or prevalence, and that the statistics we collect are very much a product of the bureaucratic structure. In learning this he will necessarily learn something about community tolerance and attitudes as well as something about the populations receiving service.

4. As psychologists become concerned about social systems, there are specific topics which must be dealt with and that are not usually taught in psychology departments. Such topics include community power and politics, the role of leadership, minority groups, social stratification, organization of community services. Each of these topics has a substantial body of literature behind it, and the trainee needs at least an overview of the subject.

5. Finally, the student should be aware of the evidence that societal reactions determine and sustain most deviant behaviors. Therefore, in addition to knowledge of the forms and content of deviant behavior, the student should know something about process. He needs to be aware of the evidence that it is not behavior per se which determines deviance but rather the interpretations others make of the behavior. "For in modern society, the socially significant differentiation of deviants from the nondeviant population is increasingly contingent upon circumstances of situation, place, social and personal biography, and the bureaucratically organized activities of agencies of control" (Kitsuse, 1962). This implies that students must have a much better understanding of the role of values than we usually transmit to them.

DESCRIPTION OF A SPECIFIC COMMUNITY MENTAL HEALTH RESEARCH TRAINING PROGRAM

For several years, we have been conducting a training program for research in community mental health at Florida State University. This is a joint effort involving doctoral sociology students and the Institute for Social Research. The institute has a staff drawn from sociology, economics, government, city planning, and psychology. It provides graduate students with an opportunity to work with other disciplines and to participate in a variety of research projects. The research conducted through the institute is such that the student can obtain a graded series of research experiences, including the analysis of data already on hand, interviewing in the field, and participating in the conceptual development and research of a given project.

Given the training assumptions and goals previously mentioned, how are these to be attained? Much of the desired content of the training program is transmitted through course work and seminars in the usual fashion. For example, the doctoral sociology student learns something about community, social systems, attitudes, etc., in his core program. Specific content relating to mental health is presented through a series of four required seminars—one in medical sociology, one in program evaluation, and two dealing with the sociology of mental health. With the exception of the seminar in medical sociology, these are new courses which deal with mental health concepts and information that is not covered by other course offerings within the university.

In line with the desire for the students to have some knowledge of mental health services, they are required to spend a minimum of two summers in field placements. These placements cover a variety of settings, including the State Department of Mental Health and local mental health centers. The purpose of this placement is twofold: (1) to acquaint the student with the culture of the agency, and (2) to provide him with some understanding of the specific problems and the types of data which are available through the agency. In most instances, the student begins a minor research project which is completed after his return to the campus.

Throughout the program the major emphasis is upon research. Starting with the first year of graduate study, the student begins receiving formal credit for directed individual research. During his entire residence on campus he attends an informal seminar in which the faculty and students present proposed research in mental health for critical evaluation. Later, the completed projects are brought back to the group for discussion of the findings. In this fashion there is a detailed exposure to methodological problems and, more importantly, an exposure to the types of community mental health questions that need to be investigated. This process also provides the more advanced students an opportunity to share in the supervision and research training of students at lower levels of competency.

Each student in the program is expected to conduct his master's research and his dissertation on a topic in the field of mental health. As indicated earlier, the interpretation of mental health is broad enough so that this has not proven to be unduly restrictive.

EXAMPLES OF COMMUNITY MENTAL
HEALTH RESEARCH

It was mentioned above that there is an attempt to involve the student in a graded series of research experiences. The research required for the M.A. and Ph.D. is designed to serve several purposes in addition to the development of skills in conceptualization and methodology. The primary goal is that of instilling in the student a continuing commitment to research in community mental health. Specific examples of investigations conducted by our students will be discussed in this section, following a description of some general considerations that are met in achieving this goal.

1. The research is expected to involve some form of field experience. The student is encouraged to leave the security of the university and to be involved in the community. This involvement is likely to take the form of interviewing and working with community leaders, program people, and agency records.

2. Considerable effort is directed toward defining a problem which has intrinsic interest for the student. We are concerned that the student complete his training within a minimum period of time, but we feel that our long-range goal is defeated if he conducts a study of limited personal interest, which simply has the advantage of being "quick and dirty" in the sense of readily available data and easily controlled variables. The hope is that in dealing with social problems and issues, the student will experience some excitement along with the necessary tedium associated with any research.

3. By attempting to set the student on a problem of some personal interest, it is felt that he is more likely to master the particular area and, in turn, he will be more likely to develop a firm base for continuing research after he has completed his training. It is our impression that in many instances the doctoral psychology student never returns to research in the area in which he conducted his dissertation.

4. If the research falls within the general framework we have been describing, it is likely to have action implications. Where this is so, the student is expected to communicate this to the appropriate people. This process of communication is seen as the final and crucial stage of research training. The response to action implications provides some of the most meaningful insights into the way in which social systems operate.

5. In addition to direct communication with appropriate people, the student is expected to publish his findings in the usual professional journals. The reinforcement which can come from early publication is provided through a series of research reports published by the Institute for Social Research.

In summary, it is expected that the research conducted by the students will in some way relate to the social process aspects of mental health and that it will have a theoretical or model testing framework. This research is likely to be a community study or program evaluation with action implications. In order to illustrate some of these points, the research of recent students will be described.

Bateman's (1965) study of a state alcoholic rehabilitation program is representative of evaluation research. He was concerned with the relation between social factors and the completion of treatment in an outpatient unit, and the outcome of treatment. In order to investigate these problems, he had to spend considerable time in the agency, familiarizing himself with its operation and philosophy. But he also gained a perspective different from that of the agency in that he was out in the community interviewing ex-patients and their families. Thus he had information about the system from both the viewpoint of the professional and the eyes of the recipient of the services. Since his major focus was on the role of social variables in alcoholism, he learned something of the significance of marital status, employment history, social status, etc., as they affected admission to the service, as well as their differential relationship to his major dependent variables—remaining in treatment and outcome of treatment. His findings made it possible to make specific recommendations to the program officials.

The research of Haney (1967) also illustrates some of the general objectives mentioned above. He focused upon the contingencies which influence the likelihood of persons being declared incompetent by the courts. This called for a systematic comparison of individuals who were declared mentally incompetent with those who escaped this judgment. In order to make these comparisons, he had to survey the county courts with regard to their judicial activity, familiarize himself with court records and procedures, and interview judges and individuals who petitioned for sanity hearings. The study involved looking at demographic and ecological variables, court procedures, and the behavior of the alleged incompetent. He found extreme variability in the various counties with regard to the outcome of competency proceedings. He also found that the behavior of the deviant in and of itself was generally not the determining factor in deciding outcome. Significant factors included such things as the role of the alleged incompetent in the family, his social status relative to that of the petitioner, the composition of the examining committee, and a number of additional nonlegal and nonmedical contingencies. The study has implications for change in the state statutes regarding mental illness and it raises questions about professional stereotypes of mental illness.

Other recent studies have included an analysis of social class differences in definitions of abnormal behavior in children, the role of ministers in community mental health, critical incidents leading to hospitalization, sociological characteristics of voluntary health agencies and comparative community studies. Most of these studies involved the guidelines mentioned above and held an intrinsic interest for the student, which increased his commitment to research in community mental health.

The importance of the setting in which the research training is to occur cannot be overestimated. In the program described here, the role of the Institute for Social Research has been critical. The faculty of this institute has had considerable experience in the community and in service agencies. Along with a commitment to research, the faculty has a concern with social problems and the action implications of research. Because of continued community involvement, they have been able to provide students with access to agencies and data which are not otherwise readily available.

Until very recently, most university departments of psychology have not had faculty members who were themselves conducting research in community mental health and until this situation changes it is unlikely that students will be doing significant work in this area. If Bergen's (1965) argument that service and research must be combined in a new way is valid, there will have to be a greater representation of these models within the training faculty.

REFERENCES

Baker, F., & Schulberg, H. C. The development of a community mental health ideology. *Community Mental Health Journal,* 1967, 3, 216–225.

Baler, L. A. Training for research in community mental health. *Community Mental Health Journal,* 1967, 3, 250–253.

Bateman, N. I. Selected factors as related to outcome of treatment for hospitalized alcoholics. Unpublished doctoral dissertation, Florida State University, 1965.

Bergen, B. J. Professional communities and the evaluation of demonstration projects in community mental health. *American Journal of Public Health,* 1965, 55, 1057–1066.

Gelfand, S., & Kelly, J. G. The psychologist in community mental health: scientist and professional. *American Psychologist,* 1960, 15, 223–226.

Haney, C. A. The adjudication of incompetency—a societal designation. Unpublished doctoral dissertation, Florida State University, 1967.

Kitsuse, J. I. Societal reactions to deviant behavior: Problems of theory and method. *Social Problems,* 1962, 9, 247–256.

Reiff, R. Mental health manpower and institutional change. *American Psychologist,* 1966, 21, 540–548.

Reiff, R. Change and ferment in psychology. Division of Community Psychology. *Newsletter,* 1967, 1, 1.

Sarason, S. B. Towards a psychology of change and innovation. Psi Chi invited address, American Psychological Association Convention, 1966.

Scheff, T. J. *Being mentally ill: A sociological theory.* Chicago: Aldine Press, 1966.

Smith, M. B. Mental health reconsidered. *American Psychologist,* 1961, 16, 299–306.

V

Summary

15

The Current Status of Training in Community Psychology

Charles D. Spielberger and Ira Iscoe

The chapters in this volume reflect a number of important general trends in psychology and raise significant questions with regard to the definition and substance of community psychology. There is little doubt that the stresses encountered in a modern industrial society place many new and different demands on the human condition, and that significant advances in psychological theory, research, and practice are needed to help man cope with these stresses. It is also apparent that graduate programs in psychology must be modified if community needs for a variety of psychological services are to be met.

Can current doctoral training programs be sufficiently altered to accommodate community psychology, or must entirely new training programs be created? In order to answer this question, it will be necessary to clarify what is meant by "community psychology." As noted in Chapter 1, the concept of community psychology emerged spontaneously at the Boston (Swampscott) Conference at which a great deal of discussion was devoted to considering its dimensions and boundaries. The concept of community psychology was also of paramount importance to the participants in the Austin Symposium on which the present volume is based. These conferences along with symposia and meetings at state, regional, and national levels, reflect an increasing general awareness of the relevance of community psychology concepts for those who are currently engaged in training in such areas as industrial, school, counseling, and clinical psychology.

In this chapter we shall consider five important aspects of community psychology: (1) definitions and conceptions of community psychology; (2) the relationship between clinical and community psychology; (3) new roles for psychologists in institutional and community settings; (4) the academic foundations that seem essential for training programs in community psychology; and, (5) the kinds of field training experiences that are needed to prepare psychologists to work effectively in the community.

We are most grateful to Dr. Patrick E. Cook for his critical comments on this manuscript, and to Mrs. Pam Harrison, Mrs. Jeanne Ray, Mrs. Helen Thomas, and Mrs. Ellen Wichman for their expert editorial and clerical assistance.

CONCEPTIONS OF COMMUNITY PSYCHOLOGY

Current concerns with defining community psychology are reminiscent of early approaches to the definition of personality. Some 30 years ago, Gordon Allport (1937) noted that the term personality was used to refer to the innermost qualities of man as well as to such superficial characteristics as may be conferred by blond hair dye or pink lipstick. To paraphrase Allport, personality is a remarkably vague, remarkably elastic, and extremely attractive term that can be used without challenge in almost any context. Most psychologists are familiar with Allport's sifting of some 49 definitions of personality, and then his setting forth number 50. Though elegant in conception, this definition has received little more recognition than its many predecessors.

Certainly by now, it is evident that no single definition of personality commands wide acceptance. Yet theory and research on personality have flourished, and an increasing number of psychologists have become strongly identified with this area. It would appear, as Hall and Lindzey (1957) have suggested, that personality can be most meaningfully defined in terms of the theories proposed to account for phenomena most relevant to this particular area of psychology.

Like personality, community psychology has many different meanings and connotations. For example, at the Austin Symposium, Bernard Bloom described what most would consider to be an extreme use of the term "community psychiatry." He related an anecdote about a colleague who regarded himself as a community psychiatrist because he was seeing one patient for psychoanalytic treatment in a community mental health center!

Within the discipline of psychology, both personality and community psychology appear to reflect broad areas that must ultimately be defined by relevant theory, research, and practice. Since community psychology is a relative newcomer striving for acceptance and respectability, many community-oriented psychologists are appropriately concerned with problems of professional identity and with the basic qualifications needed to function effectively in this field. We believe that it is premature to attempt to specify professional qualifications for the practice of community psychology, except in very general terms. Furthermore, role ambiguities are to be expected in any emerging field, especially one having relevance for so many different areas of academic, professional, and social concern. Consequently, the identity and the functions of community psychologists are understandably blurred.

The Boston Conference viewed community psychology as a movement that reflects a shift in mental health efforts from the treatment of emotional disorders to their prevention. This movement's aim is the delivery of a broad spectrum of mental health services to the entire community, not merely the diagnosis and treatment of disturbed persons. Professional activities seen as particularly appropriate for community psychologists include provision of mental health consultation to institutions and social agencies, development of new methods for working with other professional groups in support of mental health programs, and collaboration with responsible lay leaders in reducing community tensions. Thus, community psychology implies a strong commitment to the promotion of positive mental health, and to the creation of an environment that will be more conducive to human growth and development and harmonious human relations.

Whatever community psychology is, it is receiving a great deal of attention and recognition. Golann, in Chapter 3 of this volume, cites evidence for this in the establishment of the *Community Mental Health Journal*,[1] the founding of the APA Division of Community Psychology,[2] and the dramatic increase in articles and books relating to community psychology. The growth of community psychology is also reflected in Golann's own surveys of doctoral programs in clinical psychology. He found that "focused attention" on community psychology, defined in terms of identifiable course content relevant to community mental health, had increased from less than 20 percent in 1962 to 44 percent by 1967. Furthermore, in 1966/67, ten departments reported a "distinguishable curriculum or specialization" in community mental health and community psychology; only a single department reported the availability of such intensive training in 1962. The latter trend is clearly reflected in the training programs that are described in Chapters 6 through 13 of this volume.

COMMUNITY PSYCHOLOGY AND CLINICAL PSYCHOLOGY

Community psychology has evolved primarily from clinical psychology, and many psychologists who now work in the community were originally trained as clinicians. Therefore, it is not surprising that the theories and methods of clinical psychology are strongly represented in this emerging field.

[1] *The Community Mental Health Journal* was founded in 1965 under the editorship of Sheldon R. Roen.

[2] Division 27 of the American Psychological Association, the Division of Community Psychology, was founded in 1966 with Robert Reiff as its first president.

As it became evident that mental health needs could not be met with available or projected professional manpower resources (Albee, 1959), concerned clinical psychologists and other mental health professionals were stimulated to explore new procedures that would extend services to larger numbers of emotionally disturbed persons. Faced with serious manpower shortages and mounting evidence that a substantial proportion of mental health problems cannot be effectively resolved or managed through traditional approaches, clinical psychologists began to question the wisdom of the investment of a major portion of their time in direct work with patients. Instead, some began to develop consulting relationships with ministers, school teachers, policemen, welfare workers, public health nurses, and other community caregivers.

In order to work productively with community caregivers, the clinical psychologist had to augment his expertise in psychodiagnosis and psychotherapy with techniques of mental health consultation. But the development of consultation skills was not enough. Knowledge of community organization and a comprehensive understanding of neighborhoods, schools, welfare departments, and other community agencies was essential for effective mental health consultation. As the focus shifted from consultation with caregivers about the emotional problems of their clients to more general concerns about the social systems that fostered these problems, the clinical psychologist moved from community mental health into the broader field of community psychology.

Most would agree that community psychology is concerned with generating theory and research that will clarify the complex interactions between individuals and social institutions. It is also concerned with developing methods and procedures that will help individuals to cope with their environments, and with tailoring environments to better meet human needs. Thus, community psychology represents a new frontier in the study of human behavior which challenges psychology and other mental health professions to develop new techniques and skills. Many new roles have already been created by legislative responses to such pressing urban problems as poverty and increasing crime rates, and these roles require psychologists to function at the social system level, rather than to work directly with casualties of the system as dictated by traditional clinical approaches.

How essential to community psychology is training in psychodiagnosis and psychotherapy, which comprise a substantial proportion of the present professional activities of clinical psychologists? Rather than a pragmatic assessment of the value of these methods as worthwhile endeavors in their own right, the answer to this question will require an analysis of the many new and different roles that are being created by the growing involvement of psychologists in community affairs.

NEW ROLES FOR PSYCHOLOGISTS IN THE COMMUNITY

The complex new roles assumed by psychologists in recent years have been described by terms such as mental health consultant, participant-conceptualizer, social systems evaluator, social change agent, and the like. This diversity of roles would seem to indicate that community psychology does not imply a homogeneous group of psychologists with a unified body of knowledge and an established set of professional procedures. Instead, as Scribner (1968, p. 4) has recently suggested: "Community psychology represents the bringing together of various kinds of psychologists who have some concern with the broad question of 'man in society.' "

On the basis of an analysis of "interest groups" within community psychology, Scribner (1968) identifies four major roles for community psychologists which she labels "social movement psychologists," "social action psychologists," "new clinical psychologists," and "social engineers." In Chapter 7 of this volume, Cowen discusses the emergence of two roles for psychologists in community settings which are more general than those described by Scribner. He calls these the "mental health quarterback" and the "social engineer." The mental health quarterback, in consultation with other professional groups, plans and implements mental health programs, and engages in activities such as the recruitment and training of nonprofessionals to work on mental health problems. The social engineer is broadly concerned with primary prevention of mental disorders and clarification of what can be done to modify social institutions to produce a healthier and more effective society.

It is beyond the scope of this chapter to attempt an exhaustive survey and evaluation of the many potential roles that challenge the community psychologist, and it is perhaps too soon even to have a clear picture of the nature of these roles. But in order to provide perspective for evaluating training needs in community psychology, we shall consider three of the new roles in which community psychologists have come to function with some regularity. The three roles are mental health consultant, participant-conceptualizer, and social change agent. Each of these roles is defined and illustrated in the following section. It should be noted that these roles are not mutually exclusive. In working with caregivers and community leaders, a psychologist may function as both mental health consultant and participant-conceptualizer, intervene as a change agent in social systems in which he also operates as a mental health consultant, and he may, at times, function simultaneously in all three roles in the same social system.

THE PSYCHOLOGIST AS MENTAL HEALTH CONSULTANT

Mental health consultation has been defined as "a helping process, an educational process, and a growth process achieved through interpersonal relationships" (Rieman, 1963, p. 85). In essence, mental health consultation provides a mechanism whereby psychologists and other mental health specialists may assist the caregiver agents of a community to utilize mental health principles in their own work. The major goals of mental health consultation are to assist caregivers in handling certain emotional problems of their clients with greater effectiveness. Important subgoals are to help caregivers recognize the symptoms of mental illness, and to assist them in making appropriate referrals to mental health specialists when this is required. It should be noted, however, that the mental health consultant does not attempt to teach specialized professional techniques such as psychodiagnosis and psychotherapy to the caregivers with whom he works.

The practice of mental health consultation has been concerned primarily with interactions between a consultant and a single consultee (Bindman, 1959; Caplan, 1964). Typically, a relationship is established when a consultee requests assistance with a problem that has been stimulated by one of his clients. The consultant then arranges to meet with the consultee to discuss the client's problem and the consultee-client relationship. When restrictions on the consultant's time make it impractical to render on-call response to individual consultee crises, group consultation procedures have proved effective (Altrocchi, Spielberger, & Eisdorfer, 1965; Kevin, 1963; Spielberger, 1967).

The role of the psychologist as a mental health consultant may be illustrated with a problem involving a delinquent youth who has been apprehended for vandalism. The psychologist can help the juvenile court judge and the probation officer to utilize more fully all of the available community resources, as well as their own professional skills. He may also provide information that will help them understand the motivational and environmental factors that contributed to the youth's delinquent behavior. For example, in clarifying basic concepts and core problems in juvenile delinquency, the psychologist-mental health consultant might distinguish between antisocial behavior, which reflects a character disorder or emotional disturbance, and dyssocial or "gang" behavior, which generally indicates adherence to a different set of social norms.

In addition to expertise in techniques of consultation, the psychologist who functions as a mental health consultant must have a comprehensive understanding of social and developmental psychology, personality, and psychopathology and other forms of social deviance, and he must be able to use this information to clarify specific problems. He must also have consultation skills which permit him to assist caregivers to work more effectively with their clients. While he may also possess high level professional skills in techniques such as psychotherapy and behavior modification, time limitations are likely to prevent him from applying these skills in the treatment of the emotional problems of his consultee's clients.

Through mental health consultation a psychologist can help key professional workers in a community become more sensitive to the needs of their clients, and more comfortable and effective in their relationships with them. In this manner his special knowledge and skills can be applied indirectly to a broader range of problems, and he can reach a much greater number of persons who need psychological assistance than would be possible in working with individual clients or patients.

THE PSYCHOLOGIST AS A PARTICIPANT-CONCEPTUALIZER

Although the community psychologist may be called upon as an expert in the field of mental health, he must make it clear to those who seek his assistance that emotional disorders often reflect social system problems, as well as instances of individual deviance. For example, juvenile delinquency denotes not merely a set of symptoms that exist in isolation, but behaviors that occur within a social context. Consequently, the basic structure of the social system that produces the problem may require modification along with the behaviors of deviant individuals within the system.

As a participant-conceptualizer, the primary role of the psychologist is not that of an expert with special information or technical skills, but as an expert with special conceptual skills. His task is to help community leaders analyze and clarify mental health problems in terms of social system variables. After a problem is clarified, however, the psychologist may then function as a mental health consultant to formulate meaningful programs that will eliminate or alleviate the problem.

As a participant-conceptualizer, the psychologist must be aware of the dangers inherent in problem-solving to meet current emergencies. Most mental health efforts have been after-the-fact attempts to deal with immediate symptoms. Of course, solving current problems without adequate consideration of future needs is not limited to mental health; unfortunately it is a way of life in our society. Superhighways are obsolete the day they are completed and requirements for airport facilities are generally grossly underestimated. Obviously, more information and a better conceptual understanding of such problems would result in better planning and more effective solutions.

Since there will always be problems it will be increasingly important to anticipate their development, and to establish mechanisms to deal with them as they arise. This will become even more important as the population grows and interrelationships among problems become more complex. For example, what will happen to Headstart children if they come to elementary school with questioning attitudes instead of apathy? What types of teachers will be needed to work with these children? Civil rights legislation will mean increased interaction and emotional contact between blacks and whites in the United States. Our failure to prepare for this interaction has already resulted in disastrous consequences in Watts, Newark, Detroit, and Washington, and in a general heightening of racial tensions.

The difficulty of the decisions that will have to be made as our society becomes more complex staggers the imagination. Yet cooperative endeavors must be fostered if the nation is to continue to grow. The psychologist as a participant-conceptualizer can have an important, perhaps even a central role in this enterprise, but he will need to draw upon knowledge from such fields as community organization, sociology, urban planning, economics, and political science. Although most applied psychologists typically have little detailed knowledge of these areas, because of their training in science and special expertise in mental health, they can often serve effectively as a bridge between the community and other social science disciplines.

In the role of participant-conceptualizer the psychologist must be constantly aware of the possibility that any innovative solution he proposes may be threatening to those with vested interests in existing problem-solving mechanisms. For example, if it is advocated that delinquents be treated closer to their home towns, this may threaten professionals who run residential centers, as well as the economy of the communities in which these centers are located. Indeed, the economic importance of juvenile detention homes, special training schools, state mental hospitals, prisons, and facilities for the mentally retarded often perpetuates the continuance of these institutions long after they have outlived their usefulness as treatment resources.

In the solution of human problems it is generally much easier to implement physical changes in a community than it is to introduce social changes. While there will always be those who oppose new housing projects or rapid transit systems for economic or political reasons, opposition to social change will run the gamut from personal and professional jealousies to class differences and racial prejudice, all rooted in deeply ingrained emotional attitudes. Therefore, psychologists who work in the community must be sensitive to the inevitable resistances that new programs can be expected to generate because of economic, political, and personal commitments to existing mechanisms.

The Psychologist as a Social Change Agent

The psychologist who functions as a clinician generally works directly with emotionally disturbed clients or patients. As a mental health consultant, he helps community caregivers to recognize and to work more effectively with their clients' emotional problems. In the role of participant-conceptualizer, the psychologist's conceptual skills help community leaders to clarify mental health problems at the social system level and to formulate solutions to these problems. A psychologist may also attempt to bring about modifications in a social system through his own professional activities. When he does, he functions as a social change agent.

The psychologist's role as an agent of social change differs from that of a participant-conceptualizer to the extent that he attempts to solve the problems he has helped to clarify. He may do this by working directly on a problem himself, or he may train others. For example, an effective means for combating juvenile delinquency might involve working with delinquent gangs or training indigenous nonprofessionals to operate as gang members or street corner workers. The latter approach has a number of advantages. Persons who have the same sociocultural backgrounds as potential delinquents are more likely to be able to gain the confidence of young people from disadvantaged environments than professionals with middle-class backgrounds. They are also more likely to be available at times of crisis to help redirect the behavior of the potential delinquent towards socially acceptable goals.

In order to be effective as a social change agent, the psychologist will often need to work in institutions that are not generally regarded as mental health facilities. Schools, community centers, settlement houses, and storefront operations in slum neighborhoods are settings in which mental health specialists can make contact with the residents of a particular neighborhood, especially with persons from culturally deprived groups who rarely visit mental health centers. Only after the mental health specialist gains the acceptance and confidence of a community can he help its residents to discover more appropriate means for satisfying their needs.

The work of I. G. Sarason with adolescent delinquent boys (Sarason, 1968; Sarason & Ganzer, 1969) provides an excellent example of how psychologists can function effectively as agents of social change. Sarason and his colleagues first established a good working relationship with the staff of a residential diagnostic and treatment center for delinquent children. On the basis of conferences with the center staff, it was determined that delinquent boys needed special help in vocational planning, and in the development of positive attitudes toward work and education. It was assumed that if these boys were given an opportunity to observe socially acceptable behaviors in healthy persons, and to practice these behaviors themselves, their repertoire of appropriate responses could be enlarged and strengthened.

Rather than working directly with the delinquents themselves, Sarason and his colleagues trained and supervised nonprofessional personnel who carried out the remedial efforts. They experimented with a number of procedures which included the development of dialogue scripts pertaining to job interviews and on-the-job interactions with supervisors. At informal sessions, attended by delinquents and college students who served as "models," the models acted out sample scenes from the prepared scripts and the delinquents were called upon to summarize and explain the content. Then pairs of delinquents imitated and practiced the roles, and their behavior was videotaped and discussed. These modeling procedures proved to be highly effective in bringing about important changes in the behavior of the delinquents.

It should be noted that Sarason and his colleagues functioned as mental health consultants, as participant-conceptualizers, and as change agents. They assisted institutional personnel to identify and clarify some of the special problems of delinquent boys, and they suggested specific procedures for modifying the delinquents' behavior. Finally, they selected and trained additional personnel to apply these procedures. Thus, the psychologists' role as change agents also involved active participation in the program as conceptualizers, as trainers, and as consultants who served as sources of information, but not as clinicians who worked directly with individual delinquents.

The work of Cowen and Zax at the University of Rochester further illustrates the changing role of the psychologist in community settings (Cowen, Zax, Izzo, & Trost, 1966; Cowen & Zax, 1967; Zax & Cowen, 1969). The Rochester group set out to identify and prevent emotional dysfunctions in elementary school children. The first stage in the program involved consultation with school psychologists, social workers, and administrative personnel regarding selected groups of children. It was found that the potential for school maladjustment, reflected in a variety of indices such as achievement measures, classroom behavior ratings, and clinical judgments, could be observed in these children as early as the first grade. Furthermore, follow-up studies in the third and seventh grades showed that early problems persisted and often became more pronounced.

After demonstrating that it was possible to identify the potential for long-lasting emotional dysfunction in first-grade children, Cowen, Zax and their colleagues introduced several new programs designed to prevent or reduce the development of maladaptive characteristics. These programs were broadly oriented toward working with school personnel and parents rather than with the children themselves. The initial goals were to use school mental health workers as consultants rather than as professionals who rendered direct services to children. Conferences were held with teachers and other school personnel, including the principal, the school nurse, the attendance teacher, the speech therapist, special subject-matter teachers, and a psychiatric consultant who worked closely with the project. Meetings were also held with parents to discuss topics such as child development and the emotional needs of young children.

On the basis of their experiences in consultation, Cowen and Zax concluded that direct interventive contact with children was also required to maximize the probability of success for preventive efforts. Consequently, a new program for the training of teacher aides (TAs) was developed. The principle objective of this program was to make immediately available to children who needed help the attention of a warm, mature adult who was interested in working with them. It was anticipated that the TA would provide these children with special help that could not be given by the regular classroom teacher without depriving other children of the teacher's attention.

The TAs were selected and trained by Cowen and Zax, and assigned to work in the classroom with regular teachers. However, some teachers developed negative feelings toward the TAs because they felt that the TAs' working relationship with the children was more favorable than their own. Consequently, the TA was removed from her full-time classroom assignment and made available to work with children considered to have emotional difficulties only when this was requested by the classroom teacher. This modification in the format of the program succeeded in bringing teachers and TAs closer together in sharing their concerns about individual children. Not only was the friction between teachers and TAs reduced, but also each gained a better understanding and acceptance of the contributions of the other. The TA program has subsequently served as a model for other conceptually similar programs in which retired persons and college student volunteers are trained to work with children experiencing difficulties in school (Cowen, Leibowitz, & Leibowitz, 1968; Zax & Cowen, 1967).

In summary, psychologists currently function as mental health consultants, participant-conceptualizers, and social change agents. Even as these roles are clarified, new ones emerge—as might be expected for a rapidly developing area of increasing professional commitment within the field of psychology. But once community psychology has become institutionalized there is danger of complacency. Indeed, Miller, in Chapter 14 of this volume, questions whether the death knell of community psychology was sounded with the formation of Division 27. He speaks from a broad knowledge of social process and from the context of his own program which provides research training in the sociology of mental health.

Until recently, as we have previously noted, psychologists have tended to remain aloof from the realm of public affairs and they have made only limited contributions to the determination of public policy. However, as mental health consultants and participant-conceptualizers, psychologists with appropriate theoretical background and training will be called upon to play increasingly important roles in the planning and development of community services. As agents of social change, psychologists will be asked to participate in the modification of existing social structures. Effectiveness in these new roles will be determined in large measure by the adequacy of graduate training programs in psychology. Therefore, it would seem to be of critical importance to examine at this time the academic foundations on which community psychology will be built, and the practicum experiences that will enable psychologists of the future to function in the many new roles that are being created by society's needs.

ACADEMIC FOUNDATIONS OF COMMUNITY PSYCHOLOGY

As an emerging field, community psychology must draw upon the resources of a number of overlapping areas within psychology for its basic knowledge and professional techniques. Research findings and theoretical advances in social psychology, personality, abnormal psychology, developmental psychology, perception, and learning are of particular relevance to community psychology, but information from these areas will require a special kind of integration. In addition, while many of the techniques and methods of school, industrial, counseling, and clinical psychology are of potential value to the community psychologist, they will require modification and refinement if they are to be applied within a broader community context.

As community psychology has developed, there is also increasing recognition of the importance of contributions from other disciplines. Reiff, in Chapter 2 of this volume, has stated that it is no longer adequate merely to train clinical psychologists with a community orientation because the knowledge base for clinical psychology is too restricted. Since community psychology is broader than clinical psychology, it requires training inputs that should not be limited to the core courses and practicum experiences presently required of clinical psychologists. For psychologists who wish to function effectively in community settings, the contributions of such fields as sociology, anthropology, social psychiatry, economics, political science, social work, community organization, urban planning, and systems analysis are likely to be more relevant than some of the traditional areas of experimental psychology.

Among the current educational requirements in doctoral psychology programs, what content areas are most essential for community psychology? What kinds of educational inputs from other disciplines are needed? Reiff pleads for the broadest possible base as he emphasizes the need to look at old problems in new ways, to achieve new integrations of existing knowledge, and to generate new knowledge. Golann suggests that training in community psychology should adopt a generalist rather than a specialist model, and he advocates training experiences for psychology students in collaboration with other professions. Indeed, there is a clear consensus among the contributors to this volume that community psychology requires a broader range of knowledge and experience than is presently provided in most training programs.

Levine, in Chapter 5 of this volume, voices serious concern about deficiencies in psychology training programs. He expresses the feeling that students are often diverted from the significant problems of living which initially attracted them to psychology. In many graduate programs students are required to become involved with the "important problems" that academic, laboratory-oriented psychologists have identified as the ones that need to be solved first. Levine contends that university training in the social and psychological sciences is esoteric, often irrelevant and trivial, and more concerned with method than with substance. It should be noted that Levine also criticizes the prevailing orthodoxies in clinical practice which inhibit innovation by focusing upon the application of methods of limited utility.

It is apparent that the community psychologist requires, at the very least, a basic understanding of community organization and social institutions if he is to work effectively with caregivers and community leaders as a mental health consultant and participant-conceptualizer. This knowledge is particularly important to the psychologist who is called upon to intervene in complex social systems as a change agent. But in order to accommodate educational inputs from other disciplines, it will be necessary either to lengthen existing doctoral training programs or to modify their content. Since many doctoral programs in clinical psychology already require six to seven years of graduate work, the prospect of extending them is not very attractive.

Despite the objections that may be expressed to eliminating traditional courses and practicum experiences in psychology in order to make room for courses from other disciplines, training programs in community psychology will be forced to become more selective. It would seem necessary to dispense with the more molecular aspects of psychology to provide for intensive training in the most relevant areas, and to permit significant contributions from other disciplines. In effect, such changes have been incorporated into the newly established clinical psychology training program at the City University of New York which is described by Singer and Bard in Chapter 8. "Some things had to give" in this program to make room for seminars in Social Psychopathology and Small Group Dynamics and Family Interaction, which may be taken instead of courses in less relevant areas.

In addition to providing courses in appropriate content areas, it will also be important to provide training in research methods that are more pertinent to the problems of community psychology. For example, courses in epidemiology and demography, biometrics, attitude measurement, and survey research are likely to be more useful than small-sample, inferential statistics. Knowledge of computer methods for the treatment of data and the simulation of complex processes will also be essential to community psychologists who intend to carry out research on complex social system problems. In addition, the community psychologist will need to have a general understanding of the research methods in other social sciences.

PRACTICUM TRAINING IN COMMUNITY PSYCHOLOGY

One point emerges with clarity from the descriptions in this volume of community psychology training programs. All of the authors seem to agree that it is extremely important to expose graduate students to everyday problems of living in the natural settings in which these problems occur. Confrontation with problems at the scene of the action is called for, not merely academic conversations about these problems in the classroom.

To prepare students to work with real problems in community settings, Roen recommends early exposure to a broad range of applications of psychological knowledge as an integral part of graduate training. He notes that the basic question for psychology has changed from "what is the nature of man?" to the contextual question of "what happens at the interface of inner man and problem world?" In a similar vein, Levine challenges prevailing explanations of mental illness based on the concept of "intrapsychic supremacy"—the assumption that internal events are the primary determinants of emotional disorders and personality disorganization. He suggests, instead, that situational factors and the social context in which mental health problems arise are of central importance.

The active involvement of psychologists in the community poses important questions as to the nature of the settings in which practicum training may best be carried out and the kinds of practicum experiences that are required. Roen notes that many practicum facilities were originally organized as laboratories to meet the needs of academic subspecialties. Clients or patients were selected for study and treatment because they had problems that provided students with opportunities to practice special techniques. Thus, the choice of practicum agencies influences the techniques that are learned, and the professional psychological services that are available to the community. It is apparent that the basic philosophy of the agencies and institutions in which community psychologists are trained, as well as the primary functions of these agencies, will have a profound influence on the skills that are developed and, more importantly, on the psychologist's basic attitudes toward his clients and his professional work.

Golann presents a model, or general frame of reference as we would prefer to view it, within which it is possible to analyze the strategies that currently prevail in the delivery of mental health services. He proposes an ecological framework that takes into account community resources and the special nature of mental health transactions that take place between caregivers and the recipients of their services. Levine provides a number of postulates which amplify the frame of reference suggested by Golann, and emphasizes the importance of the locus of the helping agent relative to those being helped. Levine recommends that mental health programs make better use of the manpower resources indigenous to a particular setting to enhance the congruence of goals and values of the helping agent with those of the persons who receive his services.

The need to develop new facilities that permit psychologists to make more effective contributions in community settings is clearly recognized in the programs described in this volume. Roen suggests that psychology departments give serious consideration to Albee's (1964) proposal for psychological service centers, or that they establish neighborhood centers oriented toward a wide range of human problems. Levine also envisions a neighborhood center located in the midst of a densely populated urban area. He recommends that staff members and their families actually live at this center. In addition to psychologists, the center staff would consist of representatives of a variety of disciplines such as sociology, city planning, law, economics, medicine, nursing, and education. Levine would also include budding novelists, artists, poets, and indigenous nonprofessional workers as staff members.

Training in community psychology at Peabody College involves a series of unique field placements of increasing complexity. In their first practicum assignment students in the Peabody program investigate a selected aspect of the community. They often work with a citizen volunteer who has knowledge of the community (e.g., a member of the Junior League) in the collection of relevant information. The student's second placement is devoted to providing consultation to a community agency or program. In subsequent assignments, advanced students may participate in the evaluation of a community research project.

The Peabody faculty took the initiative in organizing a Center for Community Studies that provides a common ground for different academic disciplines to pursue community related research. A major goal of the center is to advance knowledge of individual and group behavior by carrying out research on topics such as poverty, the impact of health services, and the evaluation of a suicide prevention center. Staff members of the center have also worked with the mayor's office in planning urban renewal and neighborhood projects.

In Chapter 7, Cowen describes a year-long practicum experience at the University of Rochester that is required of doctoral students in clinical psychology during their final year of training. Students are provided with a broad spectrum of experiences with mental health agencies and planning groups. Students may be assigned, for example, to work in day-care programs located in elementary schools, in settlement houses in which indigenous Negro adolescents serve as companions for eight-year-old neighborhood children, or in programs for training teacher aides to work with school children who experience emotional difficulties. Such programs bring graduate students closer to the problems of the poor and to the environments in which they work and live.

The new program in clinical psychology at the City University of New York described by Singer and Bard in Chapter 8 is not constrained by the traditional values and approaches that many established clinical training programs must overcome. Recognizing the limitations inherent in traditional approaches, a Psychological Services Center located in an urban environment was developed by the City University faculty. Clients are evaluated and treated in their own milieu; they do not have to submit themselves to the scrutiny of mental health professionals on the latters' home grounds. There is a strong emphasis on field experiences in a variety of community agencies, and on developmental and longitudinal approaches. The training that is provided in consultation in this program is representative of the "new look" in clinical psychology, or perhaps more accurately, in community-oriented clinical psychology.

Sarason and Levine, in Chapter 9, describe the psycho-educational clinic that was developed as an integral part of the Yale University Psychology Department. This clinic is quite different from conventional mental health facilities in that it serves as a headquarters for students and faculty, rather than a work-setting (Sarason, Levine, Goldenberg, Cherlin, & Bennett, 1966). The staff spends its time as consultants, participant-conceptualizers, and change agents in community agencies such as public schools, centers for the mentally retarded, and various projects sponsored by the New Haven Community Action Program.

The program at the University of Colorado described by Bloom in Chapter 10 provides a two-year sequence of courses in community mental health, primarily for doctoral students in clinical psychology. Epidemiological methods, approaches to primary and secondary prevention of emotional disorders, and research problems in community mental health are emphasized. One year of clinical practicum is prerequisite for field placement in community-based action programs relevant to mental health, in comprehensive community mental health centers, and in other public and private community agencies that provide health and welfare services. Supervised experience is provided in mental health consultation, crisis intervention, mental health education, and research on a variety of topics. Students also obtain experience in action programs designed to reduce school dropouts, alcoholism and drug addiction, juvenile delinquency, and other forms of social deviance.

Students in the Community Mental Health Training Program at the University of Texas described by Iscoe in Chapter 11 obtain supervised practicum experience in a variety of community settings. They are assigned to public schools, to a juvenile court and probation department, and to the Hogg Foundation for Mental Health, a private foundation which supports programs in mental health education and applications of behavioral science to mental health. Students are also assigned to the Human Opportunities Corporation, the official municipal agency for coordinating community action programs such as Day Care, Headstart, Upward Bound, the Neighborhood Youth Corps, and other special programs. In these assignments students are supervised by university faculty and by the directors and staff at the various agencies.

The locus of the multidisciplinary field training program described by Altrocchi and Eisdorfer in Chapter 12 is a small rural county in North Carolina. The coordinating headquarters for this training program is in the county health department, but there is active involvement with the entire community. Intensive training is provided in mental health consultation in a variety of community settings and supervised field training experiences are emphasized. Trainees observe senior mental health consultants in group consultation with school teachers, nurses, policemen, and ministers, and in individual consultation with a variety of community caregivers.

The Human Relations Center at Boston University described by Lipton and Klein in Chapter 13 is a unique setting which provides training in community psychology in a multidisciplinary context. Through a fellowship program graduate students from such diverse fields as philosophy, theology, law, business, psychology, sociology, social work, nursing, and education receive stipends for one or two years of study. Frequent contact with other disciplines serves to challenge and stimulate students to examine their personal values as well as prevailing practices in their own field. All students take a practicum course in human relations in which a modified T-group approach helps trainees develop a deeper understanding and greater awareness of themselves and others.

In Chapter 14, Miller describes a research training program in sociology that draws upon a multidisciplinary faculty of economists, political scientists, city planners, and psychologists, as well as sociologists. Students in this program are required to spend a minimum of two summers in field placements such as the state department of mental health, local mental health centers, and other community agencies. These students are trained to do field research which brings them into contact with agency people and community leaders. Specific research projects have been carried out on alcoholic rehabilitation, social class differences in the definition of abnormal behavior, sociological characteristics of health agencies, and other topics relevant to the sociology of mental health.

CURRENT STATUS OF TRAINING IN COMMUNITY PSYCHOLOGY

The training programs in community psychology described in this volume by no means encompass all of the models and strategies presently in operation in this field, nor do they exhaust the many roles in which psychologists may contribute to community affairs. These programs do, however, provide outstanding examples of current training in community psychology and of the creative imagination and innovative vigor of psychologists presently involved in this area.

We have previously noted that community psychology represents a new frontier in the study of human behavior, which is broadly concerned with clarifying the complex interrelationships between individuals and their environment. In a few short years a variety of new roles have emerged for psychologists in community settings, and one may safely predict that these trends will continue. But in order to function effectively in these new roles, psychologists must have a great deal of practical information and knowledge about communities. To obtain this knowledge, the contributors to this volume recommend that psychology graduate students be exposed to a wide range of applications of psychology in both traditional and nontraditional community agencies.

The Yale Psycho-Educational Clinic, the Psychological Services Center at the City University of New York, the Peabody Center for

Community Studies, and the Human Relations Center at Boston University provide excellent examples of the kinds of innovative training, research, and service settings being developed to meet the needs of psychologists who are interested in working in the community. Such facilities permit psychologists, often in collaboration with representatives of other disciplines, to make more unique and effective contributions to the community.

Given the complexities of social institutions, it is difficult, if not impossible, to forecast the new directions in which community psychology may develop. It is likely, however, that in the future psychologists will more often be called upon to function as mental health consultants, participant-conceptualizers, and social change agents than as diagnosticians and psychotherapists. It is also to be expected that new roles for psychologists in the community will continue to emerge. Whatever these new roles and directions may be, it is apparent that the preparation of psychologists to work in the community must include academic foundations and practicum experiences that will enable them to function more effectively at the social system level.

The late Rev. Martin Luther King, in his distinguished invited address to the American Psychological Association in September, 1967, called upon behavioral scientists to lend their knowledge and skills to the civil rights movement. Little visible behavioral science activity was apparently fostered by Dr. King's appeal. It is not that he spoke to an unreceptive audience. On the contrary, he received a standing ovation. The problem then, as now, was in shifting the locus of concern from the psychology laboratory of the university to the more complex, but potentially more rewarding, laboratory of the community.

Given the press of recent events, it appears that psychology may now be more willing to accept Dr. King's challenge. The theme for the 1969 Annual Meeting of the American Psychological Association, "Psychology and the Problems of Society," suggests that a new era has begun. The next decade poses tremendous challenges for psychology and especially for community psychology.

REFERENCES

Albee, G. W. *Mental health manpower trends.* New York: Basic Books, 1959.

Albee, G. W. A declaration of independence for psychology. *Ohio Psychologist,* 1964, **10,** 2–5.

Allport, G. W. *Personality: A psychological interpretation.* New York: Holt, 1937.

Altrocchi, J., Spielberger, C. D., & Eisdorfer, C. Mental health consultation with groups. *Community Mental Health Journal,* 1965, **1,** 127–134.

Bindman, A. J. Mental health consultation: Theory and practice. *Journal of Consulting Psychology*, 1959, 23, 473–482.

Caplan, G. *Principles of preventive psychiatry*. New York: Basic Books, 1964.

Cowen, E. L., Leibowitz, E., & Leibowitz, G. Utilization of retired people as mental health aides with children. *American Journal of Orthopsychiatry*, 1968, 3 (5) , 900–909.

Cowen, E. L., & Zax, M. The mental health fields today: Issues and problems. In E. L. Cowen, E. A. Gardner, & M. Zax (Eds.), *Emergent approaches to mental health problems*. New York: Appleton-Century-Crofts, 1967. Pp. 3–29.

Cowen, E. L., Zax, M., Izzo, L. D., & Trost, M. A. Prevention of emotional disorders in the school setting: A further investigation. *Journal of Consulting Psychology*, 1966, 30, 381–387.

Hall, C. S., & Lindzey, G. *Theories of personality*. New York: Wiley, 1967.

Kevin, D. Use of the group method in consultation. In L. Rapaport (Ed.), *Consultation in social work practice*. New York: National Association of Social Workers, 1963. Pp. 69–84.

Rieman, D. W. Group mental health consultation with public health nurses. In L. Rapaport (Ed.), *Consultation in social work practice. Op. cit.* Pp. 85–98.

Sarason, I. G. Verbal learning, modeling, and juvenile delinquency. *American Psychologist*, 1968, 23, 254–266.

Sarason, I. G. & Ganzer, V. J. Social influence techniques in clinical and community psychology. In C. D. Spielberger (Ed.) *Current topics in clinical and community psychology*. New York: Academic Press, 1969, Pp. 1–66.

Sarason, S., Levine, M., Goldenberg, I., Cherlin, D. L., & Bennett, E. M. *Psychology in community settings*. New York: Wiley, 1966.

Scribner, S. What is community psychology made of? American Psychological Association, Division of Community Psychology. *Newsletter*, 1968, 2, 4–6.

Spielberger, C. D. A mental health consultation program in a small community with limited professional mental health resources. In E. L. Cowen, E. A. Gardner, & M. Zax (Eds.), *Emergent approaches to mental health problems. Op. cit.* Pp. 214–236.

Zax, M. & Cowen, E. L. Research on early detection and prevention of emotional dysfunction in young school children. In C. D. Spielberger (Ed.) *Current topics in clinical and community psychology. Op. cit.* Pp. 67–108.

Appendices

APPENDIX I

Community Mental Health Training Program, the University of Texas

An informal symposium on Training in Community Psychology was held April 20–22, 1967, in Austin, Texas, under the auspices of the Community Mental Health Training Program, Department of Psychology, the University of Texas. This symposium was supported from Training Grant 10502-01, Training Branch, National Institute of Mental Health, and the Hogg Foundation for Mental Health. A condensed version of the program is presented below and followed by the names of the key participants.

Thursday, April 20, 1967

Greetings and welcome. Gardner Lindzey, Professor and Chairman, Department of Psychology, the University of Texas.

An overview of concepts and training in community psychology and mental health. Stuart Golann, Associate Administrative Officer for State and Professional Affairs, American Psychological Association.

Is there a body of knowledge useful for the training of community psychologists? Robert Reiff, Associate Professor and Director, Division of Psychology, Albert Einstein College of Medicine, and President Pro-Tem, Division of Community Psychology (27), American Psychological Association.

Some postulates of community mental practice. Murray Levine, Director, Clinical Training Program, Department of Psychology, Yale University.

The psychological foundations of a community-oriented clinical psychology training program. Jerome Singer, Professor of Psychology and Director, Clinical Training Program, City College of the City University of New York.

A psychology for community development. James Kelly, Associate Professor of Psychology, University of Michigan.

Some preliminary thoughts on training in community mental health in departments of psychology. Bernard Bloom, Professor of Psychology, University of Colorado.

Summation. Charles Spielberger, Professor of Psychology and Director of Clinical Psychology Training Program, Florida State University.

Friday, April 21, 1967

Community centered training. Herbert Lipton, Associate Professor, Department of Psychology and Human Relations Center, Boston University, and Faculty Coordinator, Community Psychology Training.

New interpretations of the requirements in educating psychologists for professional practice and applied research. Sheldon Roen, Associate Professor of Psychology, Teachers College, Columbia University.

Community psychology, social processes, and deviant behavior. Kent Miller, Professor of Psychology and Sociology, Florida State University.

Community psychology from the point of view of trainees in a program. Linda Burke, Daniel Klein, Don Boulware, Durwood Bell, doctoral students, Community Mental Health Training Program, the University of Texas.

The community psychology trainee as seen by community and state agencies. Louis DeMoll, Acting Deputy Commissioner, Division of Community Services, Texas Department of Mental Health and Mental Retardation. Victor Ehlers, Executive Director, Community Council of Austin and Travis County. James Hubbard, Director of Guidance, Austin Public Schools. David Latz, Assistant to Director, the Hogg Foundation for Mental Health.

Key Participants

From the University of Texas, Austin:
  Ivan Belknap, Professor of Sociology
  Wayne H. Holtzman, Dean, College of Education
  Gardner Lindzey, Chairman, Department of Psychology
  Jack Otis, Director, Graduate School of Social Work
  Robert L. Sutherland, Director, the Hogg Foundation for Mental
    Health
  James Bieri, Professor of Psychology
  Charles Laughton, Professor of Social Work
  Norman Prentice, Professor of Psychology
  Fillmore Sanford, Professor of Psychology
John Altrocchi, Director of Clinical Training, Duke University

Lenin Baler, Professor of Psychology, Boston College
Louis Cohen, Professor of Psychology, University of Florida
John von Felsinger, Chairman, Department of Psychology, Boston College
John Kinross-Wright, M.S., Commissioner, Texas Department of Mental Health and Mental Retardation
David Rigler, Training and Manpower Resources, National Institute of Mental Health
David Stein, Postdoctoral Fellow of Psychology, Albert Einstein College of Medicine
Forrest Tyler, Training and Manpower Resources, National Institute of Mental Health
Shalom Vineberg, Professor of Psychology, University of Houston

APPENDIX II

Postdoctoral Fellows in Community Mental Health Assess Their Training

The programs described in this volume attest to the fact that there is an increasing emphasis on community psychology within predoctoral training programs. It is also apparent that there is much more to be learned about community psychology than can be mastered during the usual period of graduate training. To meet the needs for advanced training in community psychology, a number of postdoctoral programs have developed. It seems reasonable to expect that as psychologists become more conscious of the community they will seek the additional training and experience they require in specialized settings such as postdoctoral programs provide.

A symposium, Voices of the New Psychologists: Postdoctoral Fellows in Community Mental Health Assess Their Training, was sponsored by the Division of Community Psychology (Div. 27) at the annual meeting of the American Psychological Association in September, 1967. This symposium was chaired by Gershen Rosenblum; Sylvain Nagler, David Stein, and Robert Toal were the participants; and J. R. Newbrough and Joseph C. Speisman were the invited discussants.

In order to provide those interested in community psychology with the fresh perspective of young psychologists who have just completed a period of postdoctoral training in this area, the editors invited the participants in the Division 27 symposium to contribute their papers to this volume. The personal assessment and evaluations of the three postdoctoral fellows who participated in the APA symposium are presented in the following pages.

Reflections on the Community Mental Health Program of Albert Einstein College of Medicine, Yeshiva University

David Stein

I should like to begin this assessment of my postdoctoral fellowship with some comments about how I became interested in this general area and what I hoped to accomplish through this training experience. During my final year in graduate school, 1964/65, I had come to the conclusion that something very significant was missing from my otherwise excellent academic preparation. I couldn't quite put my finger on it at the time, but I remember feeling that the issues and concerns of academic psychology, and in particular social psychology, were not consonant with the tempo of the events taking place in our society. We were all witness to a violent civil rights struggle which impinged upon us daily through the news media, and most forcefully via television. Sheriff Clark's dogs and electric prods often held a place in our homes at night, and reports of the disappearances and deaths of civil rights workers were common. Students all around me were enlisting to serve in one capacity or another in the South. Or they participated in sit-ins at local business establishments to protest blatant discriminatory practices.

Many of these same students were also quite active in protests against the war in Vietnam. In short, the country was experiencing violent upheavals in the civil rights arena, and the war in Vietnam had begun to take its stranglehold on the lives and minds of the American people. And students were up in arms and fighting—protesting and demanding justice in a world that had turned its ears from reason and prudence. In contrast, in the ivory tower the impact of these events was muted and constrained. We spoke constantly of the tragedies in the South and in the northern ghettos, and of the futility of our position in Vietnam. But the business of the day was writing papers, preparing for exams, and discussing theories and research findings.

I need not elaborate here on the disjunctive relationship between much of academia and the problems in the outside world. But I was deeply affected by this schism and its impact tended to interact with another inconsistency—that within the domain of psychology itself. One cannot undergo a number of years of rigorous work in the study of human behavior without wondering where the "affect" went. I was quite puzzled by the absence of practically any reference to human emotion and the joys of living. With the exception of abnormal psychology, they certainly were not to be found in seminars, textbooks, or scholarly journals. It seemed that psychologists who studied human behavior had left out the very guts of the human condition.

A rare opportunity presented itself, which on a small scale helped correct this deficiency. The student unrest on campuses throughout the country found grounds not only in the civil rights struggle and in the war in Vietnam, but also right at home—in the administrations of the universities. Students were being treated indifferently and it was no exaggeration, in many cases, to compare their state to that of an IBM card. Alienation of the student was a crucial problem, and in the halls and classrooms of the psychology department a partial solution was discovered. The upper division course in group dynamics offered a laboratory section which was devoted entirely to a sensitivity training (T-group) experience for the students. Advanced graduate students in social and clinical psychology served as trainers and participated in a seminar to discuss both the practical and theoretical issues involved. The class enrollment for the course tripled and quadrupled in a little over a year, and more and more graduate students wanted a chance to gain experience as trainers.

For me the missing link had turned up, and my thinking about the issues in social psychology began to take on a whole new dimension. My ideas started to fit into a larger frame of reference which included not only cognitive and social aspects of behavior but the emotional as well. My closest friends were graduate students in clinical psychology and I envied the kind of experiential training they received in their internships. Yet I was the first to criticize them for holding such a narrow perspective in their approach. None of them paid more than cursory attention to the body of knowledge in social psychology. It seemed irrelevant to them. To me social psychology was vitally important because of its broad scope, yet it lacked the emotionality that was attendant to clinical concerns.

My thoughts were moving toward some kind of theory or system that could encompass the uniqueness of each individual and at the same time tie it to larger levels of social organization. The seminal writers in psychology and sociology who have dealt with this issue didn't seem to bring it off in a way that was satisfactory, at least to me.

About that time I began to make inquiries into postdoctoral training programs around the country and received an unusually interested reply from Bob Reiff at Einstein. He happened to be in Berkeley for a few days and we got together to discuss our interests. They coincided considerably and we agreed to undertake an "experimental" training program—one that would hopefully lead to the development of a new kind of psychologist. Since my training was in social psychology and postdoctoral fellowships of this type are given traditionally only to clinical psychologists, it was necessary for the requirement of a predoctoral internship to be waived.

I arrived in New York in September, 1965, and sat down with Bob Reiff to work out a plan for my training. He suggested that I get a good exposure to clinical psychology and psychiatry since I had had no practicum experience. We agreed that the main purpose of this experience was to get a feel for the clinical method, but to view it as a social psychologist might—in terms of its functioning as a system and its relationship to allied social systems.

I spent the first two to three months of my fellowship participating to a greater or lesser degree in some of the following activities: attending psychiatric case conferences and ward meetings, watching in-patient therapy groups through a one-way screen, learning how to give a standard clinical test battery to patients, and participating in seminars on issues in community mental health, new methods in group therapy and process, and child development. I also began to study with Bob on the selection of nursing aides. Bob and some of the other staff psychologists supervised me in these activities.

These were not happy months for me. In a way I felt as though the props had been pulled out from under me. With few exceptions everyone talked the language of the unconscious and everything was geared to psychopathology. I got particularly upset at the similarities between patients' problems and their childhood experiences and my own. Although I realized that there were basic differences between us, I found it somewhat difficult to erect barriers that would both allow me to differentiate myself from them and still be open enough to listen and to empathize with their problems. Having our offices right on the in-patient ward didn't make things easier at the time.

In addition, I had come to this setting with a strong research orientation and a tendency, perhaps pedantic, to back up my comments with research findings. I was dismayed at how most clinicians drew exclusively from the clinical literature and how uninterested they were in putting their propositions and interpretations to empirical test. I often felt thwarted in discussions in my efforts to bring in material from the social psychological literature because it seemed so out of context. So much of my academic training seemed irrelevant.

Yet at the same time I was gaining exposure to the clinical world in practical settings, I was building up a knowledge of the issues in com-

munity mental health and community psychology. To work with someone like Bob Reiff at this time and under these rather trying circumstances was of inestimable value. For Bob possesses the rare qualities of
a clinician par excellence and at the same time views society's problems
in a larger context. Our dovetailing interests in trying to conceptualize
a framework for including the individual in a larger social system led
us into many long and involved discussions.

We spent much time talking about the potential of the nonprofessional as a social force capable of significantly altering the distribution and utilization of mental health services. My time spent at neighborhood service centers helped considerably in pulling these ideas together. This theme led us into a related one regarding the different
personality styles of the nonprofessionals as contrasted with those of the
middle-class professionals and how these differences, in many respects,
influenced decisions regarding who received what type of mental health
services.

To be more specific, I was intrigued at what I call the compart-
mentalization of professionals' thinking about social-class related problems. If the "ideal" patient comes into one's Park Avenue office, one
offers psychotherapy and thinks nothing else about it. At cocktail parties
or in just chatting, the clinician talks about the injustices perpetrated
on the Negroes or poor whites. But that's as far as it goes. With mounting pressures to deal with the multifarious problems of the urban poor,
the middle-class clinician feels either that his brand of therapy is irrelevant for the poor, or that if some of these people could only be brought
into his office and learn how to free associate he could help them, or
that the problems of the poor are not within the province of psychotherapy as we know it. Because problems of middle-class neurotics are
primarily ones of self-actualization and problems of the poor, ones of
self-determination—i.e., survival issues—traditional psychotherapy for the
poor is not appropriate or must be modified drastically, following many of the suggestions made by Frank Riessman—e.g., action
therapies, role playing, etc. It is for these reasons that I am so impressed
with the promise of the nonprofessional for working with the poor. His
natural style and basic understanding of ghetto problems should be
utilized to help ameliorate the deplorable conditions that exist there.

But let me take this point a little further because I think it holds
crucial implications for the training of future psychologists. As I have
participated as a trainer in T-groups and observed and talked to therapists, I find that the psychological satisfaction derived from this activity
combined with the theoretical structure within which the therapist or
trainer operates, mitigate against adopting a public health or community
orientation to the solution of mental health problems. To assume the
stance of the latter approach is to a large degree to diffuse the nature

of one's contact with the client. The intimacy of the private office is replaced by unordered, administrative activities in a fairly chaotic situation. A community-oriented psychologist, for example, might then hold a discussion with community organizers at the local neighborhood service center, and then drive to a church to consult with a priest before returning to his office to look over some research results. Much of his time might be further spent in working with the local poverty and community action groups to help set up an integrated program that would lead to more jobs and better quality education.

What I have been describing may sound familiar to you, but many of our clinical colleagues who see the world differently may think that we have gone off the deep end. I have heard them say that the intimacy of one-to-one therapy has been violated by a senseless scrambling effort to race around in the community. What do our theories have to say about community work? Who wants to wander into dangerous neighborhoods, talk to agency personnel about problems that seem insoluble, run parent, teacher, clergy, or parole officer discussion groups, and so on? Hopefully, many of these activities can be taken over by nonprofessionals for whom these conflicts essentially are not as great. But I have often felt uncomfortable and unprepared to tackle many of these tasks. My experiences in slum neighborhoods brought me an understanding of the problems that no textbook could provide, but, in truth, I felt out of place and uneasy most of the time.

I am saying that we cannot expect most clinicians to give up what they have learned and love so dearly, i.e., psychotherapy, because the Zeitgeist impels us toward community mental health. The crux of my own training has been this and one related issue for I fervently feel that psychologists should participate in the solution of society's ills. But in order to achieve this aim, new kinds of training experiences are necessary. I am now talking about training that combines two crucial ingredients whose proper development can help us produce psychologists who can make significant contributions to this area.

First, psychologists who have a bent and a desire for doing psychotherapy should not be coerced to abandon this experience, but they should be trained to practice it within the context of a broader social program. Second, the concept of research, which states essentially that as behavioral scientists we are merely to study, describe, or analyze the existing social conditions, needs to be extended so that our research efforts can be conceptualized and implemented on the basis of theories and strategies of social intervention geared to changing the social and psychological conditions of people in need.

With regard to doing therapy within a larger program, and I think we can include sensitivity training here as well, my feeling is that one gains important psychological satisfaction and knowledge from this experience from the immediate feedback that one is helping others. I have found that it is very difficult to duplicate this feeling in other kinds of activities that may actually lead to the betterment of thousands of people, such as establishing broad-based nonprofessionally staffed neighborhood service centers. But I have discovered during these last two years that when my "clinical" activities are only a part of the services that clients receive, and that other efforts are being made concurrently to alter the social conditions that have contributed to their problems, I achieve my greatest satisfaction.

It was suggested by Bob Reiff at the Swampscott Conference that we have failed over the last 20 years in trying to integrate the scientist and clinician roles and that, at best, all we can hope for is a complementarity of functions. I think that given a different kind of training the two can be put together in a way that will be both satisfying and productive. Each individual professional may not always possess or utilize research, community organization, and clinical skills, but these kinds of skills should be used in an integrated program. I feel that to perform psychotherapy in isolation of other environmental changes and supports, and this holds for middle-class patients too, is to cater to one's own needs to the exclusion of social and professional responsibility.

Let me give an example. Last year I ran first a T-group and then a discussion group with a number of mothers and teachers of a local elementary school. Had I decided that my only obligation was to do the best I could in clarifying issues, etc. while I was present in the group, I would have been behaving in a manner that is typical of many professionals today. But I decided to go a step further and to expand the boundaries so that the administrative staff of the school and the school system in general were included. Thus, the ideas which emerged within the group were perceived in the context of a social system and efforts toward the solution of problems were directed at this more general organizational level. My own participation included meeting with the group, as well as the school principal and his administrative staff, to discuss these issues. And presently, we are trying to make an impact at the local and city levels of the Board of Education to modify certain policies and innovate others. I have decided that the effective solution to many of these problems comes about by dealing with all levels of the social structure that affect the particular domain in question and, in so doing, I can often satisfy my need to have a clinical kind of experience.

With regard to the second key issue in training, that of extending our common definition of research, I feel that one of the major sources that will contribute to our new body of knowledge in community psychology will be not only the content of our findings, but also the actual process by which we conduct research in the community. Let me elaborate. Currently there is a vast literature in the social sciences developed mainly during the last 40 years or so. If you talk to most social psychologists or sociologists, they will tell you that it is their job to do research. People in government and politics and others will implement their findings as they see fit. I think that this notion is both naive and unsound. For example, the firm body of knowledge on prejudice and discrimination has had relatively little impact on the attainment of equal rights for Negroes in the country. Or the newly emerging field of international conflict resolution gives little indication that its findings, present and future, will be utilized to achieve a world peace.

The mechanism for social change hinges on the interconnection among the researcher, a social intervention plan, and the social and political decision makers in society. I am suggesting that unless this tripartite relationship is established at the beginning, we will not be able to make headway in effecting meaningful social change.

The signs of the times suggest that political bodies and industrial concerns are more than interested in what social scientists can contribute to the betterment of society. I think that one of our most important tasks in the next few years is to reconstruct our relationship vis-à-vis these public and private establishments so that our efforts will not go in vain.

There are many implicit value judgments inherent in the suggestions being offered here. Most important is the question of the boundary between scientist and citizen roles. There is no easy answer to this question and it is one that merits serious debate at this time. My feeling is that, as social scientists, we have erred in the direction of caution and that we have made implicitly the value judgment that active participation in social change is outside our domain. This decision must be carefully examined. I think we can maintain scientific standards even as we participate in social change programs. The notion of the participant-conceptualizer is well suited to our new role. We can gain new knowledge at the same time we are helping people, and that seems to me to be the business of the day.

One final comment. There is no way to put into words the gratitude and appreciation I have for Bob Reiff who has devoted an enormous amount of time and psychological investment into my training. As a role model of clinician, supervisor, and practical humanitarian, I can imagine none finer. His very essence as a human being has been the most inspirational part of my fellowship.

RECEPTION IN PRESENT SETTING

After the completion of my postdoctoral fellowship in community mental health, I remained in the Einstein complex to work at the newly formed Soundview–Throgs Neck Community Mental

Health center. I was employed in the Consultation and Education Service of the center. My new colleagues were not entirely confused by my "breed" because I had spent an appreciable amount of time working with many of them during my fellowship. Nevertheless, there were some striking clashes of ideology and orientation during the first few months. It was obvious that my ideas for the kinds of undertakings I thought appropriate for the center were much broader and ambitious than those of my colleagues. I was kiddingly accused of being a little megalomaniacal. In fairness to their position, though, it was apparent that the wide scope of exposure to ideas and issues in my postdoctoral training experience were not moderated by an awareness of some of the practicalities and limitations imposed by most institutions.

The center faced enormous problems, having to deal with hiring, space allocation for staff, organizational structure, and program development among other things, with no time specifically allocated for planning or adequate study of the catchment area it serves. In this context, my enthusiasm for broad-based social action programs was met often with either intellectual approval or reverential fear. And my notions for more community-based programs dealing with urban problems such as housing and welfare were met with disapproval by some colleagues who thought that these areas were not within the province of community mental health centers. It soon became clear that the center had much preparatory work to do in staff development and training and that I had to learn how to curtail some of my ideas to meet both the institutional realities of the situation and the needs of my colleagues to proceed more slowly.

The nature of the internal structuring of the center did not allow me to have much contact with the psychiatrists and clinical psychologists, who deal almost exclusively with patient populations. My unit was oriented toward primary prevention programs and therefore my "fit" was fairly comfortable as I was able to bring my behavioral science perspective into program planning and implementation with less opposition than I might have received had I been working on clinical teams. My background in both social psychology and community mental health has enabled me to play major roles in the center with regard to in-service and community training and program development.

Reflections on the Postdoctoral Program in Community Mental Health of the Laboratory of Community Psychiatry, Harvard Medical School

Robert Toal

During the past academic year I was a postdoctoral student in the Laboratory of Community Psychiatry, a unit of the Department of Psychiatry of Harvard Medical School. Conducted in the Harvard School of Public Health since 1955, the program of the Laboratory was transferred to the Medical School in July, 1964. It has trained nearly a hundred psychiatrists, social workers, psychologists, and psychiatric nurses in two programs, the degree program in the School of Public Health and the certificate program in the Medical School. All four of the aforementioned disciplines were represented among last year's trainees. Fellowships were made available through funds provided by NIMH and the Grant Foundation of New York.

The training program of the laboratory includes a variety of experiences of a didactic and practical nature in the workings of communities, in planning and administration, consultation, and the philosophy and practice of community mental health. I will try to react critically to each of these experiences as I describe them, and, by way of conclusion, to evaluate the influence of the experience as a whole.

I should begin by referring briefly to certain past experiential variables which influenced my decision to undertake this kind of training, and which surely influenced my reactions to it. Most of us who come to postdoctoral training in community psychology or community mental health are rather well-used experimental animals, suitable for pilot studies out of which may come more significant future experiments, in particular, for predoctoral training in psychology.

My own rather pleasant, often exhilarating predoctoral and postdoctoral experiences in state hospitals, mental health clinics, a military hospital, a medical school, a penal institution, a university clinic, and elsewhere had led me to question the following propositions:

1. That when people face almost insurmountable problems in living they most often seek some kind of professional help.

2. That our society is, as the upper-income media always described it, abundant in opportunities to deal with life's problems, to pacify the lion unleashed by its ironies, and even to enhance significantly the quality of one's inner life. (Those of us who came of age in surges of pollyannish denial in the fifties were most passionately concerned that many Americans were denied the satisfactions of self-actualization.)

3. That when blundering parents, pathetic victims of a former and unenlightened age, planted "things that go bump in the dark" in the recesses of their children's psyches, all that was needed was intrapsychic tinkering applied with the devotion of a carburetor repairman of the twenties out of John O'Hara.

4. That the obvious fact of much human wretchedness, and even real tragedy, on my block, any block I tried to live nonvoyeuristically upon, was attributable to the frequently strange workings of chance.

5. That mental health is One-Two-Three, as the popular pamphlet implied.

These propositions and others like them have, in the sixties, lost whatever semblance of validity they may have seemed to possess in the forties and fifties. So it was with mounting concern and skepticism about a clinical psychology that should have been experiencing a revolution of rising expectations about its possible real worth, but was instead congratulating itself on increasingly successful efforts to find a dry spot under the shaky umbrella of medical insurance, that I approached postgraduate work in community mental health.

The Harvard program, under the directorship of Gerald Caplan, has, as I have indicated, a rather long history. As a pioneering program its influence has been considerable. Its relative maturity in an innovative field has not been accompanied by rigidity or any special obeisance to the past, and in fact, planned changes in the program for the coming year lend some of my remarks relevance only for the past year or two.

Its uniqueness and its most important contribution, in my view, lies in its commitment to behavioral science as a fundamental body of knowledge for mental health professionals. The resident staff of the laboratory this year included such specialties as social and clinical psychology, social psychiatry, sociology, and environmental design. Invited guests, in seminars and special programs (and there was liberal use of outside expertise of the highest quality), covered the spectrum of behavioral sciences, and also included nonprofessional social change agents.

ADMINISTRATION

The laboratory is, of course, committed to an emergent ideology of community mental health, and many invited seminar participants, in the seminar on administration and elsewhere, were administrators of new and important programs in this area. They were invited to share their experiences in the administration of innovative programs, and generally did so with bracing candor. Most were psychiatrists, nearly all were closely identified with the community mental health center concept, and nearly all were facing problems of one sort or another that might convince clinical psychology that our traditional distaste for administration (reinforced by the always present opportunity to blame lack of progress on backward psychiatrists) was well founded. It is not because if we are to have a professional impact in mental health (or any other social movement), we need an administrative breed, people who move toward executive positions, not out of professional incompetence, but because they see an opportunity to implement good things.

KNOWING THE COMMUNITY

An important element of the Harvard program consists of course work and field experience in learning how to learn about communities. I think this kind of experience is essential if we are to be more than head-scratching spectators in a period of accelerating social change. The official pieties of the fifties found many of us housed uneasily with all our exotic professional paraphernalia in comfortable and, to us, comforting mental hygiene clinics. Occasionally we ventured out to make a little talk, between songs, at Kiwanis and Rotary meetings. We were retardates—sociologically and politically—and earned another inch of obscurity for our lack of trouble. The nights we spent reading carefully edited news magazines might more profitably have been spent at city council meetings, or working precincts, or learning some barnyard urban sociology. And today we are not much better prepared, although the din raised by the sociology and politics of human need is deafening. Before the war in Vietnam it was generally conceded that all of the important legislation of the future would be concerned with the quality of human life. This goes beyond "mental health," but not beyond the realities of life in our society which we can no longer afford to ignore.

In the Harvard Community Psychiatry Program there was a year-long seminar on community dynamics, community organization, power, the pitfalls of social innovation, and the workings of change. Supplementing this was a day in the field each week—in such agencies as a poverty program, a multiservice center, a legal aid clinic, a settlement house, a welfare housing complex. My own field placement consisted of spending one day a week in the sometimes frenzied pursuit of a young, energetic, Washington-conscious mayor of an urban center in the Northeast Corridor who was attempting to implement a variety of projects to improve his community. This was an experience in the occasional euphoria, and more frequent futility, of trying to wrest a city from the iron grip of the past, to make it a good, or at least, a less pathological environment for people of the present. It was an experience in the politics of education, of health and welfare, of law enforcement, and the reclamation of the rotten urban core. It was an experience in community mental health, if indeed, community mental health means anything more than treating schizophrenics in less pastoral hideaways than we did in the past.

Didactic and supervised field experience in the organization and dynamics of communities does more than enhance one's sophistication about the way things really are in the social systems outside the clinic or hospital. It forces the practitioner to give serious consideration, perhaps for the first time, to hard issues which, as a citizen, he can comfortably avoid. Among these are the following:

1. The probability that vast numbers of nonpsychotic people who suffer are not touched in any way by mental health efforts in the United States.

2. The conflict between professional reserve and the citizen's inclination to throw oneself into community development because the need is so great.

3. Conflict between necessary accommodations to systemic evils and recognition that one is really a rather well paid agent of the system, and revulsion toward much that the system does to people accompanied by romantic aspirations to somehow invoke major social reform.

4. Finally, the issue of having to deal with intense yearning for the conceptual security of the clinic or the hospital. After all, what is one doing in the streets? What does a specialist in human behavior have to do with human behavior, except of course, in certain culturally sanctioned environments?

CONSULTATION

Mental health consultation is well represented in the program, on the basis of a seminar and extensive supervised field experience. Gerald Caplan is, of course, an early and major contributor to the theory and practice of consultation. It is taught enthusiastically and supervised skillfully.

In this method (to distinguish it from other consultative styles) the focus is on the consultee, and the terms of the case merely fuel the dialogue between consultant and consultee. A major goal early in the consultation relationship is to change the consultee. He is not to be merely a passive recipient of expert advice from a competent professional, as he may well have anticipated. He is, rather, to join with the consultant as an equal participant in the process, to enhance his competence as a person who frequently confronts human problems. Among other things, his thinking is to be complicated by counteracting the familiar tendency to conclude promptly that psychiatric intervention is necessary to prevent major catastrophe. In this sense, in consultation we try to alter a mode of thinking we ourselves helped to create in a generation of mental health education. The consultee begins to see human problems differently and to initiate problem solving on his own. He begins to feel more adequate as a potential agent of change rather than he previously felt as a dysphoric diagnostician and sophisticated buck passer.

It is a difficult process to learn, for consultant as well as consultee. Part of the difficulty lies in the fact that the student consultant is teaching while he is learning. And there is the inevitable proactive inhibition experienced by any professional who has consulted in a different way for some years. A third and, perhaps, more serious problem, is that the consultee brings to consultation the problems of individuals whose troublesome behavior is inextricably wound up in the thickets of social systems which themselves need consultation, and often much more. My own field experience with teachers and public health nurses in two white ghettos led me at times to feel like an evangelist in Hell. Too little and too late. This feeling was expressed, and not altogether pessimistically, by a nun I encountered in one of these ghettos who had witnessed an accelerating rate of physical and human dilapidation. As she viewed a particularly bleak neighborhood scene she commented: "Mental health is all well and good, but what we really need here are community organizers."

INTERDISCIPLINARY TRAINING

A comment should be made about the interdisciplinary nature of the staff and students, because interdisciplinary training under medical auspices is an issue of great concern to psychologists. My experience this year has reinforced a conviction that community psychology must move as rapidly as possible toward postdoctoral training under its own banner. This is not a negative reaction, but a positive professional response of a psychologist whose initial enthusiasm was increased by his training experience.

Yet we should not allow growing professional pride and energy to remove us from significant interdisciplinary settings, especially at a time when pride and energy (and our acceptance by other professions) make it possible for us to make more important contributions in such settings. Professional maturity and professional chauvinism do not live amicably together. A number of considerations make it likely that we shall continue to avail ourselves of existing training in psychiatric settings where these are truly committed to a multidisciplinary attack on mental health problems, however such problems may be defined. Some of these considerations follow:

1. Opportunities and money for postgraduate training in psychiatric settings exist now. We cannot wait hopefully for the expansion of similar opportunities in psychological centers of the future. We are only now engaged in the implementation of predoctoral training.

2. Medicine and psychiatry are changing, and psychology is one of several disciplines aiding and abetting this change. The suburban entrepreneurs of the medical establishment are losing their grip on the perennially inadequate medical services of the inner city. This fact, interacting with other forces, is increasing the importance of social and interpersonal dimensions in medical education. Psychiatry, too, under the impact of community psychiatry, is beginning to abandon its high cholesterol intellectual diet, and to become more actively involved in gaining some awareness of the community.

3. The new community mental health center will, in many instances, provide sanction for innovative research and service programs of psychologists. There is, indeed, a lot of old wine in this new bottle, but this could well be turned to our advantage. I am thinking now of the community mental health center with a psychiatric staff whose clinical tradition and other professional commitments make it perfectly happy to grant to the psychologist a significant burden of community involvement. New and more fruitful professional relationships could emerge from this.

OTHER EXPERIENCES

I have omitted discussion of other seminars and related experiences—in law and psychiatry, systems analysis, research, and group process, to name some—and will comment only to the effect that these were valuable, and at times, very exciting opportunities.

CONCLUSION

To conclude these remarks, I would like to indulge in some speculation about where we might be going, speculation which is directly influenced by my experiences of the past year, but which in no way reflects any working philosophy of the Laboratory of Community Psychiatry or its staff. The training arm of the laboratory, as I have tried to indicate, is dedicated to the creation of effective agents of mental health in the community, agents who, it is hoped, will lead programs and add to our knowledge.

These speculations will be advanced as predictions, all of which I would regard as conservative.

1. Professional psychologists will become more aware of social reality, and, therefore, more willing to support and even initiate new public programs. The objection is often raised that we lack bodies of knowledge of sufficient magnitude and general respectability to approach the myriad problems of wretchedness and discontent in community settings. It is this kind of alienation from life that leads so many of us to disapprove of decent and humane little programs like Head Start and Upward Bound because available data do not permit us to predict sure gains in IQ (or some other index of public worth) accruing from these programs. While I do not believe that available knowledge is in such short supply, I believe the objection can be more effectively met by pointing out that we will not get sufficient research on significant human problems until we work in settings where such problems are generated. Then we will witness new research styles and emphases, and enthusiasm for new things among our students.

2. Professional psychologists will increasingly address themselves to important human problems outside traditional psychiatric conceptualizations. It will no longer be unusual for psychologists to engage in research and service programs in such areas as loneliness and alienation, privacy, joy, communication media, the uses of leisure, and, more importantly, reciprocal relationships between social and physical environments and individual behavior.

3. Psychologists will participate actively in computer-based research on whole communities and on neighborhoods viewed as communities. Part of this activity will involve cooperative research with other disciplines on social indicators by which we will attempt to assess more accurately the quality of our society.

4. Psychologists will be actively represented in the coming revolution in elementary education. Psychological science will be taught in elementary schools as part of the regular curriculum, and we will express surprise that we did not embark on this sooner as children respond

eagerly to the opportunity to learn more about themselves and their social world.

We are moving from patients to people, from prevention of disease to promotion of human efficiency, from an obsolete pragmatism of mental health to a new romanticism of high expectation about the possible impacts of present technology on ancient problems. As with many romances, this one is destined to be quarrelsome, and at times despairing. But it is the only way to excite the imagination of those who are destined to replace us.

Experience in the Postdoctoral Training Program in Community Mental Health at South Shore

Sylvain Nagler

I spent two most productive and enlightening years at the South Shore Mental Health Center, the first as a predoctoral intern in clinical psychology and the second as a postdoctoral trainee in community mental health. I recall fairly well the initial feelings that motivated me to seek out some training in community psychology. First (but not necessarily most important), I was disenchanted with traditional mental health practices. I began seriously to question whether we were reaching enough people and, for that matter, the right people. Was psychotherapy to be our principal instrument for coping with the mental health needs of the society? I came to realize that much depended on how narrowly you defined "mental health needs."

A second source of enlightenment emanated from the civil rights struggle. I very suddenly began to understand some of the social crises that were facing our country. I began to get some measure of comprehension of what it was like to be disenfranchised, eternally frustrated, and without the power of self-determination. These issues I began to see as directly related to mental health and hence the definition broadened. My cathexes shifted dramatically and I decided to find out "What is this thing called community psychology?" and "What needs can *it* meet?" My training has enabled me to develop tentative answers to these questions and the answers have produced a favorable visceral response.

I will not describe the specific things I did as a trainee, but I will present some thoughts about community psychology and how they relate to training. These ideas are mainly a product of two years of exposure and involvement in a dynamic mental health center in Quincy, Massachusetts. As a result they will obviously reflect the biases of a clinic deeply involved in child guidance and school consultation. Hopefully, they are applicable to other institutions as well.

It is likely that at this stage of the development of community psychology a large number of individuals seeking postdoctoral training will have had only minimal exposure to community consultation and programming prior to arriving at the training institution. This suggests that the trainee may be unfamiliar with some basic considerations that underlie the community approach to mental health. Without this background information much of the initial field experience may be without meaning, the central programming may seem irrelevant, and community psychology may appear to be just another panic response to the growing awareness that traditional mental health practices have been a social bust.

Each trainee brings along with him a network of biases. In the case of a clinical psychology Ph.D., these biases most likely are predicated on the traditional medical-model approach to mental illness. While the trainee may indicate a dissatisfaction with this approach, he remains unsure with what to replace it. He has heard of community psychology, understands that its operational base is broader, agrees with the goals of serving the entire community rather than selected minorities, and is even willing to venture out into his catchment area abandoning the security of his office. But there remain the biases of past experiences.

These biases are seen in the frequently advocated compromise espoused by the traditional clinician—"let's provide more efficient clinical procedures to the community by expanding our services to include consultation. This will enable us to get out into the community, reach cases earlier, and render at least indirect services to individuals who otherwise would not ordinarily avail themselves of any direct clinical service." This hypothetical monologue best describes what is more formally called case consultation. Indeed case consultation has been going on for a long time, most popularly in the schools. While the extent of such consultation has increased in recent years, its intent remains unchanged—i.e., enhancing the psychic equilibrium of the client. Thus, coping with individual pathology has been extended from the clinic into the community. While this may represent the most common view of the nature of community psychology, the case consultation approach occupies only one small segment of the community mental health enterprise.

The other aspects of a comprehensive community mental health program, no doubt, are less known to the trainee. One effective way of introducing him to these other services is to describe them in terms of the following variables: (a) the goals of the service, (b) the targets of the service, and (c) the means by which the service will be implemented.

The goals of traditional mental health practices typically have been to provide treatment for as many patients as possible. This kind of service required that the individual be aware of a disorder, be willing to do something about it, know of an appropriate agency where he could receive help, and then be accepted for some form of assistance (usually individual, psychodynamically oriented psychotherapy). The urgent need for added service in the community prompted the clinician to leave the clinic and share his expertise with community caretakers. Children were viewed as being prime targets for such indirect services because it was reasonable to attack the problem as early in its development as possible. Thus the concentration on school consultation.

Clearly, the goal in this approach is to enhance the client's psychic equilibrium, to eliminate any aberrant behavior, and to maximize productive functioning. The principal concern is with effecting some positive change in the client—that is, the *target*. Such an intervention most often is the result of a request by a consultee for some psychological consultation. The specific means that consultees employ in making their requests vary considerably. Indeed, they are frequently presented in a disguised fashion, but the implicit message remains: "Help me to better cope with this problem." The means used by the mental health consultant to achieve these ends is case consultation. It is this type of consultation which most closely approximates the direct service associated with traditional mental health practices. The major differences are (a) there is a reaching out to the community and (b) the service is provided via the consultee and not directly to the client.

A question frequently asked by consultants of themselves (and others) is "What changes has my intervention produced?" Or put another way: "What *impact* have I, as a consultant, had on the caretakers with whom I have worked?" Insofar as the case consultant is concerned, he may point with pride to the rescued children who otherwise might well have become serious casualties were it not for his early detection and intervention. Although there may be other ancillary benefits, such as mental health education for the consultees, they represent an added bonus. The primary focus of the case consultation approach is alleviating problems in a particular client. In fact, cases are screened and selected by the consultant based on the nature and extent of the pathology in the client, much the same way most clinics accept patients.

To the trainee, it is this aspect of community involvement that appears to be most related to the graduate training he received and it is here that he will experience his greatest level of confidence. As a result, he is likely to feel most comfortable engaging in the case approach. Similarly, administrators of training programs may feel most comfortable starting trainees at this level, reasoning that case consultation skills are a prerequisite to other levels of consultation. What is communicated to the trainee is that until he masters these skills he will not be able to proceed successfully to other forms of community intervention. There appears to be no evidence to indicate that this is true *nor* is there evidence to the effect that the community requires a certain number of case consultation contacts prior to sanctioning other forms of mental health intervention. Therefore there seems to be no reason to confine trainees to learning about, or participating in, only case interventions.

A second mode of consultation has as its target the community caretakers. They include educators, police personnel, the medical profession, welfare workers, and so forth. This level of intervention seeks to enhance the functioning efficiency of such caretakers by means of educational consultation. In focusing on the caretakers, the intent is to further enlighten and sensitize these community agents so that they will be better able to cope with problem cases that were previously neglected or inappropriately referred to outside agencies. The consultation does not seek to effect any direct change in a particular client.

Whereas in case consultation case selections are left principally to the consultee, in educational consultation the consultant assumes a more active role. He screens the cases and issues in which he will consult, selecting those that seem best to serve the educational needs of the consultee. Another characteristic of consultation of this type is that it is not confined to working with a single consultee. Indeed frequent requests are made to organize and administer in-service training programs. In such instances the consultant may move beyond his more traditional role and become an active participant in the program. Here, too, there is increased maneuverability. The consultant can strategically select the subject matter and the means of presentation to effect changes in his audience of caretakers.

At this level, consultation is caretaker centered rather than case centered and its impact in terms of numbers of people helped is potentially greater. By helping to improve the skills of a community caretaker, rather than improving the behavior of a particular client, you maximize future gains. As in case consultation ancillary benefits may accrue that entail more permanent changes in the social system but these are not the result of any planned strategy. It is only at the third level of consultation that such system changes are intended.

Program or administrative consultation has as its target the social system in which the consultant operates. This may be a school system, a hospital, a town, etc. The primary goal here is to achieve some measure of system change that becomes institutionalized. In operational terms this means the change becomes a part of the system and functions independently of the consultant.

Institutional changes can be brought about by consulting with administrators of the system—e.g., a community council leader, a school superintendent; by having a demonstration project institutionalized—for example, a mental health center parent education project taken over by the local school department; or by interesting members of the community to precipitate a change. In such interventions the consultant shares his expertise with the social system and works toward the incorporation of operational innovations into the system. Such innovations are relatively permanent and affect the greatest number of people. Implicit in this approach is the value judgment that it makes more sense to concentrate on the more permanent structures within the system, rather than on the community agents who deal with the casualties of these programs and policies, or the casualties themselves. It is at this level of intervention that community psychology has its most valuable impact, and it is here where our paramount efforts should be concentrated.

Here is an example. A school consultant received a request from a school to help them deal with a number of school phobic children in the first grade. Rather than working solely on returning the youngsters to school (case consultation), the consultant very skillfully used this stressful situation for the school as a selling point to introduce a procedural change in an effort to prevent school phobias. Very briefly, the change involved instituting a spring orientation program directed at preschoolers who would be entering the first grade in the fall. The children made several visits to the school to explore the building and its facilities, meet teachers and future classmates, and participate in some sample activities. Concomitantly, a program was instituted for the mothers of these children. They, too, were introduced to the school, its facilities, and personnel, and they were given anticipatory guidance related to such issues as separation anxiety, somatic complaints in first graders, etc. The program has proved successful in reducing the incidence of first grade phobias and is now a regular school policy.

The above description of consultation levels represents a sample of what a trainee should become familiar with as early in his field training as possible. Such instruction should be introduced prior to any extensive, independent field experience; otherwise, it is likely that the trainee will revert to his previous clinical training and seek to interpret what he sees and hears in the community in a clinical framework only. This, in turn, may well lead to a near exclusive reliance on the case consultation model. In fact, we have accumulated quite a bit of evidence bearing this out.

It would be unfortunate if clinical competence became equated with consultative skills, for such a consideration might well lead to erroneous conclusions about the training and utilization of neophyte consultants. It might assume that formal training in community consultation is nonessential after completion of a clinical program of study; and it might lead clinicians to engage prematurely in independent community consultation based on their clinical experience. What is generally missing in clinical training is the study of social systems, their

dynamics, and how they can be changed. The purpose of these pre-
cautions is not so much to protect the community (for irreparable
damage is indeed unlikely) but to enhance the training experience.

The supervision could evolve from a parallel training model with
at least one senior consultant. At first the trainee would be a participant-
observer and shadow his mentor in the community. Gradually, more
and more independent responsibility could be shifted from the senior
to the junior member of the pair. This type of model for training would
have the following advantages:

1. It maximizes the supervisory experience, as the senior consultant
would have first hand knowledge of the problem or at least with the
system and its caretakers.

2. It provides an excellent avenue for the development of a role
model.

3. It facilitates the transition from student to professional status.

Mental health centers around the country are at present struggling
with the problem of manpower allocation. This is in response to the
question "How can we best serve the mental health needs of the
community?" In many instances there will be major differences of opinion among the staff. Issues such as "How much direct vs. indirect service should be offered?" "How identified with the community should we
become?" "Do we take sides?" are likely to be discussed. Such discussions on an institutional level present in microcosm the issues facing the
mental health professions. As such, they provide an invaluable arena of
learning for the trainee. Trainees should be encouraged to attend community meetings and, as much as possible, to participate in the exchange of ideas. Participation in decision-making meetings of this type
is an important step in motivating trainees to become interested in
major issues and in later assuming administrative positions in the community mental health endeavor.

This symposium is titled Voices of the New Psychologist, yet my
remarks are not meant to be limited to psychologists alone. The clinical
case model is not the exclusive domain of psychology, it is shared by
other disciplines as well. These other disciplines are also training community mental health workers and their trainees ask many of the same
questions we ask. Most of these questions, I think, can be subsumed
under a single major one: "Am I doing justice to my aspirations to
help people combat misery, blight, and illness and to the clinical training I have received?" The more one ventures out into the community,
the more one gets involved in community health projects, the more one
sees efforts rewarded, the more emphatically one answers: "Yes!"

Name Index

Adams, H. B., 38
Addams, Jane, 78
Albee, G., 7, 34, 66, 71, 100, 103, 230, 241
Allport, Gordon, 228
Altrocchi, John, 191–205; 14, 45, 192, 195, 197, 199, 232, 243, 250
Anderson, Luleen S., 12, 177, 196
Andrews, Thomas, 92, 94

Baker, F., 216, 217
Baler, Lenin A., 218, 251
Bandura, A., 44
Bard, Morton, 125–141; 14, 134, 240, 242
Bateman, N. I., 223
Batton, Lois, 192
Beach, D. R., 107
Belknap, Ivan, 250
Bell, Durward, 250
Benne, K., 208
Bennett, C. C., 12, 177, 196
Bennett, E. M., 5, 71, 72, 73, 104, 121, 122, 143, 242
Bennis, W., 208
Bergen, B. J., 224
Berken, G., 196, 197, 198
Berkowitz, Bernard, 134
Bieri, James, 250
Bindman, A. J., 232
Bloom, Bernard L., 163–177; 14, 54 n, 228, 243, 250
Bockoven, S., 34
Boulware, Don, 250
Brayfield, A., 3
Breiter, D. E., 39
Burke, Linda, 250

Campbell, Ernest, 93 n
Caplan, Gerald, 8, 45, 101, 103, 192, 199, 232, 263, 265
Carlisle, Robert L., 108 n
Carney, Dennis, 108 n

Chave, S., 168
Cherlin, D. L., 5, 71, 72, 73, 104, 121, 122, 143, 242
Chin, R., 208
Chinsky, Jack, 118 n, 120 n
Cohen, J., 100, 103
Cohen, Louis, 251
Cooper, James, 87 n, 94
Cooper, S., 12, 177, 196
Cowen, Emory L., 99–124; 5, 14, 99, 100, 103, 107, 108, 110, 115, 117, 121, 122, 231, 236, 237, 242
Cumming, E., 74, 197
Cumming, J., 74, 100, 197

Davis, J. A., 33
De Marche, D. F., 6, 7
De Moll, Louis, 250
Denny, J. P., 46, 48
De Tocqueville, Alexis, 27
Dohrenwend, Barbara, 132
Duhl, L., 9
Dunham, H. W., 103, 169
Dworkin, Earl, 110 n

Ebner, E., 42
Ehlers, Victor, 250
Eisdorfer, Carl, 191–205; 14, 45, 192, 195, 196, 197, 198, 232, 243
Eisenberg, L., 71
Elam, Lloyd, 93 n
Elkes, C., 39
Ewalt, J., 6, 7
Eysenck, H. J., 71

Farberow, N. L., 49, 50
Feld, S., 6, 7, 101
Flint, A. A., 39
Fougerousse, Myra, 108 n
Frankel, Gail, 108 n
Frankel, Mark, 121 n
Freeman, R. W., 39
Freidenburg, E., 208

Subject Index